MUSHROOMS *of* HAWAI'I

MUSHROOMS *of* HAWAI'I

An Identification Guide

DON E. HEMMES
AND
DENNIS E. DESJARDIN

EPBM
ECHO POINT BOOKS & MEDIA, LLC

Published by Echo Point Books & Media
Brattleboro, Vermont
www.EchoPointBooks.com

Mushrooms of Hawai'i
ISBN: 978-1-62654-182-5 (paperback)

Cover images courtesy of the authors.

Front, *(top, left to right)*:

Chlorophyllum molybdites appears on lawns throughout the Hawaiian Islands during rainy periods. These large mushrooms have toxins that will cause severe gastrointestinal problems and send people who ingest them to the emergency ward.

Dictyophora multicolor is a phallic-looking fungal fruiting body with a lemon-yellow net or indusium hanging down. These "netted stinkhorns" appear in composted woodchip piles and on lawns.

Bright red, star-like fruiting bodies of *Aseroe rubra* appear in composted woodchips and *Eucalyptus* forests. The black slimy gleba on the upper surface contains the spores and gives off an odor resembling feces or dead animals to attract flies for spore dispersal, thus the name "stinkhorn."

The famous morel mushroom, *Morchella* species, are uncommon in Hawai'i, but have been found every month of the year, from sea level to 8,000 ft. on Mauna Kea, in such diverse habitats as on tree ferns in the native forest and in conifer groves.

Back:

A cluster of *Lepista tarda* on the lawns at the University of Hawai'i at Hilo. These lavender mushrooms appear in fairy rings and arcs on lawns and are considered first rate edibles.

Interior design by Betsy Stromberg

Cover design by Adrienne Núñez
Editorial and proofreading assistance by Ian Straus,
Echo Point Books & Media

*This book is dedicated to those teachers
who inspired us to become mycologists—
Drs. Salomon Bartnicki-Garcia, Hans Hohl,
Don Huffman, Ron Petersen, and Harry Thiers—
and to R. Philip Hanes, gentleman scholar,
notorious fungophile, and mutual friend
of the authors and publisher.*

Coprinus disseminatus, a common inhabitant of the wet alien rainforests in Hawai'i, forms spectacular clusters of crumbly, gray-capped mushrooms on stumps and logs.

CONTENTS

Acknowledgments   ix

Introduction   1
     Fungal Kingdom   2
     Organisms Classically Studied by Mycologists   6
     History of Mycology in Hawai'i   6
     Seasonality of Hawaiian Mushrooms   9
     Collecting Sites   11

CHAPTER 1 Identifying Mushrooms   15

CHAPTER 2 Mushrooms in Hawaiian Vegetation Zones   21
     Lawns   24
     Compost Piles and Wood Chips   32
     Flowerpots   44
     Pastures   48
     Guava Thickets   58
     Wet Windward Alien Forests   60
     Coastal *Casuarina*   82
     Coastal Coconut   90
     Arid Leeward Coastal Habitats   94
     Arid Leeward Montane Habitats   98
     Conifer Forests   104
     Eucalyptus Forests   114
     Montane *Casuarina* Forests   122
     Mesic Montane Native Forests   126
     Wet Montane Native Rainforests   142
     Sphagnum Bogs   156

CHAPTER 3 Other Hawaiian Fungi   159
     Rust Fungi   160
     Lichens   162
     Mycetozoans—The Slime Molds   164
     Animals That Feed on Fungi   170

CHAPTER 4 **Medicinal Mushrooms**   173

CHAPTER 5 **Poisonous Hawaiian Mushrooms**   175

CHAPTER 6 **Hallucinogenic Hawaiian Mushrooms**   181

CHAPTER 7 **Culturing Mushrooms at Home**   183

CHAPTER 8 **Edible Mushrooms**   185

Glossary   191

**Common and Scientific Names
of Mushrooms and Trees in Hawai'i**   194

Hawaiian Terms   195

Bibliography   196

About the Authors   203

Index   205

ACKNOWLEDGMENTS

PROFESSIONAL CONSULTANTS:

The authors would like to thank the following professional mycologists for help and collaboration on various groups of Hawaiian fungi: Uno Eliasson, Göteborg University, Göteborg Sweden, for help with the myxomycetes; Don Gardner, University of Hawai'i, with the rust fungi; Robert L. Gilbertson, University of Arizona, with the polypores and other wood-rotting fungi; Roy Halling, New York Botanical Garden with *Collybia*; Egon Horak, ETH, Zürich, Switzerland, with *Galerina, Entoloma, Crepidotus,* and other selected agarics; Richard Korf, Cornell University, with ascomycetes; Orson Miller, Virginia Polytechnical Institute, with *Amanita*; Kristin Peterson, Harvard University, with *Agaricus*; Jack D. Rogers, Washington State University, with the Xylariaceae; Clifford Smith, University of Hawai'i, with the lichens; Else Vellinga, University of California, Berkeley, with *Lepiota*; George J. Wong, University of Hawai'i, Manoa, with the jelly fungi; and Jorge Wright, University of Buenos Aires, Buenos Aires, Argentina, with the Tulostomataceae.

COLLECTORS:

We also thank the following individuals who took time out to collect specimens and call us when the mushrooms were out: John Allen; Mike and Lei Au; Roger Baldwin; Kealii Bio; Earl Bolkan; Susan Cate; John Chan; Michelle Clapper; Martin Doudna; Tony Fernandez; Grant, Sharon, Hattie, and Emma Gerrish; John Giffin; Marlene Hapai; Calvin Harada; Helen Hemmes; Curtis Hintz; Grant Hirata; Marianne Humm; Ed Johnson; Kyle Kaaa; Ed Katahira; Jack Lockwood; Richard Matsunaga; Karla McDermid-Smith; Bill Mull; Greg Nielsen; Dave Paul; Brian Perry; Kristin Peterson; Kate and Nevin Reinard; Ryan Resquer; Carol Severance; Sabre Shehata; Russell Shioshita; Richard Short; Pete Sparks; Walter Steiger; Lani Stemmerman; Fred Stone; Dennis Suenobu; Ann Tanimoto; Bob Tanoue; Mashuri Waite; LaVanda Warren; and George Wong.

FACILITATING ACCESS:

We thank the following people for facilitating access to collecting permits and acting as guides: Ed Misaki, Paul Higashino, and Guy Hughes (The Nature Conservancy of Hawai'i); Betsy Gagne and Randy Kennedy (Natural Area Reserves); Ralston Nagata (Koke'e State Park); Charles Stone and David Foote (Volcanoes National Park); Lloyd Loope (Haleakala National Park); Randy Bartlett and Hank Oppenheimer (Maui Land and Pineapple Co.); Dick Wass and Jack Jeffrey (Hakalau Forest National Wildlife Refuge); and George Wong (University of Hawai'i at Manoa). We also thank Dr. David Lorence and Ken Wood (National Tropical Botanical Garden, Kaua'i) for providing housing while on Kaua'i.

HAWAIIAN LANGUAGE EXPERTS:

We are grateful to Dr. Kalena Silva, Chairman of the Hawaiian Studies Program, University of Hawai'i at Hilo, and his colleagues for supplying the appropriate Hawaiian names for the newly described species.

SPECIAL PEOPLE:

Special thanks go to people who provided constant companionship on field trips and prevented us from getting lost and hurt most of the time: Merton J. Goldsmith, Debbie Scott, and Randy Walker. Finally, we thank Helen Hemmes, who has been a delightful hostess to many visiting mycologists in Hilo and for her constant encouragement during this project.

FUNDING:

We thank the National Science Foundation for funding the majority of fieldwork and scientific analyses (Biotic Surveys and Inventories Grant # DEB-9300874).

Mushroom hunters with the Green-spored Parasol, *Chlorophyllum molybdites*, found growing in macadamia nut orchards on the Big Island.

A spectacular fruiting of *Lentinus bertieri* on a log in the woods around Hilo on the Big Island.

INTRODUCTION

With all the sunny weather and white sand beaches a common experience in Hawai'i, a visitor or resident might think that conditions are not conducive for mushroom growth in the islands. But one day while working in the garden or backyard you may notice a cluster of Inky Caps, *Coprinus lagopus,* popping up in a compost pile or some sulfur-yellow Flower-pot Parasols, *Leucocoprinus birnbaumii,* in nursery pots. If you are up early strolling on a damp, cool morning, you may see dozens of little Cone Heads, *Conocybe lactea,* scattered in the grass on the front lawn or in the park. Hikers in the forests and mountains of Hawai'i often come upon the brilliant red and obnoxiously stinky Starfish Stinkhorn, *Aseroe rubra,* or discover a log covered with hundreds of little gray mushrooms called Creeping Crumble Caps, *Coprinus disseminatus.* We have to admit that a common reaction by most

is to assume these mushrooms are poisonous and to deal with these critters by stomping them into oblivion. Surely, some education is needed to understand what these delicate and beautiful creations are all about.

This guidebook illustrates the more common mushrooms and other fungi found in selected Hawaiian habitats, whether these vegetation zones consist largely of introduced plants or native plants. If you are considering a mushroom found on your lawn, look in the first habitat chapter titled "Lawns." If you wish to identify a fungus in a native rain forest, look for that chapter heading, and so on. Edible, hallucinogenic, and poisonous species are noted, and strange and wonderful forms such as stinkhorns, earthstars, and bird's nest fungi are also included.

This field guide is the result of over ten years of research on all the major Hawaiian

Islands, from mountaintop to seashore. All of the species found in each habitat are not included, but we have included the most common, large, fleshy mushrooms and other fungi that observers might encounter in their lawns and gardens, in pastures, and in the various forests throughout the islands. We do hope you find enjoyment in these pages and gain a better understanding of these elegant and colorful organisms.

THE FUNGAL KINGDOM

Fungi are unique among living organisms and are placed in a kingdom with a rank equal to plants and animals. Fungi are *heterotrophic,* unable to produce their own food through photosynthesis like green plants, and must extract food and energy from the substrates on which they live. They may be *saprobic* and absorb nutrients from fallen logs, stumps, leaves and other detritus; or they may be

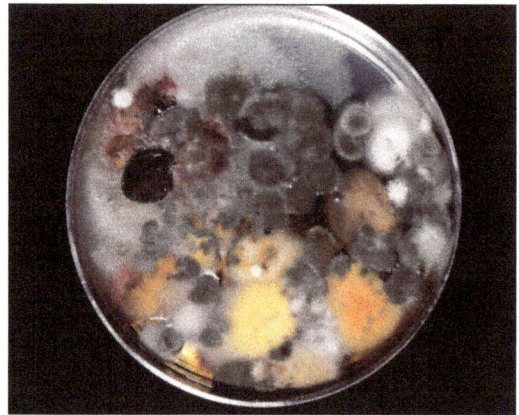

(clockwise from upper left) *Fomitopsis nivosa* destroying a mailbox post; various molds from leaf litter; *Penicillium* mold on fallen tangerine; *Dacryopinax spathularia* on plywood lanai.

parasitic and live on other living organisms, including plants, animals, or other fungi. These habits often make fungi nuisances, because they rot the railing on our lanais and appear as mildew in our showers, on photographic slides, and leather shoes.

Fungi play a critical role in our environment, however, by breaking down and digesting leaves, branches, fallen trees, and stumps in the forest. Fungi also live in the ocean, in streams, and in ponds, where they digest organic debris and recycle nutrients to the environment. Some fungi are *mycorrhizal* and live in close association with the roots of vascular plants and capture and deliver scarce nutrients to the plants. Fungi are obviously critical to the well-being of the tropical rainforest, where they quickly return nutrients to the ecosystem, and to agricultural crops in Hawai'i, where heavy rainfall can leach essential minerals from the soil.

Fungi grow as thin threads or tubes called *hyphae* that colonize a wide variety of organic substrates from the welcome mat

A mycelium and mushroom primordia growing out of a welcome mat during rainy weather in Hilo.

shown on page 3 to the wooden cabinets shown below. Many intertangled hyphae form a *mycelium,* the white cottony growth you recognize as mold growing on stale bread or on a jar of jelly that has been left open. Hyphae will grow on almost any substrate that is not toxic to them and that supplies some nutrition. For example, fungal hyphae grow on the surfaces of leaves in the Hawaiian rainforest and serve as a food source for Hawai'i's endemic Achatinellid tree snails. On the downside, University of Hawai'i researchers groan in disbelief when they find hyphae growing in the thin film of grease on optical lenses, which causes the lenses of their favorite microscopes and cameras to become occluded and etched.

Fairy rings (menehune rings in Hawai'i) demonstrate the radial growth of a fungal mycelium in the soil from a point of inoculum. Perhaps a mushroom dropped spores in the leaf mulch at the center of the ring, or some cow dung supplied the energy for the initiation of a mycelium in a pasture. Each year the mycelium grows outward radially, and then, after a heavy rain and when the temperature is right, mushrooms are produced at the outer

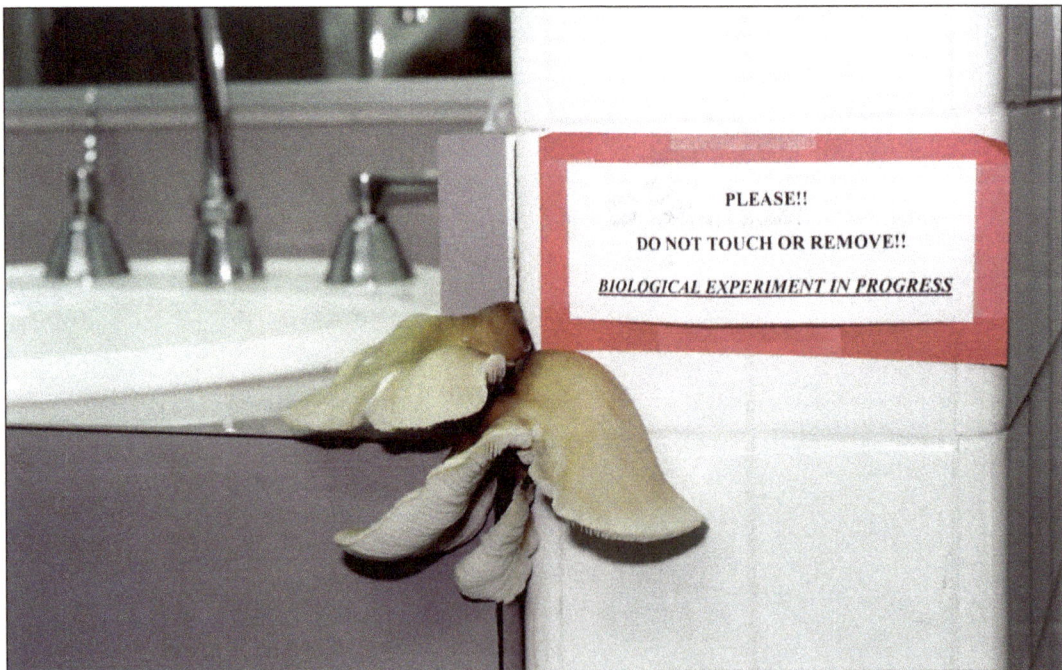

Oyster mushrooms fruiting out of the wooden sink cabinet in a restroom at the University of Hawai'i at Hilo.

edge of the mycelium. Fairy rings over 30 meters wide, which must be many years old, have been observed in pastures on the Kona side of the Big Island.

Most fungi produce spores of some type. A typical mushroom will drop millions of tiny spores that are then dispersed by wind, rain, insects, or other animals. If the conditions are right, the spores falling from the underside of a large mushroom or shelf fungus will appear like smoke swirling in the air currents. The students below are reacting to the cloud of spores released from a single mature puffball.

Fairy ring of *Chlorophyllum molybdites* in a pasture on the Big Island. The far side of the fairy ring is visible in the distance.

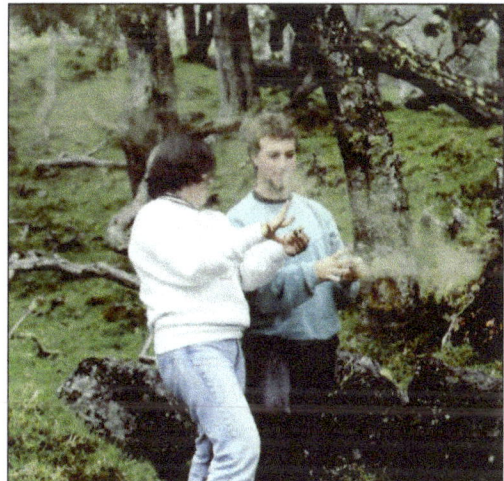

ORGANISMS CLASSICALLY STUDIED BY MYCOLOGISTS

PROTISTA

Protosteliomycota (Protostellads)

Amoebae form tiny fruiting bodies on dried leaves and twigs. Fruiting bodies usually consist of a stalk and single spore, about 10–40 micrometers tall.

Acrasiomycota and Dictyosteliomycota (Cellular Slime Molds)

Individual amoebae stream to form a pseudoplasmodium. Fruiting bodies consist of a tiny stalk and elevated spore mass, usually only one to two millimeters tall.

Myxomycota (Plasmodial Slime Molds)

A wet, glistening mass of cytoplasm (plasmodium) forms miniature sporangia, 3–7 millimeters tall, on logs and leaves.

Oomycota (Water Molds)

Microscopic fungi that live in ponds, lakes, streams, and damp soil. Many are plant pathogens; some are fish pathogens.

TRUE FUNGI

Chytridiomycota (Chytrids)

Microscopic fungi that live in ponds, lakes, and streams. Saprophytic on plant debris, especially pollen grains.

Zygomycota (Zygote Fungi)

Microscopic terrestrial fungi. Common food contaminants because of wind-blown spores. Produce ornate sexual spores called zygospores.

Ascomycota (Cup Fungi)

Large group of fungi that produce asexual spores called conidia. Sexual spores (ascospores) borne in asci in cup- or flask-shaped fruiting bodies. Includes yeasts and members that cause plant diseases such as ergot and powdery mildew. Large edible species include morels and truffles.

Basidiomycota (Club Fungi)

Sexual spores (basidiospores) borne on a club-shaped basidium. This group produces a variety of fruiting bodies known as mushrooms, toadstools, earthstars, stinkhorns, bird's-nest fungi, and others. Some fruiting bodies are edible; others are hallucinogenic or poisonous. Plant pathogenic species are rusts and smuts.

For more details, see these mycology textbooks: Alexopoulos, Mims, and Blackwell, *Introductory Mycology*, 1996; Deacon, *Introduction to Modern Mycology*, 1997; Kendrick, *The Fifth Kingdom*, 1992; Moore-Landecker, *Fundamentals of the Fungi*, 1996; Webster, *Introduction to Fungi*, 1980; or a botany text such as Moore, Clark, and Vodopich, *Botany*, 1998; Raven, Evert, and Eichhorn, *Biology of Plants*, 1999.

HISTORY OF MYCOLOGY IN HAWAI'I

The earliest significant papers documenting fungi of the islands are those of Stevens (1925) and Parris (1940). Both of these papers dealt almost exclusively with plant pathogenic fungi. Recently, a number of plant pathogenic taxa have been added to these early lists by Raabe et al. (1981) and Farr et al. (1989). Gardner, at the University of Hawai'i at Manoa, continues to study the rust fungi of Hawai'i (Gardner, 1988, 1994, 1997; Gardner and Hodges,

1989). Reports on selected fungi imperfecti from Hawai'i are those of Anastasiou (1964), Goos (1970b, 1978, 1980), and Baker (1977), whereas Goos and Anderson (1972) documented the Meliolaceae (Pyrenomycetes) from the islands. Recently, the distribution and ecology of vesicular–arbuscular mycorrhizal fungi (Zygomycetes) in Hawai'i have been analyzed (Koske, 1988; Koske and Gemma, 1990; Gemma and Koske, 1990). Concerning nonpathogenic Basidiomycota, to date only selected groups of Gasteromycetes have received attention. Lloyd reported on a number of Hawaiian Gasteromycetes in his *Mycological Notes and Letters* (Lloyd, 1898–1919); and the occurrence and distribution of bird's-nest fungi (Nidulariales) (Brodie, 1972; Goos, 1977), earthstars (Smith and Ponce De Leon, 1982), and stinkhorns (Goos, 1970a; Dring et al., 1971) have also been documented. Studies are currently in progress concerning the presence of wood-rotting fungi (Aphyllophorales) (Gilbertson and Hemmes, 1997a; 1997b) and Xylariaceous fungi (Rogers, Ju, and Hemmes, 1992; Rogers, Ju, and Hemmes, 1997) in the various vegetation zones of Hawai'i.

Gladys Baker and Roger Goos served as mycologists at the University of Hawai'i at Manoa over the years. Dr. Baker was on the staff in Botany from 1962 to 1973 and published on a wide range of mycologial subjects from the distribution of fungi in Hawai'i (Baker, 1964) to fungi on leaves of native plants, which serve as a food source for native tree snails (Baker, Dunn, and Sakai, 1979). Dr. Goos served as a researcher and visiting colleague in the Department of Botany from 1969 to 1970 and specialized in the Meliolaceae (Goos, 1978; Goos and Anderson, 1972) and published on the phalloid fungi of Hawai'i (Goos, 1970; Dring, Meeker, and Goos, 1971). Dr. Goos also served as president of the Mycological Society of America in 1986. Together, Baker and Goos wrote about the endemism and evolution of Hawaiian fungi (Baker and Goos, 1972).

Because of limited collecting historically, only a few taxa of fleshy Basidiomycetes, like the Agaricales (agarics and boletes–mushrooms) have been reported in the literature. Prior to 1973, only 24 species of agarics had been reported from the Hawaiian Islands (Berkeley and Curtis, 1851; Curtis and Berkeley, 1862; Hennings, 1900; Cobb, 1906, 1908; Peck, 1907, Burt, 1923; Parris 1940; Arnold, 1944; USDA, 1960; Raabe and Trujillo, 1963; Chun, 1965; Hesler, 1969, Meredith, 1969). In 1973, Ueki (unpublished undergraduate honors thesis) and Ueki and Smith (1973) increased the total by an additional 44 species. Between 1973 and 1985 only three additional species of agarics were reported from the Hawaiian Islands (Singer, 1975, 1976; Redhead, 1979; Redhead and Ginns, 1980), while in 1985, Doyle (unpublished Masters thesis)

cited an additional 22 species as first reports. A number of these species were reported again by Raabe et al. (1981) and Farr et al. (1989). By 1990, fewer than 100 species of agarics and boletes had been reported from the islands.

In the 1990s a systematic survey of the mushrooms of Hawai'i was initiated by Desjardin and Hemmes with the support of the National Science Foundation (Grant #9300874). Final analysis of all specimens collected during the course of this project has not been finished, but to date 310 species of Agaricales representing 83 genera in 14 families have been recorded. Of these, 44 have so far been described as new to science, including two new genera (Desjardin and Baroni, 1991; Desjardin, Wong, and Hemmes, 1992; Horak and Desjardin, 1993; Desjardin, 1993; Miller, Hemmes, and Wong, 1996; Horak,

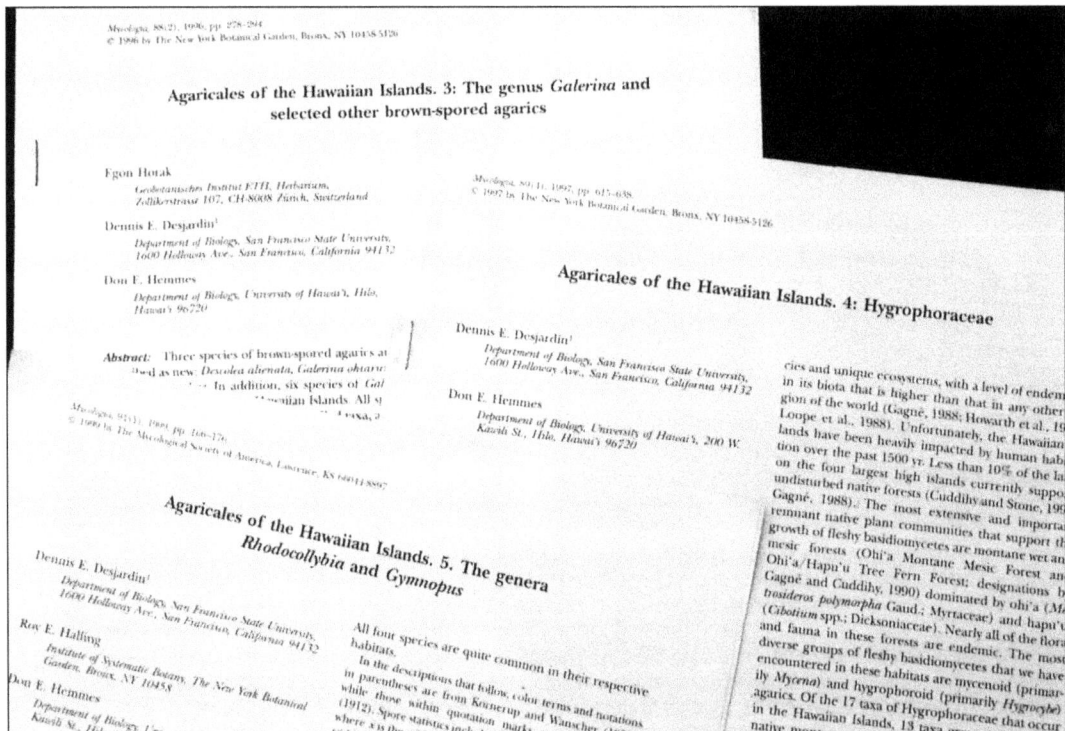

Recent scientific publications on mushrooms of Hawai'i.

Desjardin, and Hemmes, 1996; Desjardin and Hemmes, 1997; Desjardin, Halling, and Hemmes, 1999; Desjardin and Horak, 1999; Peterson, Desjardin and Hemmes, 2000; Desjardin and Hemmes, 2001). Two hundred ninety-one species (94%) represent saprotrophic organisms, whereas only 19 (6%) represent ectomycorrhizal taxa. The ectomycorrhizal taxa are all associated with alien trees. Two hundred fifty-eight taxa are putatively introduced species, whereas only 52 taxa (17%) are considered to represent native Hawaiian species. Of these 52 native species, however, 46 represent putative endemic species. That represents 88% endemism in native Agaricales, a level slightly less than that reported for vascular plants.

SEASONALITY OF HAWAIIAN MUSHROOMS

The subtropical environment of Hawai'i pales in the numbers and types of mushrooms found when compared to the tropical forests of Southeast Asia, the coniferous forests of the Pacific Northwest, or the deciduous hardwood forests of the eastern United States. But there are a good number of mushroom species in the various vegetation zones of the islands, some alien and brought in with vegetation and soil from distant locations, others native. What Hawai'i lacks in diversity and abundance, it makes up for in beauty and uniqueness.

Mushrooms pop out of shaded wood-chip and compost piles from July through January when rain is plentiful and the temperatures are warm.

If you look hard, fungi can be found any time of the year in Hawai'i, especially on the rainy windward sides of the islands, with their prevalent trade winds and showers. If you roll a small log or rotting branch you are almost assured of finding several different types of wood-rotting fungi. Actual mushrooms are more difficult to find. It is not uncommon to hear avid hikers say, "Where do you find mushrooms in Hawai'i? I was out all day and didn't see one."

Our collecting over the past ten years indicates that there is a prime time to locate Hawaiian mushrooms. Both in alien habitats, such as wood-chip and compost piles, as well as in the native rainforests, mushrooms make their debut for the season around July and then increase in abundance and diversity all the way to December and January, when they hit their peak. In the new year, the number of mushrooms falls to a low level and then increases again in July.

Relative Abundance
1 = 1–4
2 = 5–9
3 = 10–24
4 = 25+
(Fruiting bodies per kilometer transect)

Relative Abundance of Selected Hawaiian Rainforest Mushrooms (1992–1995)

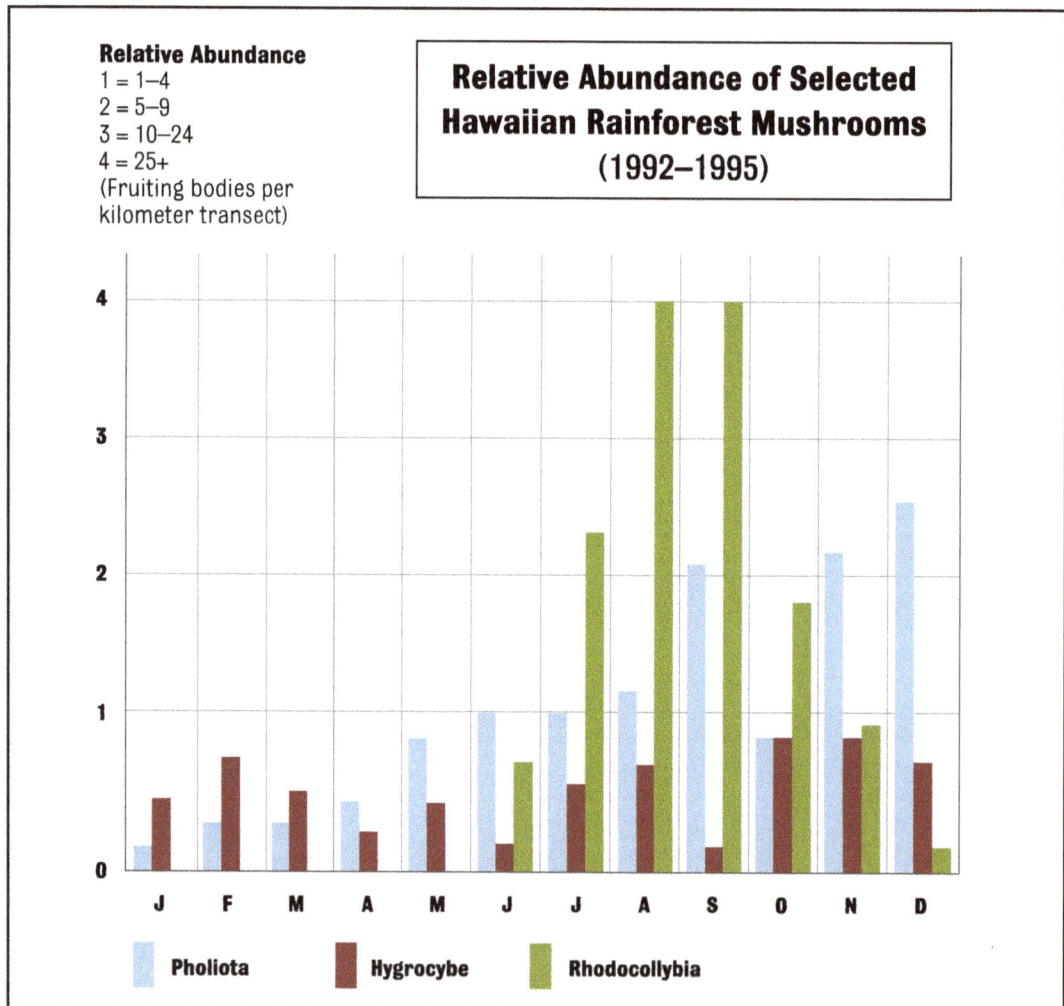

Legend: Pholiota, Hygrocybe, Rhodocollybia

This graph shows the relative abundance of native Hawaiian *Pholiota*, *Hygrocybe*, and *Rhodocollybia* species monthly over a three-year period in three different native forests on the Big Island.

The data on page 10 show that if you walk on paths through the native rainforest in Hawai'i from January through June, you might not see a single mushroom on a two-mile hike. The forest is always damp to dripping, so there seems to be plenty of moisture available for fungal growth. Fallen leaves, twigs, and tree-fern trunks are available substrate, but somehow the conditions are just not right for the production of fruitbodies.

Even in the best of conditions, the native mushrooms are relatively small, and few and far between, but they are often brightly pigmented and their contrasting colors should catch one's eye. On one or two of those special days in November or December, native mushrooms will be out in profusion.

On a two-mile hike in one of our study sites we might see over 100 solitary *Pholiota*, a half-dozen large clusters of *Rhodocollybia*, three or four different populations of *Hygrocybe*, and several species of *Entoloma*, *Mycena*, and *Marasmiellus* lining the senescent petioles of tree ferns.

COLLECTING SITES

Listed here are some of our favorite places on the various islands to find mushrooms and other types of fleshy fungi. Notice that these are forest areas within national and state parks, natural area reserves, and other protected habitats. *Collecting is not allowed without a permit.*

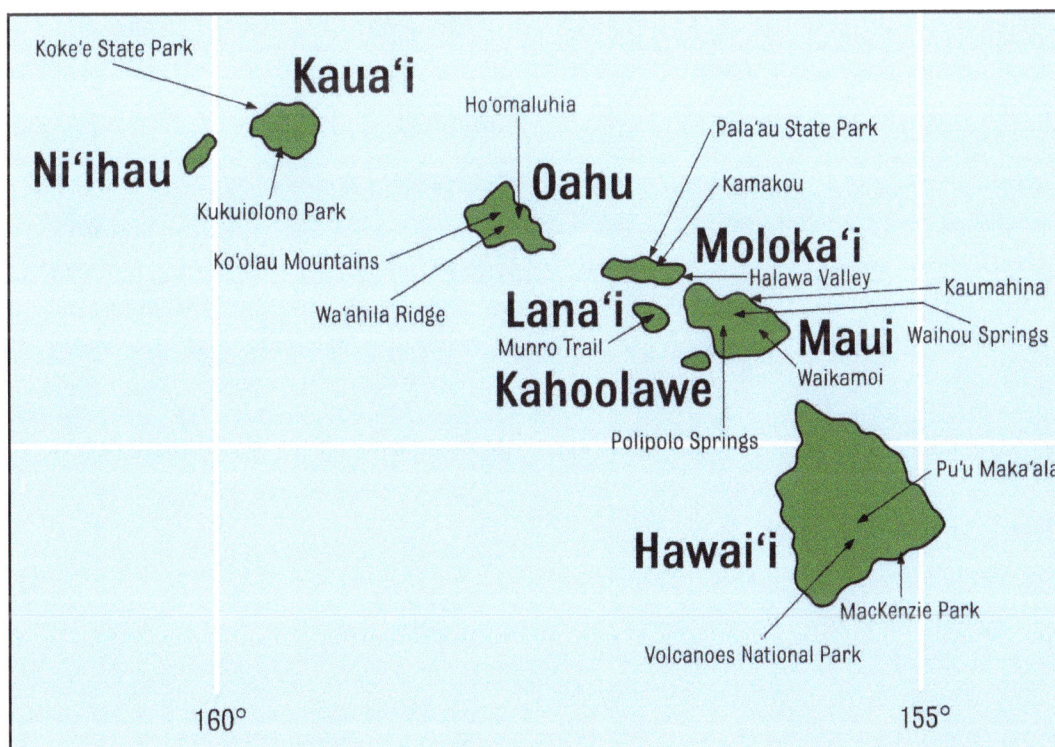

KAUA'I

Koke'e State Park

Koke'e State Park and the surrounding areas on the mountainous areas of western Kaua'i are covered with a mixture of native forests and trees alien to Hawai'i. You will find extensive *Eucalyptus* and pine plantings, Monterey cypress, redwoods, and Chinese fir. The native ohi'a and koa are intermixed with karakanut trees from New Zealand. These forests are criss-crossed with a number of excellent hiking trails where, from September through January, you can observe an extensive array of mushrooms from *Armillaria* to *Xylaria*. Look for the Starfish Stinkhorn *(Aseroe rubra)*, earthstars, and coral fungi. The lawns in the state park include *Agaricus* and *Lepiota*, while the pines support *Suillus* species and *Amanita muscaria*. The *Eucalyptus* groves feature *Pisolithus*, *Scleroderma,* and the deadly *Amanita marmorata*.

Kukuiolono Park

Kukuiolono Park near Kalaheo includes a short circular nature walk through a *Eucalyptus* grove. In the fall when the heavy rains soak this arid parcel, the ground will erupt with *Amanita marmorata*, a number of *Lepiota* species, *Pisolithus,* and many more interesting fungi.

O'AHU

Ho'omaluhia Botanical Garden

Ho'omaluhia Botanical Garden is the most extensive of several Honolulu Botanical Gardens managed by the City and County of Honolulu, located near Kaneohe on the windward side of O'ahu. The wood-chip and sawdust compost used around the trees and shrubs provides a wonderful substrate for *Coprinus, Lepiota,* and myriad other mushrooms in the shady, damp habitats. The stinkhorns *Aseroe rubra* and *Phallus rubicundus* will delight the keen observer.

Wa'ahila Ridge Park

Wa'ahila Ridge Park requires a curvy drive up St. Louis Heights in the Ko'olau Range above Honolulu, but the vistas of Manoa Valley and city below are worth the trip. A walk on the trails under the towering Norfolk Island Pines is often rewarded with *Lepiota, Agaricus,* and other mushrooms.

The Ko'olau Mountain Range

The Ko'olau Mountain Range is traced with many good hiking trails that begin in nearly every valley. These are great places to spy all types of interesting mushrooms and other fungi on O'ahu. (See one of the many guides to hiking trails of O'ahu for directions.)

MOLOKA'I

Pala'au State Park

Pala'au State Park in central Moloka'i, the site of the famous phallic rock and overlook of Kalaupapa, contains mature stands of *Casuarina* (ironwoods) and *Eucalyptus* that are kept damp by the prevailing tradewind showers. The *Casuarina* duff and fallen trees support the growth of bracket fungi and a variety of mushrooms.

Kamakou Forest Preserve

Kamakou Forest Preserve requires a four-wheel drive vehicle and special permission from the Nature Conservancy for access. Many alien mushrooms typical of *Eucalyptus* and coniferous forests can be found along the road through Kamakou. The brightly colored

Hygrocybe so characteristic of the Hawaiian rainforests can be spotted in the native plant communities.

Halawa Valley

Halawa Valley is a huge valley facing the tradewinds on the eastern side of Moloka'i. The trail to the falls at the back of Halawa passes through some private property, so inquiries should be made about the accessibility of the trail. The trees are typical of the alien, wet, windward forests of Hawai'i and include monkey pod, mango, and kukui nut with an understory of noni, guava, and other alien species. Jelly fungi, bracket fungi, and a host of wood-rotting fungi are easily spotted in these wet, shady habitats.

MAUI

Polipoli Springs State Recreation Area

Polipoli Springs State Recreation Area, on the slopes of Haleakala above Kula, features a large coniferous reserve including a variety of pines, Monterey cypress, and redwoods. During the wet winter months the pine needles are carpeted with *Mycena*, while *Suillus, Leucopaxillus,* and other conifer-associated mushrooms abound. Polipoli probably has the largest population of morel mushrooms of any place in Hawai'i—unfortunately still not a very abundant crop.

Waihou Springs State Recreation Area

Waihou Springs State Recreation Area, just above Makawao, also features alien trees including *Eucalyptus,* pines, Monterey cypress, tropical ash, and other plantings. During hikes on the lovely trails through the area a variety of mushrooms and other large fleshy fungi can be observed.

Waikamoi

Waikamoi, just below Haleakala National Park, is managed by the Nature Conservancy and features pine forests and other conifers near Hosmer's Grove, and native rainforests in the lower elevations. The Nature Conservancy offers hikes on the extensive trails in those areas where a good number of mushrooms and other fungi can be spotted and photographed.

Kaumahina Wayside Park

Kaumahina Wayside Park is one of many good mushroom hunting spots along the winding Hana highway. Steep trails pass through *Eucalyptus,* bamboo, and a variety of forest types where mushrooms and other fungi abound during wet periods.

LANA'I

The Munro Trail

The Munro Trail winds through extensive *Eucalyptus* groves in the mountainous region of the small island of Lana'i, just above Lana'i City. Look for *Amanita marmorata, Dermocybe clelandii,* and various species of *Scleroderma,* typical of *Eucalyptus* forests.

HAWAI'I (BIG ISLAND)

Hawai'i Volcanoes National Park

Hawai'i Volcanoes National Park offers numerous hiking trails through native ecosystems. One has a good chance to run into groupings of *Rhodocollybia laulaha* or one of the native *Hygrocybe* on the hapu'u tree ferns in the rainforest around Thurston Lava Tube or on the Crater Rim Trail that encircles Kilauea Crater. In Kipuka Puaulu (Bird Park) or Kipuka Ki, *Agrocybe parasitica* or clusters of *Coprinus truncorum* may be seen on manele trees, and huge conks of *Ganoderma australe* and *Laetiporus sulphureus* jut out from koa logs.

MacKenzie Park

MacKenzie Park, on the southeastern coast of the Big Island, provides a scenic view of the spectacular lava-cliff shoreline where waves crash and pound high in the air. The park is partly *Casuarina* (ironwood) forest and partly coconut grove, trees that cover the lava benches with deep duff and fronds, producing substrates ideal for fungal growth. Look for everything from the poisonous *Chlorophyllum molybdites* to the edible *Pulveroboletus xylophilus.* After a few days of good tradewind showers, the park can be covered with mushrooms of many types, including earthstars, puffballs, and netted stinkhorns.

Kahaualea and Pu'u Maka'ala Natural Area Reserves

Kahaualea and Pu'u Maka'ala Natural Area Reserves, both in the Volcano area of the Big Island, are native forests with extensive trail systems. Even though the native mushrooms of Hawai'i are fewer and smaller than the large ectomycorrhizal species found in coniferous and *Eucalyptus* forests, it is quite a thrill to see a pink *Hygrocybe noelokelani* or bright yellow *Hygrocybe lamalama* in all its glory on tree ferns in these native rainforests. Remember, you can only observe and photograph mushrooms in these native reserves: *A permit is required for any collecting.*

CHAPTER ONE

IDENTIFYING MUSHROOMS

A short course featuring the basic morphological characteristics of mushrooms will allow interested parties to identify the more common genera of mushrooms. An excellent identification guide is the series of manuals by Dr. David L. Largent and other authors on how to identify mushrooms to genus (Largent, 1986; Largent and Thiers, 1977; Largent, Johnson, and Watling, 1977; Largent and Baroni, 1988). For additional information, an extensive list of mushroom field guides from around the world, with keys and photos of the various genera, is provided in the bibliography. The next step, identifying the mushroom to species, requires more work. The following pages show how a mycologist goes about the identification process.

A collection of mushrooms for the day. How do you identify them?

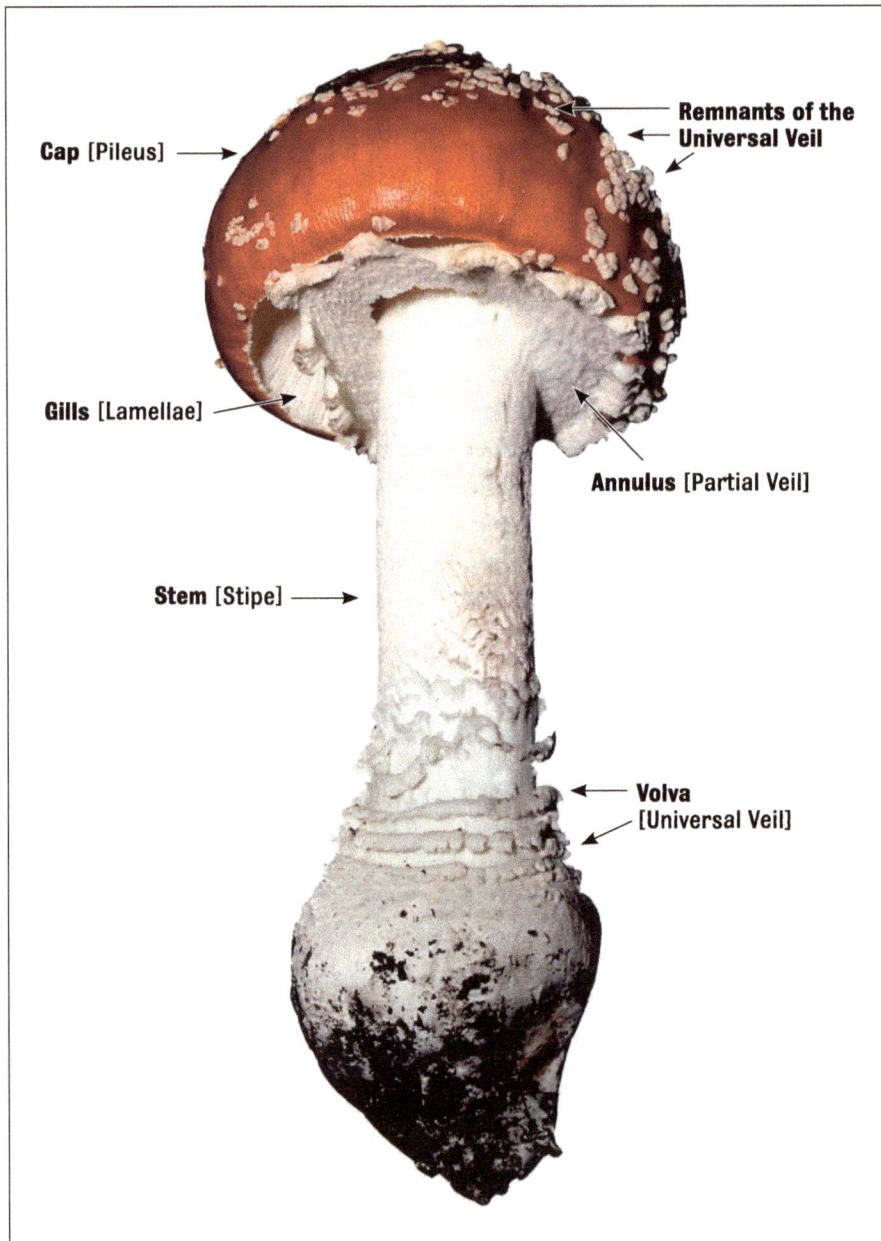

A photograph of *Amanita muscaria*, which displays many of the macroscopic characteristics that mycologists observe at first glance—the shape of the cap, presence of ornamentations or coloration on the cap, and the presence or absence of a volva and annulus. In most cases these macroscopic characteristics, plus the color and attachment of the gills, are enough for an experienced mycologist to determine the genus of the mushroom in question.

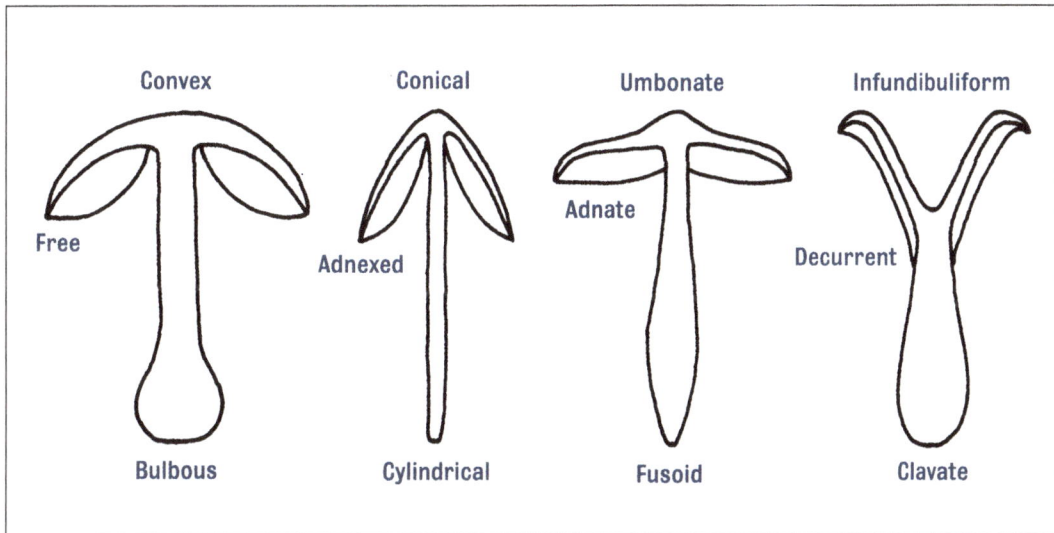

The basic shape of the cap and stem, and how the gills are attached to the stem, are important characteristics for genus/species determination. Above are just a few examples. A much more extensive list of cap and stem shapes and the various types of gill attachments can be found in the identification manuals by Largent and coworkers.

A color guide, such as the *Methuen Handbook of Colour* by Kornerup and Wanscher, is used to determine the precise color of the mushroom. Obviously, there are many shades of brown, from grayish brown to reddish brown, and yellow, from reddish yellow to golden yellow. Each color has a code and name such as "6B5, grayish orange," so that the investigator can come back to that exact color when making a species determination.

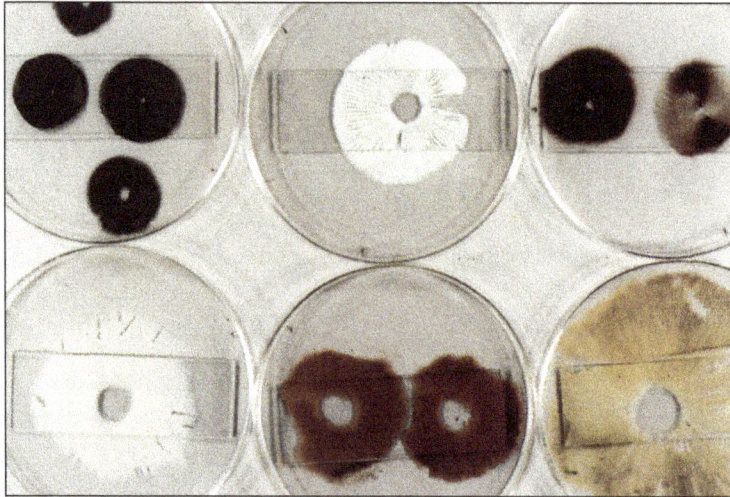

A spore print is made on white paper or on a glass slide. The cap of a fresh mushroom is cut off and placed over the slide and allowed to sit for several hours or overnight. "What color is the spore print?" is often the first question on an identification key. Common spore print colors are white, yellow, pink, black, and various shades of brown. Spores on glass slides can be examined easily with the microscope to determine spore size, shape, and ornamentation.

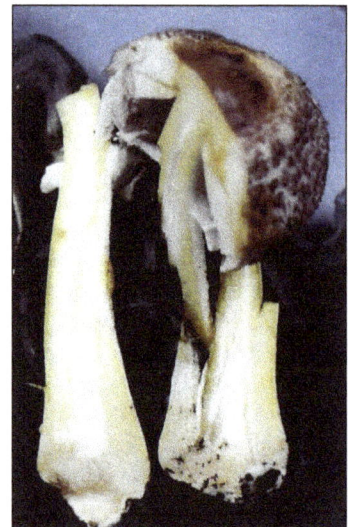

Staining reactions are also important in species determination. The surface of the cap or base of the stalk may bruise yellow or brown upon touch. The gills of *Lepiota besseyi,* above left, turn orangish-red upon contact. Other mushrooms turn color when a 3% potassium hydroxide (KOH) solution is added. Drops of the KOH solution added to the outside and cut surfaces of *Agaricus* collections may stain yellow (as in *Agaricus subrufescens,* above right); in other genera tissues may stain green, red, brown, or black. The species can then be segregated into yellow-stainers, brown-stainers, and the like. Odor and taste are also important taxonomic characters. They can be sweet, spicy, pungent, like radishes (raphanoid) or fresh ground flour (farinaceous), like garlic (alliaceous), almonds, phenol, or bleach. It is important to smell and taste the specimen when it is young and fresh. When tasting a mushroom, place a small piece of cap tissue on the tip of your tongue, taste it, then spit all of it out and rinse your mouth with water. No harm will come from tasting a potentially poisonous mushroom as long as you do not swallow the tissue.

Species: _Hygrocybe noelokelani_   Collection Number: _DED 6035_

PILEUS: Size — 10–30 mm diam.

Shape (young & old) — Convex, soon broadly convex to plano-convex with a shallow central depression

Surface Features (young & old) — striate, glabrous, glutinous becoming viscid in age

Color: young — deep pink (9–12 A3–4) to pale red (7–8 A4) or with a slightly paler margin

old — fading to pale greyish pink or greyish red (8–9 B3–4) on the disc, to pink or pinkish white (7–8 A2) on margin

CONTEXT: Thickness in Pileus— 0.75–1.5 mm

Color in Pileus — watery-concolorous with pileus surface   Color in Stipe — white; hollow; no staining rxn's

LAMELLAE: Attachment — broadly arcuate or adnate to subdecurrent

Spacing — distant

Breadth — 2–3 mm   • edges subgelatinous, translucent

Lamellulae: number of series — 2–3   Intervenosity? none

Color: young — pale pinkish white (7–8 A2) to pink (9–10 A2)

old — same or slightly faded

STIPE: Size — 25–35 × 2–4 mm ; central or slightly eccentric

Shape — terete, ± equal, sometimes w/ a slightly enlarged base

Surface Features (young & old) — glabrous, covered w/ a thick layer of unpigmented glutin, becoming viscid in age

Color: at apex (young & old)— yellow overall when young (3–4 A5), apex fading in age to pale yellowish white (3–4 A2), base remaining

at base (young & old) — yellow in age.

Attachment to substrate — non-insititious   Rhizomorphs? none

Annulus or Cortina? — none

Volva? — none

ODOR: none   **TASTE:** none, not distinctive

HABIT and SUBSTRATE: Scattered among mosses (mainly R. hizogonium) on forest floor under ōhia.

HABITAT: Ōhia Montane Wet Forest dominated by ōhia (Metrosideros) and hapu'u (Cibotium).

LOCATION: Moloka'i, Kamakou Forest Preserve; Lat. 21°07'27.0"N, Lon. 156°55'05.1"W

DATE COLLECTED: 11 Jan. 1994   **COLLECTOR:** Desjardin & Hemmes

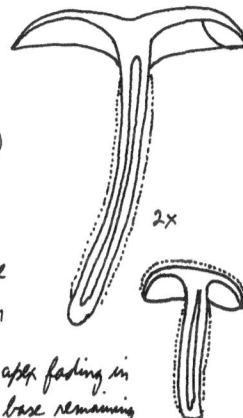

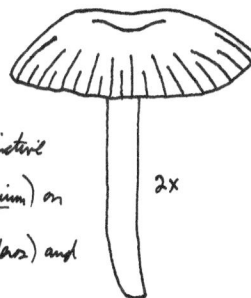

2x

2x

2x

Work sheets are used to record the measurements, colors, and other macroscopic characteristics of fresh specimens. Dates, locations, and habitats are recorded. If you have a good collecting day, you must quit quite early in the afternoon or you will be working into the wee hours of the night recording the data. After recording the data, dry the mushrooms overnight on a fruit drier and temporarily store in sealable plastic bags.

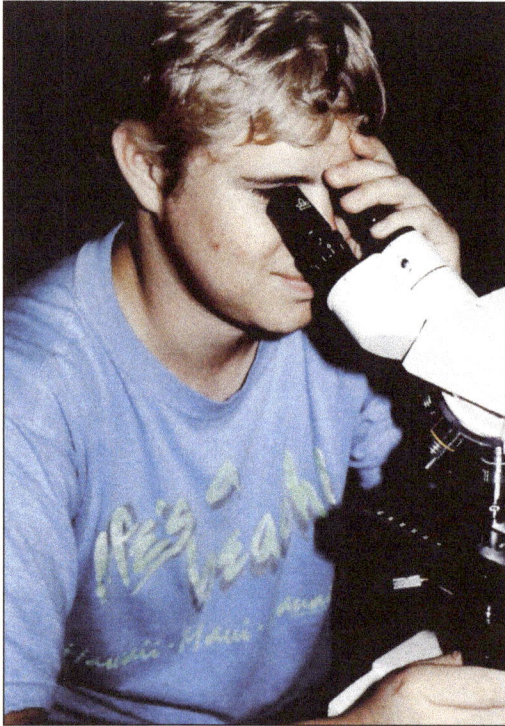

The microscope work is done later, back in the laboratory. The dried specimens are rehydrated and all tissues are examined and analyzed. Special attention is given to the arrangement and type of cells that form the cap, gills, and stem surfaces; to sterile cells called *cystidia;* to fertile cells called *basidia;* and to the spores. The shape, size, ornamentation, and pigmentation of each of these cell types is recorded. Without the microscopic data, definitive species diagnosis is often impossible.

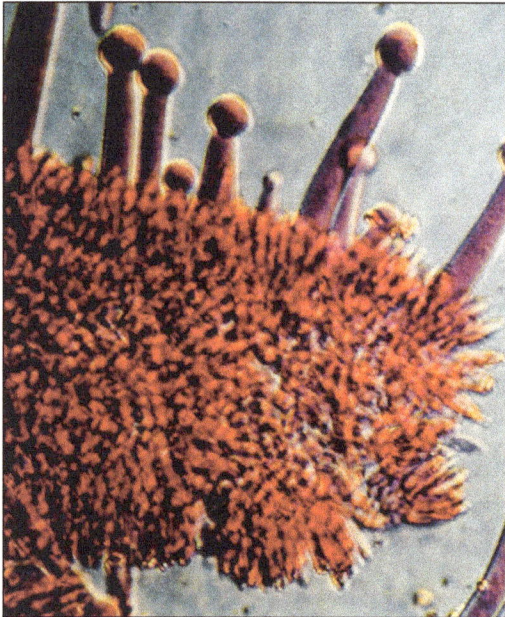

Cystidia on *Gloiocephala epiphylla.*

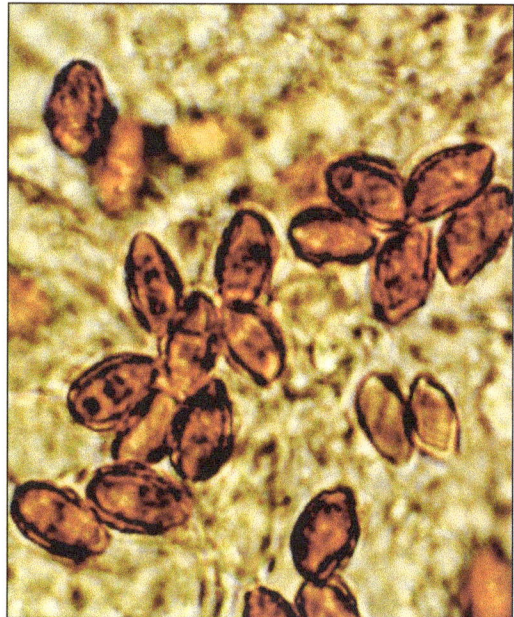

Ornamented spores of *Galerina velutipes.*

CHAPTER TWO

MUSHROOMS IN HAWAIIAN VEGETATION ZONES

The Hawaiian archipelago is the largest and most isolated oceanic island group in the world. Located between 18° and 22° North latitude in the central Pacific Ocean, the islands are more than 4,000 km from the nearest continent and about 3,200 km from the nearest high-island group. They are volcanic in origin, with the oldest of the main islands, Kaua'i, being about 5.6 million years in age, and the youngest and still volcanically active Hawai'i being about 0.1 to 0.5 million years in age (MacDonald and Abbott, 1979; Carlquist, 1980). Because of their isolated nature and relatively recent volcanic origin, the Hawaiian Islands are excellent natural laboratories of considerable interest to scientists investigating biodiversity, biogeography, species dispersal mechanisms, and evolutionary processes. On these islands there has evolved a spectacular array of species and unique ecosystems, with a level of endemism in its biota that is higher than that in any other region of the world. The influences of geology, climate, evolutionary processes, and human activities have resulted in a diverse array of habitats that support the growth of fleshy fungi. For more information on Hawai'i's natural history, vegetation, and conservation biology see Carlquist (1980), Cuddihy and Stone (1990), Gagne and Cuddihy (1990), Stone and Scott (1985), Stone and Stone (1989), Wagner and Funk (1995), and Wagner, Herbst, and Somer (1990).

The bulk of this field guide is dedicated to documenting the more common species of fleshy fungi that can be observed in easily recognizable and readily accessible habitats. Undoubtedly more mushroom species occur in these habitats than those included in this field guide, but we have tried to include those species that are most frequently encountered in each habitat. In the descriptions that follow, each species is identified by its scientific Latin or Greek name. You will immediately notice that we do not use many common names. This is because there are no common names for most tropical species, and also because some common names apply to more than one species of mushroom and are therefore potentially confusing. However, a few common names for fungi and trees have been used, and we provide an annotated list of these at the back of this book. In the species descriptions each scientific name is followed by abbreviations of the name of the mycologist who first formally described the species or who transferred it to its currently accepted genus (i.e., the authorities). Standardized abbreviations for authorities are those of Kirk and Ansell (1992). Scientific terms are used in the descriptions and some Hawaiian terms are used in the commentaries. Separate glossaries for these terms are also provided. We have included data on the edibility of each species, and we report on which islands they have been collected. Island abbreviations are as follows: HA, Hawai'i; KA, Kaua'i; LA, Lana'i;

MA, Maui; MO, Moloka'i; OA, O'ahu. Some species of Hawaiian mushrooms occur commonly in more than one habitat. We have included their descriptions with the habitat in which they are most frequently encountered, and we have added a cross-reference to additional habitats at the end of each chapter. For example, *Gymnopilus subtropicus* typically grows in wet windward alien forests, but may occur occasionally in flowerpots, in coastal *Casuarina,* and in *Eucalyptus* forests. At the end of each of the latter chapters there is a thumbnail photo and a directive to proceed to the chapter on wet windward alien forests to find a description and commentary.

A view of the Alaka'i Swamp area (foreground) and Waimea Canyon from the Mohihi Waialae Trail, Koke'e, Kaua'i.

LAWNS

In Hawai'i, lawns around homes, schools, and parks support a characteristic group of mushrooms and puffballs. The early morning jogger is certainly familiar with mushrooms peeking through the dew-covered grass along jogging paths, and golfers will spot mushrooms along fairways, or even sometimes on greens, in the early morning light. Some of the larger lawn mushrooms, the deadly Marbled Amanita (*A. marmorata*), and the viscid-capped Slippery Jack *(Suillus brevipes)* are actually associated with landscaping trees but are mentioned here because they frequently appear on nearby lawns.

Although not considered a lawn species, the poisonous *Amanita marmorata* subsp. *myrtacearum* occurs frequently in lawns in association with *Eucalyptus* and *Melaleuca* trees, as shown here on Hawai'i Community College campus in Hilo.

Conocybe lactea (J. E. Lange) Métrod

Cap 10–25 mm broad, rounded-conical to bell-shaped, glabrous, often radially wrinkled, not hygrophanous, whitish cream, often with a pale ochraceous center, becoming grayish white when wet. Gills adnexed, becoming free, crowded, narrow, cinnamon. Stem 70–100 x 1–2 mm, equal above a bulbous base, fragile, minutely pruinose-striate, white. Spore deposit rusty brown. Edibility: edible but not recommended.

Conocybe lactea, the Cone Head or Dunce Cap mushroom, with its distinctive conical, light-tan colored cap and cinnamon-colored gills is commonly seen on lawns in the early morning after warm, damp evenings. When the sun first peeks out, the fragile fruiting bodies dehydrate and collapse. Is: HA, KA, MO, OA.

The conical cap and cinnamon-colored gills are characteristic of *Conocybe*.

Leucocoprinus fragillissimus (Ravenel) Pat.

Cap 20–40 mm broad, at first conical to bell-shaped but soon plane, radially pleated, surface covered with yellow powder when young, glabrous in age, pale lemon yellow overall when young, becoming white with a yellow center in age; flesh very thin, delicate, translucent. Gills free, close, narrow, white. Stem 50–100 mm, cylindrical with an enlarged base, fragile, powdery, pale yellow, with a membranous annulus near the apex that becomes free and movable in age. Spore deposit white. Edibility: unknown.

A cluster of *Leucocoprinus fragillissimus* on the lawn at the University of Hawai'i at Hilo campus.

One surely needs to get up early on wet, drizzly mornings to see these delicate agarics. Any hard rain shreds the caps and direct sun will dry them up in minutes. Fruiting bodies on lawns are pure white with only a hint of yellow in the center of the cap. Those individuals found in the deep shade are usually pale yellow. As the name implies, these mushrooms are fragile and difficult to collect without having them stick together and collapse in your hands. Is: HA, OA.

Coprinus plicatilis (Fr.) Fr.

Cap 5–15 mm broad, convex but soon becoming plane with a depressed disc, radially pleated, glabrous, at first ochraceous to tawny, becoming grayish white to gray with a rusty or cinnamon center; flesh very thin, translucent. Gills free, narrow, remote, attached to a thin collar of tissue at stem, gray to black. Stem 50–70 x 1–2 mm, equal, fragile, glabrous, white. Spore deposit black. Edibility: edible but why bother?

The adjectives delicate and beautiful certainly apply to the Japanese Parasol, *Coprinus plicatilis*. The dainty little fruiting bodies are often found on lawns in the early morning with the Dunce Caps, *Conocybe lactea*. This is another ephemeral species that quickly disappears with the first strong morning sunlight. Is: HA, KA.

The Japanese Parasol, *Coprinus plicatilis*, in a park in Hilo.

The Green-spored Parasol mushroom, *Chlorophyllum molybdites,* on a fairway of a Kona golf course.

Chlorophyllum molybdites (Meyer: Fr.) Massee

Cap 70–120 mm broad, at first hemispherical, becoming broadly convex then flattened in age. When young covered with a thin, smooth, brown to pinkish-tan skin that breaks up as the cap expands to form concentric brown scales on the disc; remainder of cap white. Gills free, crowded, broad, at first off-white but soon becoming grayish green. Stem 80–140 (–200) x 8–15 mm, cylindrical with a bulbous base, fibrous, white to pale grayish brown, with a large, membranous annulus near the apex that becomes free and movable in age; stem flesh staining red where bruised. Spore deposit olive to green. Edibility: poisonous.

The Green-spored Parasol grows on lawns after rains or heavy lawn watering. Look for them on golf courses, school yards, public parks, and pastures. The large cap size (as big as a salad plate) and the presence of brown scales on the cap (somewhat like corn flakes) are diagnostic characteristics. These large, elegant mushrooms have tempted a number of people to toss them in the pot for dinner. But watch out, this species is poisonous to most and sends a number of people to the emergency ward each year with acute gastrointestinal upsets (see section on Poisonous Mushrooms). This species looks very similar to the edible Shaggy Parasol, *Macrolepiota rachodes,* which does not occur in Hawai'i. The latter species differs from *Chlorophyllum* in having white instead of green gills and spores. For additional photos, see Pastures and Coastal *Casuarina.* Is: HA, KA, MA, OA.

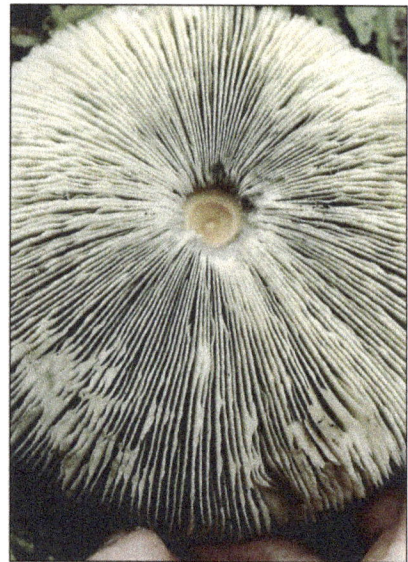

Look for the greenish gills and a green spore deposit to identify *Chlorophyllum.*

Lepista tarda Peck

Cap 30–90 mm broad, broadly convex becoming plane, with wavy and folded margin, glabrous, hygrophanous, violet to grayish purple, fading to purplish white; flesh thin (1–3 mm), purplish white. Gills adnate to subdecurrent, close, narrow, violet to purplish white. Stem 15–110 x 5–10 (–30) mm, cylindrical or with an enlarged base, twisted-fibrous, streaked, grayish purple. Spore deposit pale pinkish white. Edibility: edible and esculent.

Lepista tarda is very similar to *Lepista (Clitocybe) nuda*, the Blewit, a well-known and choice edible mushroom common to Europe and North America but unknown in

These purple fruiting bodies of *Lepista tarda* are fruiting on a fairway at the Volcano Golf Course on the Big Island.

Hawai‘i. *Lepista tarda* differs from the Blewit in forming more delicate, thin-fleshed caps, but like *L. nuda* is an excellent, tasty mushroom. This medium-sized mushroom is easily identified by its vivid purple color in young, moist specimens. Besides lawns, *L. tarda* is also found in banana patches, bamboo thickets, around compost piles, and in montane pastures. Is: HA, KA.

Agaricus comptuloides Murrill

Cap 30–55 mm broad, convex to broadly convex, dry, satiny, white on the margin with pale reddish brown to purplish brown, appressed fibrils in the center; flesh yellowing slightly where bruised; odor of almonds. Gills free, close, broad, pink when young, becoming dark brown in age. Stem 45–60 x 3–5 mm, cylindrical or gradually enlarged downward, satiny, white, with a white, membranous annulus near the apex. Spore deposit dark brown. Edibility: edible.

This small *Agaricus* species can be found in arcs and fairy rings snuggled in lawn grass. We have collected it on lawns at the University of Hawai‘i at Hilo and on the ground of the Iolani Palace in Honolulu. *Agaricus comtulus* is another edible, small white *Agaricus* with an almond odor that grows in lawns in Hawai‘i, but it differs from *A. comptuloides* in having a pure white cap, lacking reddish or purplish brown fibrils in the center. Is: HA, OA.

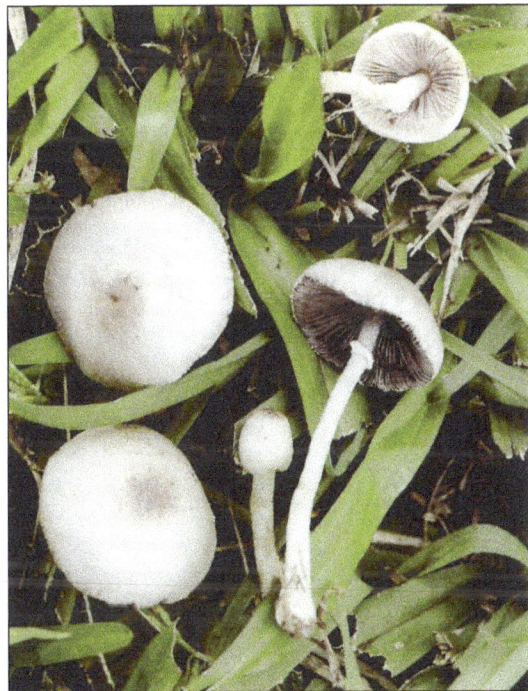

These specimens of *Agaricus comptuloides* were found on well-watered lawns at beach-side hotels on the Kona Coast of the Big Island.

Agrocybe retigera (Speg.) Singer

Cap 30–45 mm broad, convex or bell-shaped to broadly convex or plane, strongly rugulose to pitted-reticulate, glabrous, dry, ivory with a pale yellowish brown to yellow center or off-white overall. Gills adnexed, subdistant, broad, grayish orange becoming grayish brown in age. Stem 40–50 x 3–5 mm, gradually enlarged downward to a bulbous base, streaked, pubescent, off-white. Spore deposit grayish brown. Edibility: not recommended.

Agrocybe retigera is frequently found scattered on lawns during the summer months. This species can be recognized by it rugulose (wrinkled) cap, which is at first convex, but then planar at maturity. This species tastes bitter and is not good to eat. Is: HA, MA, OA.

Agrocybe retigera on a cemetery lawn near Paia, Maui.

Agrocybe pediades (Fr.) Fayod

Cap 15–30 mm broad, hemispherical to convex or broadly convex, smooth, glabrous, viscid when young, cream or yellow to pale yellowish brown overall. Gills adnate, subdistant, broad, dull brown (sepia) with pale edges. Stem 30–50 x 2–4 mm, cylindrical, dry, striate, pruinose, pale ochraceous to yellowish brown. Spore deposit brown. Edibility: not recommended.

Another little brown mushroom of lawns, *Agrocybe pediades,* has a convex cap that often becomes cracked with age. This species is smaller than *A. retigera* and lacks the rugulose–pitted cap surface. Although edible, we recommend against eating this mushroom because it can be confused with similar looking poisonous species. Compare with *A. semiorbicularis* in the chapter on pasture fungi. Is: HA, KA.

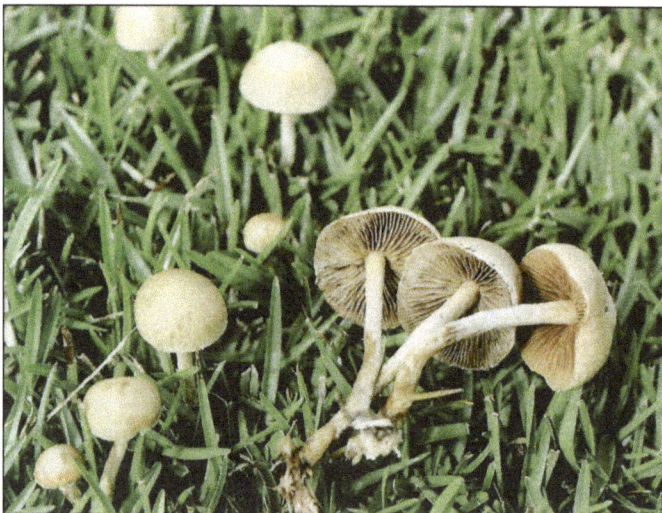

Agrocybe pediades from lawns at Koke'e State Park on Kaua'i.

Entoloma umbiliciforme Hesler

Cap 15–40 mm broad, convex with a depressed to umbilicate center, striate, dry, slightly scurfy and brown in the center, silky and orangish brown to pinkish tan on the margin. Gills adnexed to adnate, subdistant, broad, white with reddish brown edges when young, becoming pink to pale orangish brown in age. Stem 25–60 (–100) x 1–2 mm, cylindrical, apex pruinose, glabrous below, white to pale yellow or grayish yellow. Spore deposit pale pinkish brown. Edibility: unknown.

Entoloma umbiliciforme on lawns at the University of Hawai'i at Hilo.

This small, tan-colored *Entoloma* will be found scattered on lawns through Hilo during the hottest months of the summer. The spore print is pink. Is: HA.

Hygrocybe conicoides (P. D. Orton) P. D. Orton & Watling

Cap 10–15 mm broad, acutely conical, becoming broadly conical when expanded, glabrous, dry to greasy, yellow to reddish orange, blackening where bruised. Gills free, subdistant, broad, white to yellow with a hint of red, drying salmon. Stem 20–25 x 1.5–2 mm, cylindrical, dry, striate-fibrous, bright yellow to orangish yellow above a white base. Spore deposit white. Edibility: not recommended.

Macroscopically, *H. conicoides* looks much like its close relative *H. conica*, which also occurs in the Hawaiian Islands. The fruiting bodies of *H. conicoides* do not turn entirely black upon drying as do those of *H. conica*. *Hygrocybe conicoides* grows in lawns, whereas *H. conica* is found under pine and cypress trees. Both species form fruiting bodies that range from yellow to reddish orange. Is: HA, KA.

H. conicoides on a lawn at the Allerton Estate at Lawai, Kaua'i.

A gelatinous primordium of *Dictyophora cinnabarina* nestled in lawn grass (left) and cutaway view showing the stinkhorn primordium inside (right).

Dictyophora cinnabarina Lee

Unexpanded fruiting body ovoid, 25–35 mm broad, spiny, gray to grayish brown. Expanded fruiting body 70–140 mm tall. Head conical with an apical hole surrounded by a white ring, surface netted and covered by an olive brown, gelatinous spore mass (gleba). Stem 8–20 mm broad, cylindrical or narrowed upward, netted and perforate, white with cinnabar-orange tones. Indusium attached at base of cap, well-developed and pendulous, bright orangish pink. Volva gray to grayish brown. Odor strongly fetid. Spores olive brown. Edibility: edible when young and unexpanded.

This spectacular orange-netted stinkhorn springs up on lawns in Hilo during the rainy winter months. No one is sure why fruiting bodies appear on particular lawns each year and not on others. Perhaps the soil for the lawn comes from a certain location or fertilization with manure is essential for the growth of this fungus. The head and stalk of the stinkhorn grow out of an egg-like peridium consisting of a tough, outer skin and a gelatinous interior. The delicate orange veil or indusium is dropped from the base of the head. The greenish, slimy spore mass (gleba) covering the head is smelly and attracts flies and other insects to disseminate the spores. *Dictyophora cinnabarina* also appears in great clusters in wood-chip–manure compost at the University of Hawai'i at Hilo agriculture farm near Hilo. The bright orangish pink indusium in combination with a gray volva are characteristics that distinguish this beautiful *Dictyophora* from other species. Is: HA.

Dictyophora cinnabarina appears each year on lawns in the Hakalau District of Hilo on the Big Island.

Vascellum floridanum A. H. Smith

Fruiting body 10–25 (–35) mm broad, turbinate to pear-shaped with a sterile stem-like base; fertile portion white to dingy yellow and covered when young with small, white to brown granules and spines up to 1.5 mm long; these are easily washed off in age, leaving a smooth, yellowish brown peridium; opening by an irregularly split pore. Gleba initially white becoming olive-brown in age. Spores olive-brown. Edibility: edible when gleba is white.

The grass-loving puffball, *Vascellum floridanum,* on a lawn in Hilo.

When young, the clusters of fruiting bodies of *Vascellum floridanum* resemble marshmallows, soft and solid white within and covered with white to brown granules and tufted spines. With age, the spores mature to yellowish brown, the surface spines often wash off, and the spore sac eventually ruptures by a broad apical pore that releases spores in puffs as rain hits it or when it is squeezed or stepped on. *Vascellum floridanum* is similar to the common western North American species *V. lloydianum* (*Vascellum subpratense*), but differs in forming smaller fruiting bodies with ovoid spores and no pigmented capillitial hyphae. Is: HA.

Additional Species on Lawns

Amanita marmorata subsp. *myrtacearum*

Paperbark or bottlebrush trees, (*Melaleuca* spp.), and *Eucalyptus,* all introductions from Australia, are common landscaping trees on lawns, golf courses, and parks in Hawai'i. *Amanita marmorata,* a deadly poisonous mushroom, has accompanied these trees from Australia to Hawai'i. The hyphae of this fungus surround the root systems of these trees and produce crops of white mushrooms on lawns in the vicinity of these trees (see *Eucalyptus* Forests for full description).

Suillus brevipes

These large Slippery Jacks will be found on neighboring lawns where Monterey pines *(Pinus radiata)* are planted in the landscaping. This fungus is mycorrhizal and associated with the root systems of these trees (see Conifer Forests for full description).

Suillus salmonicolor

Another mycorrhizal species, *S. salmonicolor,* will be associated with slash pines *(Pinus elliottii)* when they are planted as landscaping trees at the edges of lawns (see Conifer Forests for full description).

COMPOST PILES AND WOOD CHIPS

Piles of wood chips, grass clippings, and other decaying vegetable matter produce a succession of mushrooms, especially when the composting material is in shady areas where it is cool and damp. *Coprinus, Agrocybe, Lepiota,* and *Agaricus* are common compost inhabitants.

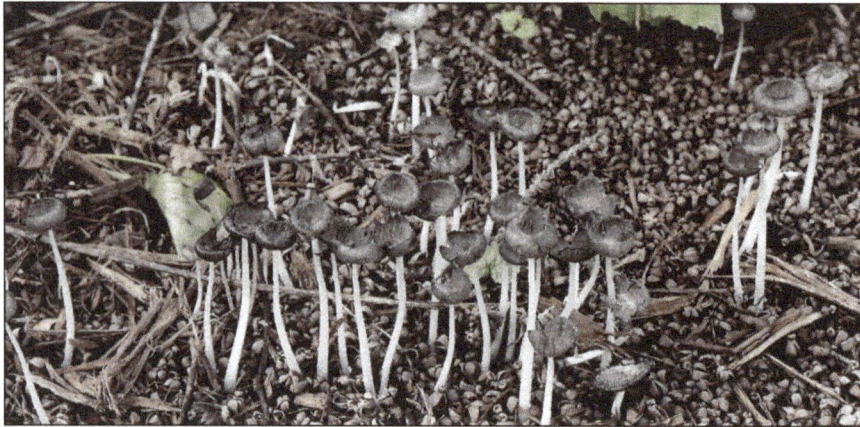

Coprinus lagopus, fruiting in wood chips at Ho'omaluhia Botanical Gardens on O'ahu. The thin caps are already rolling up and will soon deliquesce and wither away.

Coprinus lagopus (Fr.) Fr.

Cap 10–25 mm tall x 1–15 mm broad when young, ovoid and covered with white to grayish brown fibrillose-stringy scales, expanding at maturity to broadly conical then plane, striate, gray, glabrous or with grayish brown veil fibrils on the center. Gills free, crowded, white or gray then becoming black, quickly deliquescent. Stem 45–75 x 2–5 mm, gradually enlarged downward, not rooting, pubescent to fibrillose, white. Spore deposit black. Edibility: edible.

These caps of *Coprinus lagopus* show the short fibrillose-stringy scales typical of the species.

Coprinus lagopus appears on wood chip and compost piles as forests of delicate little mushrooms with gray fuzzy caps and white stems. *Coprinus lagopus* often grows together with *C. cinereus,* and can be distinguished from the latter species by having dark gray rather than white fibrillose scales on dried mature caps, by lacking a rooting stem base, and by having caps that deliquesce more slowly. Is: HA, OA.

Wooly Caps of *Coprinus cinereus* peeking out of wood-chip mulch in the late afternoon.

Fruiting bodies of *Coprinus cinereus* develop at night and must be collected early in the morning before they autodigest.

Coprinus cinereus (Schaeff.: Fr.) S. F. Gray

Cap 10–30 mm tall x 5–20 mm broad when young, elongate-conical to ovoid and covered with white floccose-fibrillose tufts of "hairs," expanding at maturity to obtusely conical to campanulate, 30–50 mm broad, glabrous and often devoid of veil hairs, striate, grayish brown to brown centrally, margin gray. Gills free, crowded, narrow, white or gray then becoming black, quickly deliquescent. Stem 50–150 x 3–4 mm (apex) x 5–10 mm (base), gradually enlarged downward, then tapered to a rooting base below ground, fibrillose, white. Spore deposit black. Edibility: edible.

Both common names Wooly Cap and Inky Cap apply to *Coprinus cinereus*. These mushrooms are usually spied the day before they fruit as hairy, wooly caps peeking out of compost or wood-chip piles. During the night or early morning, the stems elongate and the caps expand. Within hours, however, the caps roll back and deliquesce into black ink, leaving white stalks in the morning as the only evidence of their presence the night before. Although *C. cinereus* typically grows in dung, in Hawai'i the species is more commonly found in wood chips. The Hawaiian form with long rooting stem is also known as *Coprinus macrorhizus*. Is: HA, OA.

Caps of *Coprinus cinereus* deliquescing into "ink."

Coprinus curtus Kalchbr.

Cap 5–10 mm broad, obtusely conical to convex expanding to broadly convex with a flattened center, striate to radially pleated, covered with brown, powdery granules when young; white becoming grayish white in age but retaining the brown granules on the center. Gills free, close, narrow, white to gray becoming black in age. Stem 20–30 x 0.5–1 mm, cylindrical, fragile, glabrous, white. Growing in dense clusters. Spore deposit black. Edibility: unknown.

This *Coprinus* resembles *Coprinus disseminatus* in size, color, and clustering habit. Look for the brown granules at the apex of the cap to distinguish these two species. These delicate mushrooms quickly shrivel up and disappear in the early morning light. Is: HA.

A cluster of *Coprinus curtus* on wood chips at the Prince Kuhio Mall in Hilo. Note the brown granules at the center of the cap.

Agaricus subrufescens Peck

Cap 50–150 mm broad, at first cylindrical-convex, becoming convex to plane in age, dry, white with reddish brown flattened squamules especially on the disc; odor strongly of almonds. Gills free, close, broad, at first white to pink, becoming dark brown in age. Stem 60–150 x 15–25 mm, cylindrical or subbulbous, white, staining yellow where bruised; with a persistent, white, membranous annulus near the apex. Spore deposit dark brown. Edibility: edible and choice.

Agaricus subrufescens, the Almond Mushroom, has a strong odor and taste similar to almond extract. The cap is covered with fine reddish brown, flattened squamules, and the lower half of the stalk bruises yellow when touched. This species is edible and adds a wonderful flavor to pasta and other foods. It is widespread and also has been found under coastal *Casuarina* (ironwoods) and in ginger fields, but it is more commonly collected on compost piles. Is: HA.

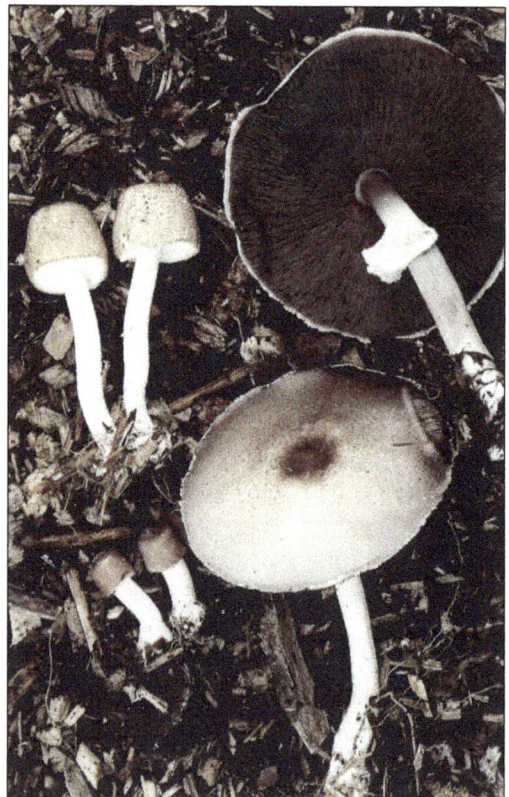

The marshmallow-shaped primordia and reddish brown disc on the cap, along with the strong almond odor, are identifying characteristics of *Agaricus subrufescens*.

Bolbitius coprophilus (Peck) Hongo

Cap 30–40 mm broad, conical or bell-shaped becoming plane in age; subviscid, hygrophanous, translucent-striate to the center, pinkish gray to grayish brown with pink tones, often with a darker center. Gills adnexed to free, close to crowded, narrow, at first yellowish brown, becoming reddish brown in age. Stem 70–100 x 3–5 mm, cylindrical or gradually enlarged downward, fragile, glabrous, striate, white with pink tones. Spore deposit reddish brown. Edibility: unknown.

Although *coprophilus* means "dung-loving," in Hawai'i this tall, fragile mushroom is one of the first to appear on wood-chip piles. At first conical and viscid, the mature cap loses its stickiness, quickly flattens, and becomes translucent-striate when moist. Is: HA, KA.

Bolbitius coprophilus growing in wood chips under coconut trees along the bay front in Hilo.

Leucoagaricus meleagris (Sowerby) Singer

Cap 60–80 mm broad, convex or bell-shaped, expanding to flattened bell-shaped; dry, white with small, cinnamon brown to dark brown scales concentrated on the center. Gills free, crowded, broad, white. Stem 70–120 x 8–15 mm, gradually enlarged downward to a subbulbous base, white with reddish brown squamules especially near the base; surface quickly staining orangish red where bruised; with a white, membranous evanescent annulus near the apex. Spore deposit white. Edibility: unknown.

Leucoagaricus meleagris is readily recognized by its habit of growing in large clusters on piles of wood chips and by the orange-red blushing at the base of the stalks when touched. The entire fruiting body turns rosy pink upon drying. The edibility of this species is unknown to us. Is: HA, OA.

A typical huge cluster of dozens of fruiting bodies of *Leucoagaricus meleagris* in wood-chip mulch on Coconut Island at Hilo Bay (left). See how the stems bruise a bright orange-red immediately after they are touched (right).

Notice the characteristic yellow disc at the center of the cap of these fruiting bodies of a *Leucoagaricus hortensis* that appeared in an organically grown herb garden in Hilo.

Leucoagaricus hortensis (Murrill) Pegler

Cap 40–60 mm broad, hemispherical expanding to plano-convex with a central umbo in age; dry, glabrous at first, outer surface breaking up into small flattened scales that are easily removed; margin striate under the scales, white with a yellow to pale yellowish brown center. Gills free, close, broad, white. Stem 40–60 x 4–8 mm, cylindrical with a small bulbous base, glabrous, fibrous, white to pale pinkish gray; surface quickly staining burgundy red where bruised; with a white, membranous, persistent annulus near the apex. Spore deposit white. Edibility: unknown.

The stalk of this compost-loving species, also listed in some field guides as *Lepiota humei* Murrill, bruises red upon contact and sometimes even bleeds red droplets when the stalk is broken. Little is known about its edibility, so it should be avoided. *L. hortensis* has also been spotted on fairways of golf courses on Maui and the Big Island. Is: HA, MA.

Stropharia variicolor in wood chips around the Prince Kuhio Mall in Hilo.

Stropharia variicolor Desjardin & Hemmes

Cap 50–90 mm broad, convex to broadly convex, becoming flattened in age; dry, glabrous, deep wine-red to dark reddish brown when young, changing to yellowish brown or tan in age, with white flocculose remnants of a partial veil on the margin when young. Gills adnate, close, broad, dingy buff to tan at first, becoming brown in age, lacking purple tones. Stem 50–80 x 8–14 mm, cylindrical, longitudinally grooved, flocculose, white becoming yellowish brown; base of stem with coarse white rhizomorphs; with a white, membranous, flocculose partial veil that ruptures upon cap expansion and remains as tatters on the cap margin. Odor and taste unpleasant. Spore deposit brown (Vandyke brown). Edibility: edible but not recommended.

Stropharia variicolor looks similar to *S. rugosoannulata,* a good edible and cultivated species native to North America. *Stropharia variicolor* differs, however, in lacking a persistent annulus, and in forming much smaller and differently pigmented spores and different cheilocystidia. This robust *Stropharia* grows in dense clusters in wood chips, binding the chips together with coarse white rhizomorphs. The cap is wine-red at first then fades to yellowish brown upon expansion. Local reports state that, although edible, this species tastes bad and is not recommended for eating. Is: HA.

Volvariella volvacea growing out of wood-chip mulch at Ho'omaluhia Botanical Garden on O'ahu.

Volvariella volvacea (Bull.: Fr.) Sing.

Fruiting bodies initially egg-shaped, 30–50 mm broad x 40–90 mm tall, dark gray or grayish brown to black on upper portion, white at the base; upon development forming a cap 70–120 (–160) mm broad, convex to obtusely conical at first, becoming plano-convex with a central umbo, dry, radially fibrillose, center and fibrils dark gray to black, paler towards the white margin. Gills free, close, broad, white becoming pinkish brown. Stem 80–145 x 10–15 mm, equal or gradually enlarged towards the bulbous base, silky-striate, white; volva sacklike, gray and white. Spore deposit pinkish brown. Edibility: edible and choice.

This large *Volvariella* species is the well-known Paddy Straw Mushroom, a species cultured in rice straw in the Philippines and Southeast Asia and included as an ingredient in many Asian soups. *Volvariella volvacea* favors wood chips and sugar cane bagasse piles and is collected by local field workers and prized in ethnic dishes (see section on edible mushrooms). This species is known in Hawai'i as the Bagasse Mushroom. The primordium stage, which is the favored stage to collect for the table, is nearly indistinguishable from the primordium stage of the potentially deadly *Amanita marmorata*. Both species may co-occur in horticultural areas where the myrtaceous tree associates of *A. marmorata* grow. A word of caution: Do not eat primordia collected near *Eucalyptus* or *Melaleuca* trees. Is: HA, KA, OA.

Agrocybe aff. *procera* Singer

Cap 25–60 (–80) mm broad, convex to obtusely conical to broadly bell-shaped, eventually plano-umbonate; dry, glabrous, brownish-yellow overall when young, center remaining brownish yellow in age, margin becoming cream to pale yellowish-white. Gills adnexed, close, broad, ivory when young, becoming grayish brown to brown at maturity. Stem 65–125 x 5–8 mm, cylindrical with a clavate base (up to 18 mm broad), glabrous, slightly striate, satiny, white. Spore deposit dull brown to pale reddish brown. Edibility: unknown.

Agrocybe aff. *procera* grows in wood chips, such as this mulch under swings at a children's play school in Hilo.

The overall look of this species suggests it belongs in *Conocybe* or *Psathyrella*; however, the spore print is dull brown to pale reddish brown, not bright rusty brown or black. Although we are unable to identify this species with certainty, it is very similar to *Agrocybe procera*, described from Chile. It is distinctive in forming two-spored basidia, large vesiculose hymenial cystidia, large spores, and no caulocystidia. Troops of this tall *Agrocybe* frequent wood-chip mulches in parking lots of shopping centers and around playground equipment in parks. Is: HA, OA.

Hypholoma fasciculare (Huds.: Fr.) Kummer

Cap 20–50 mm broad, convex to bell-shaped, sometimes umbonate, dry, glabrous, orange centrally and sulfur yellow towards the margin. Gills covered at first by a pale yellow cobwebby partial veil, adnate, close, broad, greenish yellow becoming grayish green. Stem 40–60 x 2–4 mm, cylindrical, fibrillose, sulfur yellow. Spore deposit reddish brown. Edibility: poisonous.

Hypholoma fasciculare in a wood-chip pile near Haleakala National Park on Maui.

Look for the distinctive greenish yellow gills on the yellow-capped *Hypholoma*. This species usually grows in large clusters on wood chips and buried wood, and is a poisonous species. Is: MA.

Pseudocolus fusiformis (Fischer) Lloyd

Fruiting bodies initially subglobose, 10–25 mm broad, white, opening along three sutures, developing into three distinct erect arms that arise from a short stem; base of "egg" attached to white, cordlike rhizomorphs. Arms 15–45 mm long, fusiform, wrinkled and pitted, united at their tips, apex orange to pale orange, base white. Gleba lining upper portion of arms, gelatinous, grayish green. Stem 10–25 x 10–20 mm, cylindrical, hollow, pitted, white. Volva sacklike, white to gray. Odor strongly fetid. Spores grayish green. Edibility: edible.

Pseudocolus fusiformis growing in wood-chip mulch at the College of Agriculture farm near Hilo on the Big Island.

Also known as *P. schellenbergiae* and *Anthurus javanicus*, this three-armed stinkhorn appears solitary or in large clusters in wood-chip mulch during wet periods. The three arms usually remain attached. The odor given off by fruiting bodies is wretched, much like fresh pig manure! Is: HA, OA.

Phallus rubicundus (Bosc.) Fr.

Fruiting bodies initially egg-shaped, 15–30 x 10–15 mm, white, base attached to white, cordlike rhizomorphs. Head 15–30 mm tall x 10–15 mm broad, conical to fusiform, wrinkled to longitudinally ridged, apex truncate, pink to red. Gleba covering the head, gelatinous, dark grayish olive. Stem 50–150 x 8–15 mm, cylindrical or gradually enlarged downward, hollow, wrinkled to pitted, pink to salmon at the apex grading to white at the base. Volva sacklike, white. Odor strongly fetid. Spores grayish olive. Edibility: poisonous.

The detachable, conical head at the apex places this slender stinkhorn in the genus *Phallus*. This species is found in wood-chip mulch and well-manured soil in gardens and on farms. The peridia, or "eggs," of most stinkhorns, such as P. *rubicundus*, will mature overnight in the laboratory if covered with a beaker or jar and kept moist and humid. This species is reported to be poisonous. Is: HA, OA.

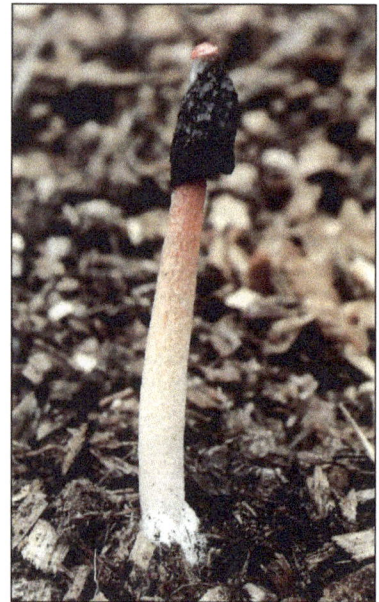

Phallus rubicundus in a garden in Manoa Valley on O'ahu (above), and fruiting in a bowl in the laboratory (left).

A cluster of *Mutinus bambusinus* growing out of wood-chip mulch at the University of Hawai'i at Hilo (left). Close-up (right) showing clear demarcation line between red and pinkish color zones.

Mutinus bambusinus (Zoll.) E. Fisch.

Fruiting bodies initially egg-shaped, 15–30 x 10–20 mm, white, base attached to a white, cordlike rhizomorph. Stem 70–100 x 10–15 mm, hollow, upper half wrinkled, tapered to a narrow apex, reddish orange to deep red; lower half densely pitted, cylindrical, white. Gleba covering the upper red portion, gelatinous, olive green. Volva sacklike, white. Odor strongly fetid. Spores olive green. Edibility: unknown.

The upper half of the thin stalk of *Mutinus bambusinus* is dark red (after the gleba is washed off), whereas the lower half is white. The demarcation line between the colors is abrupt and clear. *M. bambusinus* frequents wood-chip mulch and rotten stumps. Is: HA.

Mutinus elegans (Mont.) E. Fisch.

Fruiting bodies initially egg-shaped, 20–30 x 10–20 mm, white. Stem 10–150 x 15–20 mm, hollow, strongly wrinkled overall, cylindrical below, gradually tapered to a narrow apex, upper half bright red to reddish orange, grading into pinkish white below. Gleba covering the upper third, gelatinous, greenish brown. Volva sacklike, white. Odor strongly fetid. Spores greenish brown. Edibility: unknown.

Mutinus elegans, known as the Headless Stinkhorn, is similar in size and shape to *Mutinus bambusinus,* shown above, except that there is no distinct color demarcation between the upper and lower parts of the stem; instead the entire stem shows red pigments. The species is commonly found in garden and farm areas enriched with manure. Is: HA.

Flies are attracted to these fruiting bodies of *M. elegans* appearing on a farm at Laupahoehoe on the Big Island.

Cyathus pallidus
Berk. & M. A. Curtis

Fruiting bodies crucible-shaped, 5–7 mm tall and broad, exterior covered with pale buff or straw-colored hairs, interior glabrous, smooth, white to silvery. Operculum white with straw-colored hairs. Peridioles silvery gray, attached by a thin cord. Edibility: unknown.

The Bird's-nest Fungus, *Cyathus pallidus*, grows on fallen twigs in the forest, but is most commonly seen where it appears in huge clusters on wood-chip mulches. The tiny "nests" (peridia) have lids that pop off to reveal egglike peridioles, small cases that contain spores. Raindrops splash the peridioles into the surrounding substrate. Is: HA, KA, OA.

The Bird's-nest Fungus, *Cyathus pallidus*, covering the wood-chip mulch at the Prince Kuhio Mall in Hilo.

Peziza arvernensis Boud.

Fruiting bodies cup-shaped, 50–70 mm broad, irregularly wavy, brittle, thin-fleshed; interior smooth, chestnut brown; exterior finely hairy to glabrous, slightly paler. Edibility: unknown.

This large, chestnut brown Discomycete appears on wood-chip piles found in shady, damp locations. The spore-forming surface, called the *hymenium*, covers the interior of the cup. If you breathe on the hymenium of fresh specimens, the resulting change in temperature and humidity will stimulate the spores to be forcibly discharged and you will see a cloud of spores released. Is: HA, OA.

Peziza arvernensis on wood chips at the Ho'omaluhia Botanical Gardens on O'ahu.

Additional Species on Compost Piles and Wood Chips

Agaricus rotalis

This species develops in large clusters in wood-chip piles. The caps of the young fruiting bodies are black, resembling charcoal briquets. The black cuticle breaks up in a radial fashion as the cap expands, giving a pinwheel appearance (see Coastal *Casuarina* for a full description).

Gymnopus menehune

This small *Gymnopus* appears in fairy rings in wood-chip compost. It is easily recognized by its small size and the indentation at the top of the cap (see Coastal *Casuarina* for full description).

Gymnopus luxurians

Look for the longitudinal grooves and swollen base on the stem of this *Gymnopus*. It grows in clusters rather than fairy rings (see Coastal *Casuarina* for full description).

Dictyophora cinnabarina

Hundreds of fruiting bodies of this Netted Stinkhorn appear in wood-chip compost at the University of Hawai'i at Hilo agriculture farm during prolonged rainy periods (see Lawns for full description).

Lepiota besseyi

All parts of this mushroom, especially the gills, will blush pinkish-orange immediately upon contact (see Coastal *Casuarina* for full description).

Leucocoprinus birnbaumii

This bright-yellow agaric is commonly observed in the potting soil of flowerpots, but it will appear in great numbers in composting wood chips (see Flowerpots for full description).

Lepista tarda

This strikingly lavender mushroom will also appear in large clusters in wood-chip piles. It is a deliciously edible species. (See Lawns for full description.)

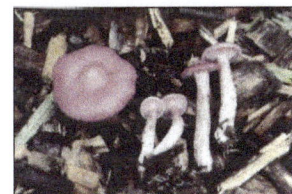

FLOWERPOTS

Backyard gardeners and plant nursery workers in Hawai'i are familiar with crops of mushrooms popping up with their potted plants. Mushrooms have even been seen fruiting inside bags of potting media before they are opened.

Note the lilac-colored granules near the center of the cap of these fruiting bodies of *L. lilacinogranulosus*.

Leucocoprinus lilacinogranulosus (Henn.) Locq.

Cap 20–50 mm broad, conical expanding to plano-umbonate, margin striate to pleated, center covered with lilac-brown granules, margin white with scattered lilac granules. Gills free, close, narrow, white. Stem 30–50 x 2–4 mm, cylindrical with an enlarged base, granulose to glabrous. White with a pink tone; with a delicate, membranous white annulus near the apex. Spore deposit white. Edibility: unknown.

A delicate *Leucocoprinus* that frequents nursery pots, *L. lilacinogranulosus* is white with powdery lilac granules scattered on the surface of the cap. This species also appears in wood-chip mulch at Lili'uokalani Park in Hilo. Is: HA.

The Flowerpot Parasol, *Leucocoprinus birnbaumii*, makes a lovely addition to this hanging basket.

Leucocoprinus birnbaumii (Corda) Singer

Cap 30–50 mm broad, bell-shaped to rounded-conical, expanding to plano-umbonate, covered with sulfur yellow powder, margin striate and splitting, sulfur-yellow overall. Gills free, close, broad, yellow. Stem 30–50 x 3–4 mm, cylindrical above an enlarged base, powdery and yellow overall; with a small, membranous, yellow annulus near the apex. Spore deposit white. Edibility: poisonous.

The dainty Yellow Parasol or Flowerpot Parasol, also known as *Leucocoprinus luteus*, commonly appears in nursery pots where it may outshine its orchid or house plant partner in elegance and beauty. Unfortunately, the fruiting bodies only last for a day or less and rapidly wither with bright sunlight. This species also appears on lawns and in compost under trees in shady locations. It could cause gastrointestinal upsets and should not be eaten. House pets have been known to be poisoned from ingesting *L. birnbaumii*. Is: HA, KA.

Conocybe fragilis
(Peck) Singer

Cap 8–15 mm broad, obtusely conical expanding to bell-shaped, short-striate, dry, hygrophanous, dark reddish brown to chestnut brown when moist, fading to light brown or pinkish brown with moisture loss. Gills narrowly adnate, close, narrow, edges fimbriate, cinnamon brown. Stem 30–50 x 1 mm, cylindrical, glabrous to pruinose, same color as cap. Spore deposit cinnamon brown. Edibility: unknown.

Dozens of fruiting bodies of *C. fragilis*, with their conical caps and cinnamon-colored gills, are common companions of germinating seeds in shade house nurseries. Is: HA.

A stand of *Conocybe fragilis* in a nursery pot with germinating cycad seeds.

Conocybe aff. hadrocystis
(Kits van Wav.) Watling

Cap 15–30 mm broad, convex to obtusely conical, expanding to plano-umbonate, wrinkled, short-striate, dry, hygrophanous, brown with a yellowish brown margin, fading to ochraceous buff with a darker center with moisture loss. Gills narrowly adnate, close, broad, brown to rusty brown. Stem 50–60 x 3–4 mm, cylindrical or slightly enlarged at the base, glabrous, ochraceous to brown, with a pale yellowish white, cufflike annulus in the center. Spore deposit rusty brown. Edibility: unknown.

This *Conocybe* grows in nursery pots imported from the mainland and demonstrates how fungi are being imported to Hawai'i almost on a daily basis. The Hawaiian species shows a close affinity (aff.) to *Conocybe hadrocystis* but differs in forming larger spores with a distinct germ pore. *Conocybe* aff. *hadrocystis* differs from *C. fragilis* (above) in forming larger fruiting bodies with a well-developed annulus on the stem, and in forming different-shaped cystidia on the gills and stem. Is: HA.

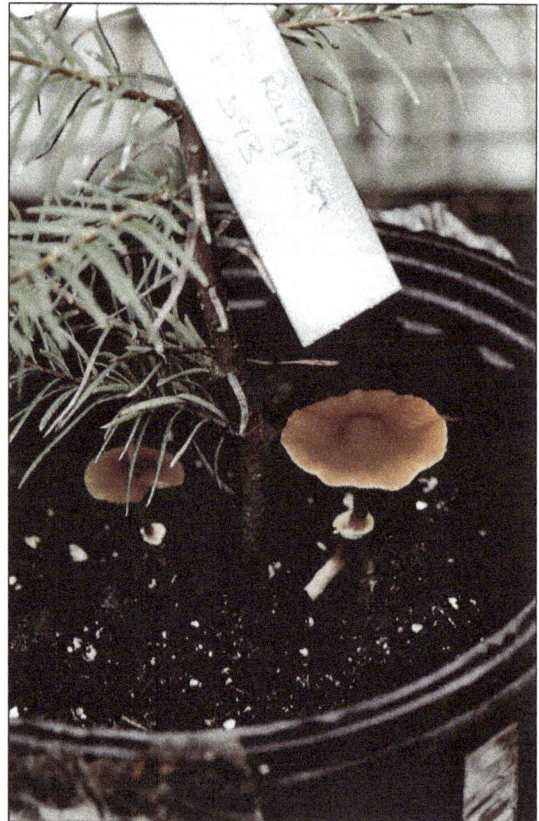

Conocybe aff. *hadrocystis* growing in a nursery pot with an imported conifer.

Hygrocybe mexicana forma *defibulata* **Desjardin & Hemmes**

Cap 5–10 mm broad, convex becoming plano-convex with a central depression, striate, moist to dry, deep red fading to pink. Gills adnate, distant, broad, pinkish white when young, orangish red to red in age. Stem 4–10 x 0.5–1 mm, cylindrical, glabrous, dry, deep red. Spore deposit white. Edibility: unknown.

Even though tiny, the bright-red fruiting bodies of *H. mexicana* are easily spotted against the dark green background of mosses in shady areas. This species also loves flowerpots and planters, especially those kept damp and laden with moss. Hundreds of fruiting bodies were seen peeking out from under bark mulch in planters at the University of Hawai'i at Hilo student center. *Hygrocybe mexicana* forma *defibulata* differs from the typical form that occurs in Mexico and the Caribbean region in lacking clamp connections and in forming primarily bisporic basidia. Is: HA.

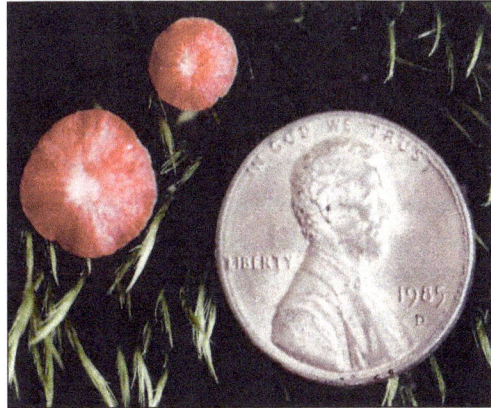

Although less than the size of a penny, this *Hygrocybe* is easily spotted in nursery pots because of its bright red color.

Additional Species in Flowerpots

Galerina velutipes

Clusters of this medium-sized *Galerina*, with a tiny point in the middle of the translucent cap, frequently sprout up in nursery pots and crowd their green plant partners (see Wet Windward Alien Forests for full description).

Gymnopilus subtropicus

This distinctly orangish mushroom with a bright orange spore print is also a common inhabitant of nursery pots (see Wet Windward Alien Forests for full description).

Cyathus pallidus

These tiny Bird's-nest Fungi love the ground-up bark usually found in nursery pots (see Compost Piles and Wood Chips for full description).

PASTURES

The extensive high mountain cattle ranches that encircle Mauna Kea and Kohala Mountain on the Big Island and flank Haleakala on Maui support luxurious pasture grass during rainy seasons and a variety of mushrooms. Look in tall clumps of grass for coprophilous species of *Panaeolus, Stropharia,* and *Psilocybe* growing directly in "cow pies." *Agaricus* and *Lepiota* are found in open areas. The hallucinogenic Magic Mushroom *(Copelandia cyanescans)* is found in lowland and coastal pastures and paddocks throughout the islands.

The vast pasture lands of Parker Ranch that surround Mauna Kea support a variety of grass-decomposing and coprophilous mushrooms.

Agaricus campestris L.: Fr.

Cap 50–100 mm broad, convex becoming plano-convex in age; dry, glabrous or minutely scaly on the margin, white; flesh white and unchanging when bruised; odor mild (not of almond nor of phenol). Gills free, close, broad, pink when young, becoming blackish brown in age. Stem 20–100 x 10–15 mm, cylindrical or narrowed downward, glabrous above and slightly scaly below, white; with a white, membranous, flaring annulus above the middle of the stem. Spore deposit dark brown. Edibility: edible and choice.

The meadow mushroom, *Agaricus campestris*, fruits in pastures on the slopes of Mauna Kea. It is a choice edible species.

Most mushroom connoisseurs would agree that wild meadow mushrooms are much more flavorful than their commercially grown relatives sold in grocery stores. Look for *A. campestris* year round in pastures a few days after rainy periods. *Agaricus campestris* differs from other grassland *Agaricus* species in lacking yellow or red staining reactions and in lacking either an almond or phenolic odor and taste. Is: HA, MA.

Leucoagaricus leucothites (Vittad.) Wasser

Cap 60–120 mm broad, hemispherical to convex, expanding to broadly convex or plane with a broad umbo, dry, glabrous, white. Gills free, close, broad, white, and remaining so in age. Stem 60–120 x 10–15 mm, cylindrical above a club-shaped or bulbous base, glabrous, white; with a white, membranous annulus near the apex that may fall off in age. Spore deposit white. Edibility: poisonous.

Leucoagaricus leucothites is a common resident of pastures on the slopes of Haleakala on Maui and around Waikii and Kohala on the Big Island.

This large, pure-white *Leucoagaricus* is common in pastures on the slopes of Haleakala on Maui and Mauna Kea on the Big Island. It also appears on lawns and along the edges of the roads at Koke'e State Park on Kaua'i. This species is likely to cause stomach upsets and should not be collected for food. Be careful when collecting large white "meadow mushrooms" for the table. *Leucoagaricus leucothites* looks very similar to some good edible *Agaricus* species, differing mainly in forming white gills and spores when mature instead of pink to brown gills and brown spores as in *Agaricus*. This species is known as *Leucoagaricus naucinus* in most other field guides. Is: HA, KA, MA.

Magic Mushrooms, *Copelandia cyanescens,* in cow manure at Maluhia, Maui.

Copelandia cyanescens (Berk. & Bromme) Sacc.

Cap 20–40 mm broad, convex to bell-shaped, dry to moist, pale brownish gray when young, fading in age to off-white with yellowish brown or grayish brown tones in the center. Gills adnexed, close, narrow, mottled grayish black. Stem 80–100 x 2–3 mm, cylindrical, fragile, fibrillose, gray to yellowish gray, bruising bluish where handled. Spore deposit black. Edibility: strongly hallucinogenic.

A coprophilous (dung-loving) and strongly hallucinogenic species, *Copelandia cyanescens* is widely known in Hawai'i as the Magic Mushroom. Clusters of fruiting bodies with light-gray caps can be found in tall clumps of grass in pastures where a "cow pie" has been deposited. This species bruises blue within minutes of handling, evidence of the hallucinogenic drug inside (see section on Hallucinogenic Mushrooms). *Copelandia cyanescens,* also known as *Panaeolus cyanescens* (but not *Psilocybe cyanescens,* which is a different species altogether), is nearly indistinguishable from three other grassland and dung-loving *Copelandia* species known to occur in the Hawaiian Islands. Is: HA, KA, MA, MO, OA.

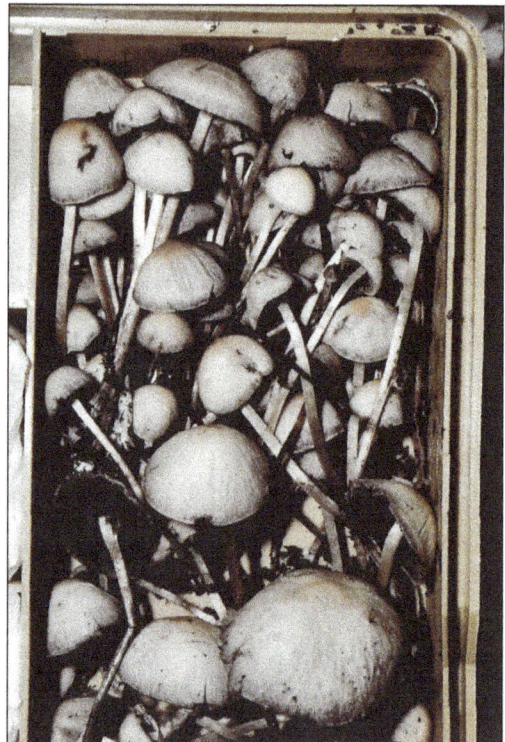

A collector's box of Magic Mushrooms picked fresh from cow dung after rainy days.

Panaeolus papilionaceus (Bull: Fr.) Quél.

Cap 20–30 mm broad, convex to bell-shaped, dry, glabrous, often wrinkled, grayish brown to grayish cinnamon or grayish cream with a white fringe (from partial veil) on the margin. Gills adnexed, close, narrow, mottled grayish black. Stem 60–100 x 2–3 mm, cylindrical, fibrous, pruinose, grayish brown; partial veil not remaining as an annulus. Spore deposit black. Edibility: not recommended.

Panaeolus papilionaceus (also known as *P. campanulatus* and *P. sphinctrinus*) has tall, gray, thin-stalked fruiting bodies that grow directly in dung in pastures. The cap is gray when growing in the shade, but will become brown or bronzed in direct sun. This species does not bruise blue and is not hallucinogenic. Is: HA, KA, MA, MO, OA.

Note the tattered veil remnants at the edge of the cap of these specimens of *Panaeolus papilionaceus* growing in dung in a pasture on Mauna Kea.

Panaeolus antillarum (Fr.) Dennis

Cap 40–50 mm broad, hemispherical to broadly convex, dry, glabrous, white overall, sometimes becoming silvery gray and cracked when sun dried. Gills adnexed, close, broad, mottled grayish black. Stem 70–100 x 3–6 mm, cylindrical or enlarged downward, solid, pruinose, longitudinally striate at the apex, white. Spore deposit black. Edibility: edible but not recommended because of toxic and hallucinogenic mimics.

Panaeolus antillarum, also known as *Anellaria phalaenarum* and *A. sepulcralis,* is a tall, white to silvery gray-capped species that grows in clusters of a half dozen or more

This large *Panaeolus* is a common dung-inhabiting mushroom at the University of Hawai'i at Hilo's Panaewa agriculture farm and in pastures around Hilo.

fruiting bodies in well-rotted cow or horse manure. It is distinguished from other black-spored dung inhabitors by its pure white cap, more robust and solid white stem that does not stain blue when bruised, and the absence of a partial veil. Also, look for distinct, fine lines or grooves (striae) on the apex of the stalk. Is: HA, MA.

PASTURES

Panaeolus subbalteatus
Berk. & Broome

Cap 30–40 mm broad, convex expanding to
broadly convex, moist to dry, hygrophanous,
glabrous, sometimes centrally wrinkled,
cinnamon brown in the center, surrounded
by a grayish buff or tan zone and a ring of
brown to dark brown at the margin. Gills
adnexed, close, broad, mottled grayish black
with white edges. Stem 40–60 x 2–3 mm,
cylindrical, twisted-fibrous, grayish brown to
pinkish brown beneath white fibrils; no partial veil. Spore deposit black. Edibility: poisonous when raw, mildly hallucinogenic.

Panaeolus subbalteatus growing in cow dung—enriched soil.
Notice the characteristic band of dark brown at the cap margin.

Another coprophilus species, *Panaeolus
subbalteatus* grows directly in dung or
in the surrounding grass. This species is
reported to have minimal hallucinogenic properties. Is: HA, MA.

Panaeolus semiovatus (Fr.) Lundell

Cap 20–40 mm broad, parabolic to obtusely conical, subviscid, glabrous, wrinkled, cinnamon buff when young,
fading in age to white. Gills adnexed, close, broad, mottled
grayish black with white edges. Stem 60–100 x 4–7 mm,
cylindrical above a subbulbous base, solid, fibrous,
pruinose, white to cinnamon buff; with a persistent,
membranous, white, flaring annulus near the apex. Spore
deposit black. Edibility: edible but not recommended
because of toxic and hallucinogenic mimics.

The ringed *Panaeolus*, with its distinct annulus,
grows out of cow and horse dung in pastures at
high elevations. This species is not hallucinogenic
and most reports list it as edible. Is: HA.

These specimens of *Panaeolus semiovatus* are growing in
horse dung near the Humuhula sheep station in the Saddle
area between Mauna Kea and Mauna Loa on the Big Island.

Psilocybe semiglobata (Batsch.: Fr.) Noordel.

Cap 20–50 mm broad, hemispherical to convex expanding to broadly convex, viscid, glabrous, yellow to straw-colored or ochraceous. Gills adnate, close, broad, purplish black. Stem 50–80 x 4–8 mm, cylindrical above a slightly enlarged base, dry and white above, viscid and yellow below, with a viscid, fibrillose partial veil that remains as an annulus or only a zone of fibrils near stem apex, often blackened by spores. Spore deposit dark purplish brown. Edibility: edible.

Psilocybe semiglobata in cow dung at Parker Ranch on the Big Island. This is easily the most commonly seen coprophilous mushroom in the high mountain pastures in Hawai'i.

This yellow-capped *Psilocybe*, also known as *Stropharia semiglobata*, is one of the more common dung inhabiting mushrooms in high mountain pastures, along with *Panaeolus*. As the name implies, the caps are strikingly hemispherical and are viscid and slimy when wet. Some consider *Psilocybe semiglobata* to be edible but of poor quality. It should be noted that not all *Psilocybe* species contain hallucinogenic compounds, including this species. Is: HA.

Psilocybe coprophila (Bull.: Fr.) Kummer

Cap 10–25 mm broad, convex to obtusely conical, hygrophanous, glabrous, viscid, translucent-striate, brown to reddish brown when moist, fading to brownish tan with moisture loss. Gills adnate, subdistant, broad, brown, mottled at first. Stem 30–50 x 2–4 mm, cylindrical or narrowed downward, dry, pale brown above, reddish brown below, with white fibrils; no partial veil. Spore deposit dark purplish brown. Edibility: edible but not recommended because of toxic and hallucinogenic mimics.

The reddish brown cap helps distinguish *Psilocybe coprophila* from other black-spored mushrooms growing directly in dung.

Psilocybe coprophila is also found growing in high-elevation pastures throughout Hawai'i. Ten to fifteen fruiting bodies per "cow pie" are common. At first reddish brown with translucent radial striations, the caps fade to a lighter tan color with moisture loss. This species of *Psilocybe* does not contain hallucinogenic compounds. Is: HA, KA, MA.

Bolbitius variicolor G. F. Atk.

Cap 30–40 mm broad, conical to bell-shaped, becoming flattened in age, viscid, glabrous, often strongly wrinkled or pitted in the center, yellow to olive yellow becoming gray in age. Gills adnexed to adnate, moderately broad, yellowish brown to cinnamon. Stem 60–80 x 3–4 mm, cylindrical, fragile, dry, minutely floccose, yellow above, white at the base. Spore deposit rusty brown. Edibility: edible.

Bolbitius variicolor is another dung-loving agaric. It differs subtly from the more common grassland species *B. vitellinus*, in having a more olive yellow instead of bright lemon yellow cap that is often strongly wrinkled or pitted, and in having slightly larger spores. *Bolbitius variicolor* is considered by some as merely a variety of *B. vitellinus*. Is: HA.

Bolbitius variicolor fruiting near dung in pastures on Mauna Kea.

Coprinus cothurnatus Godey apud Gillet

Cap at first 10–20 mm tall x 5–10 mm broad, ovoid, white and covered with white to grayish brown fluffy granules, expanding to obtusely conical or bell-shaped in age, 10–30 mm broad, striate, gray with clay-colored to pinkish brown veil granules remaining on the center. Gills free, crowded, narrow, white becoming black and deliquescent. Stem 50–130 x 2–5 mm, cylindrical or enlarged downward, fragile, white, covered with white to clay-colored fluffy granules. Spore deposit black. Edibility: unknown.

Coprinus cothurnatus grows directly in cow dung and first appears as an ovoid, fluffy-granulose primordium that quickly expands into a tall mushroom with a gray cap and white stem. The cap quickly deliquesces (self-digests) and the mushroom withers away, often during the same day as it appears. This beautiful *Coprinus* is distinguished from other species by the clay-colored to pinkish brown veil granules on the cap and stem at maturity, and by producing very large, mitriform (shield-shaped) spores. Is: HA.

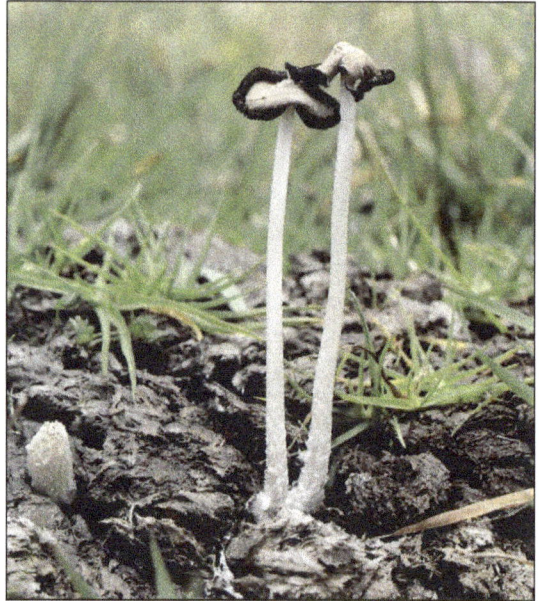

Coprinus cothurnatus fruiting in cow manure in Parker Ranch pastures on Mauna Kea.

The plaques of a universal veil are readily apparent on these specimens of *Coprinus picaceus* growing in cow dung in a pasture near Hilo Medical Center.

Coprinus aff. *picaceus* (Bull.: Fr.) S. F. Gray

Cap 30–40 mm tall x 20–30 mm broad at maturity, at first elongate-ovoid, expanding to obtusely conical, brown to dark grayish brown covered with large, white to pale brown plaquelike scales. Gills free, crowded, moderately broad, white becoming black and slowly deliquescent. Stem 35–60 x 3–5 mm, gradually enlarged downward to a subbulbous base, fibrillose, white. Spore deposit black. Edibility: possibly poisonous.

This relatively large *Coprinus* is readily identified by its habit of growing directly in dung and exhibiting large plaques of universal veil material on the cap, even on mature specimens. It shows close affinities to *C. picaceus*, a species that grows in Europe and is primarily associated with beech forests. The Hawaiian species differs from *C. picaceus* in forming smaller fruiting bodies with mitriform spores and no clamp connections, and in growing directly from dung. *Coprinus picaceus* has been reported as poisonous. Is: HA.

Coprinus stercoreus Fr.

Cap 5–10 mm broad at maturity, at first ovoid, expanding to broadly convex, margin striate and splitting along the striate in age and becoming uplifted, white to gray and covered with white, powdery to wooly veil particles. Gills free, close, narrow, white but soon black and slowly deliquescent. Stem 6–20 x 0.5–1 mm, cylindrical, fragile, granulose, white to gray. Spore deposit black. Edibility: unknown.

This tiny *Coprinus* is common on cow dung found in pine groves and other shady locations in pastures. The cap is ovoid and covered with wooly powder at first; it then expands into delicate, little umbrellas only 10 mm wide. Is: HA.

This primordium of *Coprinus stercoreus* is only 2 mm tall.

Conocybe rickenii
(Jul. Schaff.) Kühner

Cap 10–25 mm broad, ovoid to obtusely conical, dry, glabrous, orangish brown, fading slightly with moisture loss. Gills narrowly adnate, close, broad, cream to cinnamon. Stem 60–80 x 1–2 mm, cylindrical, pruinose, orangish brown. Spore deposit cinnamon to rusty brown. Edibility: unknown.

Look for the orangish color, conical cap, and thin fragile stem of this dung-loving *Conocybe*. The spore print will be a cinnamon-brown color. *Conocybe rickenii* differs from other coprophilous *Conocybe* in forming two-spored basidia, very large spores, and in lacking lecythiform caulocystidia. Is: HA.

Conocybe rickenii in cow manure in Parker Ranch pastures flanking Mauna Kea on the Big Island.

Agrocybe semiorbicularis
(Bull. ex. St.-Amans) Fayod

Cap 20–50 mm broad, hemispherical expanding to broadly convex, glabrous, viscid when wet but soon becoming dry, orangish brown fading to cream. Gills adnate, subdistant, broad, grayish brown to brown (sepia). Stem 30–50 x 2–5 mm, cylindrical, tough, glabrous, dry, yellowish cream. Spore deposit brown. Edibility: not recommended because of toxic and hallucinogenic mimics.

Yet another dung-loving mushroom is *Agrocybe semiorbicularis*. This species usually grows directly in dung, but also may appear in grass surrounding cow droppings. The cap and stem are orangish brown

A cluster of *Agrocybe semiorbicularis* from the Parker Ranch cattle pastures on Mauna Kea.

and there is no annulus on the stem. Under the microscope the spores are very large and formed on two-spored basidia, and the sterile cells on the edge of the gills (cheilocystidia) are capitate. *Agrocybe semiorbicularis* is difficult to distinguish from *A. pediades* in the field. In Hawai'i, *A. pediades* grows typically on lawns, not in dung, has much smaller spores formed on four-spored basidia, and has noncapitate cheilocystidia. See the chapter on lawn fungi for a description and photo. Is: HA.

Calvatia gigantea (Pers.) Lloyd

Fruiting bodies 100–300 mm broad, globose to subglobose, outer surface (peridium) dry, glabrous, smooth, breaking into irregular flakes in age and sloughing off, white when young, becoming grayish white then mottled brown, finally brown in age. Gleba (interior spore mass) soft and spongy, white when young, becoming olive brown to brown at maturity. Spores brown to dark olive brown. Edibility: edible when gleba is white.

Giant Puffballs appear in the high mountain pastures surrounding Mauna Kea on the Big Island during the rainy season, usually near stock tanks or corrals where animals loiter. When young, about the size of a softball and white throughout, these puffballs are choice edibles. Is: HA.

This Giant Puffball, about the size of a basketball, was growing in a horse corral above Kailua-Kona on the Big Island.

Cyathus stercoreus (Schwein.) De Toni

Fruiting bodies crucible-shaped or like an inverted cone, 5–10 mm tall x 4–6 mm broad, exterior covered with golden brown shaggy hairs, interior glabrous, smooth, lead gray. Operculum cream to pale straw-colored. Peridioles black, attached by a thin cord. Edibility: unknown.

This coprophilous Bird's-nest Fungus will grow by the dozens in a choice, aged "cow pie." In the genus *Cyathus,* the individual "eggs" or peridioles are attached to the cup by a long cord or funiculus. Each peridiole, which is dispersed by a rain drop splashing inside the cup, contains a large number of spores. Is: HA, MA.

A group of *Cyathus stercoreus* growing in cow dung in Parker Ranch pastures on the Big Island.

ADDITIONAL SPECIES IN PASTURES

Chlorophyllum molybdites

The green-spored *Chlorophyllum* appears in giant fairy rings in pastures near Kailua-Kona on the Big Island (see the Fungal Kingdom for a photo and Lawns for full description).

Lepista tarda

This species grows in arcs and fairy rings in pastures where the fruiting bodies are usually hidden between the blades of grass and just barely peek out (see Lawns for full description).

PASTURES

GUAVA THICKETS

Guava, especially the waiawi or strawberry guava *(Psidium cattleianum)*, has escaped cultivation in Hawai'i and forms dense stands in the wet lowlands along the windward coasts of the islands. Guava thickets play host to a variety of fleshy fungi including a chanterelle relative, *Gomphus pallidus,* a coral fungus, *Ramaria fragillima,* and an Oyster Mushroom, *Pleurotus cystidiosus.*

Strawberry guava thickets, such as this stand near MacKenzie Park on the Big Island, are nearly impenetrable (left). The guavas shade out most other vegetation. A cluster of young fruiting bodies of *Xylaria psidii* on a rotting guava fruit (right).

Xylaria psidii J. D. Rogers & Hemmes

Fruiting bodies 30–50 mm tall, needlelike, gradually narrowed to an acute apex, upper portion white, base dark grayish brown to black; in age entire fruit body black with upper fertile portion slightly swollen. Spores black. Edibility: unknown.

The thin stalks of *Xylaria psidii* grow in clusters from seeds of decaying guava fruit. The species name refers to the guava genus *Psidium,* and was described from Hawai'i. Is: HA.

Pleurotus cystidiosus O. K. Miller

Cap 20–60 mm broad, fan-shaped, broadly convex and centrally depressed in face view, dry, with gray to pale grayish brown fibrils or tiny squamules over a white background. Gills decurrent, often netlike where they meet the stem, close, broad, white. Stem 5–20 x 5–10 mm, strongly eccentric to lateral, solid, tough, white to gray. Spore deposit white. Edibility: edible and choice.

Pleurotus cystidiosus, one of several Oyster Mushroom species in Hawai'i, grows in decaying crotches or holes on living guava trees in wet, windward valleys of Maui and the Big Island. When put into culture, small black-headed coremia covered with cysts are produced on the mycelium. *Pleurotus cystidiosus* is easy to grow and fruits readily on wood chips (see section on Edible Mushrooms). Is: HA, KA, MA.

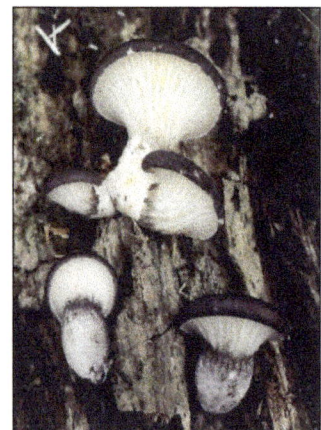

Pleurotus cystidiosus on strawberry guava at Maluhia, Maui.

Gomphus pallidus
(Yasuda) Corner

Cap 30–100 mm broad, curved, fan-shaped like half a funnel, with an irregularly wavy to lobed margin, dry, glabrous to suedelike, yellowish white to white when young, becoming cream in age. Gills veinlike, corrugated, interconnected and netlike, decurrent, thick, edges rounded, cream to brownish cream often with reddish spots in age. Stem 20–40 x 8–15 mm, lateral, narrowed downward, white. Spore deposit cream-colored. Edibility: edible but not esculent.

Unfortunately, the large fleshy *Gomphus pallidus* is not a good edible species. It fruits in large numbers in guava thickets during the rainy season.

Gomphus pallidus is found growing out of leaf mulch in strawberry guava thickets during wet periods. Close relatives of this species are called Pig Ears, and if you have ever seen a skinned pig in a market, you would know why. The fruiting bodies are fan-shaped and expand into cauliflowerlike clusters. The hymenial surface consists of wavy veinlike ribs instead of bladelike gills. Is: HA, MA.

Ramaria fragillima
(Sacc. & Sydow) Corner

Fruiting bodies coralloid, 60–100 mm tall x 40–80 mm broad, with numerous erect branches arising polychotomously to dichotomously from a short solid stem. Branches 2–4 mm thick, orangish brown to cinnamon brown with orange tips. Stem 20–40 x 10–25 mm, cinnamon brown, covered at the base with white mycelium; all parts of fruiting body bruising vinaceously. Spore deposit rusty brown. Edibility: unknown.

This Coral Fungus is often found with *Gomphus pallidus* in guava thickets. Fruiting bodies grow out from under lava rocks with only the smallest amount of leaf litter present. Is: HA, KA, OA.

Spores are produced on the coral-like branches of *Ramaria fragillima*.

WET WINDWARD ALIEN FORESTS

The forests in low elevation valleys and gulches along the windward coasts of the Hawaiian Islands are now a mixture of trees alien to Hawai'i: tropical American monkey pod *(Pithecellobium saman)*, Java plum *(Eugenia cumini)*, Indian mango *(Mangifera indica)*, and a Polynesian introduction, the kukui nut tree *(Aleurites molucca)*. Noni, the Indian mulberry *(Morinda citrifolia)*, and strawberry guava *(Psidium cattleianum)*, introductions from South America, are common understory trees.

In other wet, lowland areas, especially around Hilo on the Big Island, the gunpowder or charcoal tree *(Trema orientalis)* and trumpet tree *(Cecropia peltata)*, both from South America, and the Philippine basswood *(Melochia umbellata)* predominate. These areas were actually seeded from airplanes with these fast-growing alien trees to reduce chances of the forest fires that were a threat in the drier native forest.

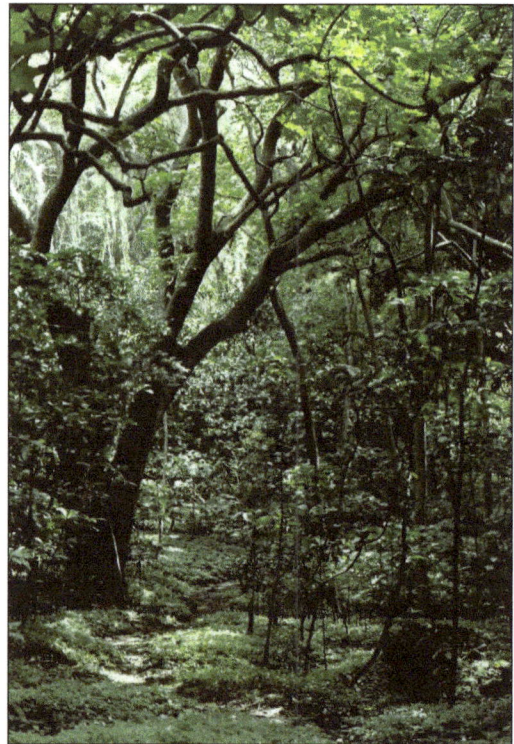

Jelly fungi, such as Pepeiao, and wood-rotting polypores are common on fallen branches and logs in wet alien forests like in Waihe'e Valley on Maui (left) and Waipi'o Valley on the Big Island (right).

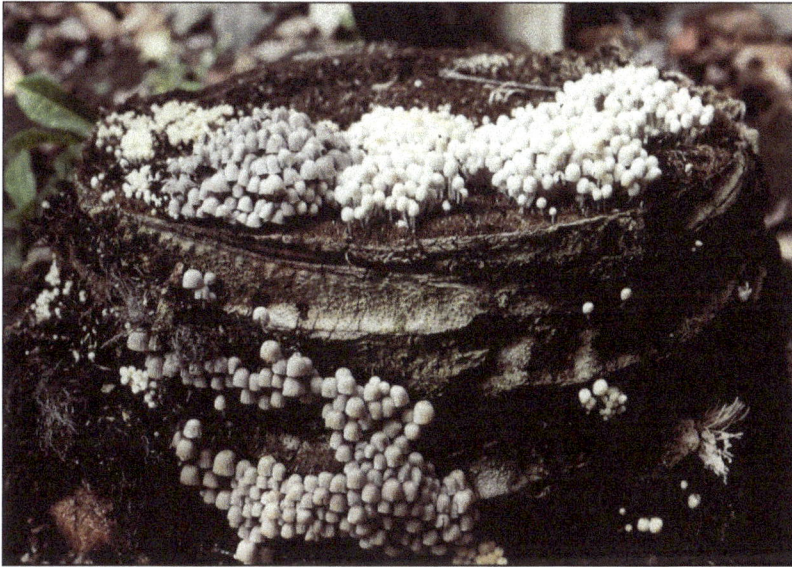

Coprinus disseminatus appears to creep over a coconut stump as the fruiting bodies develop in great numbers.

Coprinus disseminatus (Pers.: Fr.) S. F. Gray

Cap 8–20 mm broad, obtusely conical to bell-shaped, plicate nearly to center, dry, covered overall when young with a white, granulose veil, glabrous in age, white to cream at first with a pale cinnamon center, becoming gray at maturity. Gills adnexed to free, subdistant, narrow, white then gray-ish black, not deliquescing. Stem 20–40 x 1–2 mm, cylindrical, fragile, minutely pubescent to glabrous, white to pale gray. Spore deposit black. Edibility: edible.

Coprinus disseminatus is sometimes placed in the genus *Pseudocoprinus* because the caps do not deliquesce as do those of other *Coprinus* species.

A troop of hundreds of Creeping Crumble Caps growing over a stump or log is a memorable sight. A large fallen monkey pod log at the Hawai'i Tropical Botanical Garden in Onomea on the Big Island had an estimated 10,000 fruiting bodies on it one cool, damp morning. At first creamy white and then turning gray, the tiny pleated caps are very brittle and crumble upon contact. A second species, *Coprinus curtus,* also grows by the hundreds in large troops on wood chips in Hawai'i and looks quite similar to *C. disseminatus. Coprinus curtus* can be distinguished by the slightly smaller caps covered with brown instead of white universal veil granules (see Compost Piles and Wood Chips for a photo of *C. curtus*). Is: HA, KA, MA, MO, OA.

Cyptotrama asprata
(Berk.) Redhead & Ginns

Cap 8–25 mm broad, globose in primordia, bright orange to golden yellow and covered overall with erect conical spines formed from clusters of orange fibrils joined at their tips, convex to broadly convex in age, remaining orange or fading through yellow to nearly white. Gills adnate, subdistant, broad, white. Stem 10–40 x 3–4 mm, cylindrical above a bulbous base, covered with small spines like the cap when young, becoming pubescent in age, ranging from deep orange to yellow to white in age. Spore deposit white. Edibility: unknown.

Young fruiting bodies of *Cyptotrama asprata* displaying their bright golden orange spines.

Cyptotrama asprata is another common agaric that grows on fallen branches in the nonnative forest and which catches your eye because of its bright color. The Golden Scruffy *Cyptotrama* lives up to its name when young with its golden yellow cap covered with tufts of fibrils. The golden fibrils wash off in the rain so that the cap may appear nearly white when mature. Is: HA, KA, MA, MO, OA.

Rickenella fibula (Bull.: Fr.) Raithelh.

Cap 3–7 mm broad, convex to bell-shaped with a shallow central depression, striate, minutely roughened or hairy in the center, dry, reddish orange, orange or brownish orange with a yellowish orange margin. Gills decurrent, distant, narrow, orangish white to white. Stem 10–25 x 1 mm, cylindrical, pliant, pruinose overall, white to pale orangish white. Spore deposit white. Edibility: unknown.

One needs to get on hands and knees to see this tiny orange Moss Agaric. Fruiting bodies peek out of moss in shady places in the forest and may be found on lawns where moss has invaded the grass. Is: HA.

The Moss Agaric, *Rickenella fibula,* growing on moss-covered rocks near Waipio Valley on the Big Island.

There are both white and grayish green species of *Campanella* in Hawai'i, such as *Campanella* aff. *alba* (left) and *Campanella* aff. *eberhardtii* (right).

Campanella aff. *eberhardtii* (Pat.) Singer

Cap 10–25 mm broad, convex then plano-convex, sulcate to wrinkled, dry, glabrous, white when young but becoming grayish green in spots or discoloring grayish green overall in age. Gills distant, anastomosing and intervenose, often forming a net, narrow to broad, white then discoloring grayish green. Stem absent, fruiting body attached by the side of the cap. Spore deposit white. Edibility: unknown.

Soft, shelving fruiting bodies of *Campanella* species line twigs and small branches in wet alien woods and are easily identified to genus by their lack of a stem and by their veinlike and reticulate gills. There is currently much confusion in the taxonomy of *Campanella* and most described species are poorly documented. In Hawai'i, there are several species: A pure white species is close to *Campanella alba* described from South America, while our grayish green species is close to *C. eberhardtii* described from Vietnam. Is: HA, MA, MO.

Marasmiellus pacificus Desjardin

Cap 10–20 mm broad, convex expanding to plano-convex with a central depression in age, wrinkled-striate, pruinose to glabrous, white. Gills adnate to short-decurrent, distant, broad, white. Stem 8–16 x 1–2 mm, cylindrical above a subbulbous base, glabrous and white above, pruinose and white to pale gray below. Spore deposit white. Edibility: unknown.

The pure white fruiting bodies of *Marasmiellus pacificus* stand out in the gloom of the dark, alien forest. This species fruits singly or in clusters on fallen twigs and branches on the forest floor. There are a number of white *Marasmiellus* species that occur in the Hawaiian Islands and fit the description given above, so a specialist should be consulted for correct identification. Is: HA.

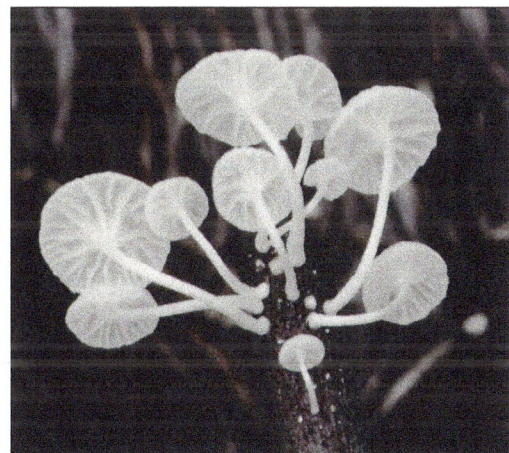

Marasmiellus pacificus is a common species in wet windward forests around Hilo and was described originally from Hawai'i.

Galerina velutipes growing on coconut husks at Honua, Hawai'i on the Big Island (left) and in woody debris (right). Note the characteristic pellucid, striate nature of the cap.

Galerina velutipes Singer

Cap 6–20 mm broad, convex with an acute papilla when young, expanding to plano-depressed with an acute papilla, striate, glabrous to pruinose, hygrophanous, brown, fading to brownish orange or orange with moisture loss. Gills adnate to decurrent, distant, narrow, light orange becoming brownish orange in age. Stem 10–20 x 1–3 mm, cylindrical or gradually narrowed downward, pruinose to velvety overall, brownish orange. Spore deposit rusty brown. Edibility: unknown.

Galerina velutipes is a widespread species that occupies a number of habitats in wet areas. It grows on rotting wood, on wood-chip debris, and in the ground bark media in nursery pots. The cap often ends in a tiny, abrupt point. Is: HA, MA.

Hydropus semimarginellus Singer

Cap 8–30 mm broad, convex to broadly campanulate, expanding to plano-depressed with a shallow umbo, centrally wrinkled, striate, dry, pruinose to velvety overall, grayish brown to dark yellowish brown or pale olive brown. Gills decurrent, close, moderately broad, white to pale grayish white. Stem 10–20 x 1–3 mm, cylindrical, tough, minutely pruinose, white above, pale gray to pale yellowish brown below. Spore deposit white. Edibility: unknown.

Hydropus semimarginellus is similar to North American *Hydropus marginellus*, differing primarily in microscopic features and in forming white stems on monocotyledonous plants. This small, rubbery mushroom has a grayish brown cap that contrasts nicely with white decurrent gills and a pale stem. In Hawai'i, it fruits singly or in clusters on bamboo and coconut in wet windward alien forests. Is: HA.

Hydropus semimarginellus fruiting on bamboo in a wet alien forest near Hilo.

Gymnopilus subtropicus Hesler

Cap 30–50 mm broad, convex to plano-convex, dry, orange to yellowish orange with tiny reddish orange scales in the center. Gills adnate, close, broad, bright yellowish orange. Stem 30–40 x 3–5 mm, cylindrical above an enlarged base, striate, dry, solid, yellowish orange to brownish orange, with remnants of a cobwebby partial veil forming a thin ring near stem apex. Spore deposit bright rusty brown. Edibility: unknown.

The yellowish orange fruiting bodies of *Gymnopilus subtropicus* are sure to catch your eye. This species grows on rotting logs in the wet forest and has been seen growing directly in *Casuarina* duff under coastal ironwoods. It was described originally from specimens collected in Hawai'i and from along the Gulf Coast of North America. Is: HA.

Gymnopilus subtropicus showing off its color in a large fruiting on a fallen log. This species loves to grow on coconut stumps.

Hohenbuehelia atrocaerulea var. *grisea* (Peck) Thorn & G. L. Barron

Cap 10–30 mm broad, shell-shaped to fan-shaped, minutely velvety, rubbery, hygrophanous, gray to grayish brown near point of attachment with a pale gray to off-white margin. Gills radiating, close, narrow, pale yellowish white. Stem absent. Spore deposit white. Edibility: edible but of poor quality.

Hohenbuehelia atrocaerulea is a soft, shelving agaric with a gray cap and white gills. The fruiting bodies resemble an Oyster Mushroom, but they are usually smaller. This genus is known for its nematode-trapping ability, wherein the mycelium captures and digests these small wormlike animals. Is: HA, KA.

This fruiting body of *Hohenbuehelia* is just a couple centimeters in diameter.

A cluster of *Mycena alphitophora* growing on the underside of a log in Halawa Valley on Moloka'i.

Mycena alphitophora (Berk.) Sacc.

Cap 2–8 mm broad, hemispherical, and covered with tiny white granules in primordia (like sugar grains), convex to obtusely conical and expanding slightly in age, striate, white to gray with scattered white granules. Gills adnexed, close, narrow, white. Stem 5–25 x < 0.5 mm, cylindrical, fragile, pruinose to hispid overall, white; lacking a basal disc. Spore deposit white. Edibility: unknown.

Mycena alphitophora is a tiny white *Mycena* commonly found on fallen sticks and logs in the wet alien forest. It is indistinguishable from *M. spinosissima* and *M. brunneospinosa* when mature, so primordia must be collected to observe veil tissue on the cap for correct species identification. This species has also been found in duff under coastal *Casuarina*. Is: HA, MO.

Gloiocephala epiphylla Massee

Cap 1–4 mm broad, convex, soon expanding to plane or funnel-shaped, dry, covered especially on the margin with tiny resinous hairs, white but often drying reddish or with reddish brown spots. Gills absent. Stem 2–8 x 0.1 mm, wiry, glabrous, or minutely pruinose, white at first, base becoming brown in age. Spore deposit white. Edibility: unknown.

This tiny mushroom can be found on the petioles and leaf blades of fallen leaves in the wet forest. The identifying feature of this species is the small size, the lack of gills, and the presence of hairs covering the cap and stem. Is: HA, KA.

Note the tiny "hairs" or cystidia covering the tiny fruiting bodies of *Gloiocephala epiphylla*. The fruiting body is only about 8 millimeters tall.

Tetrapyrgos nigripes (Schwein.) E. Horak

Cap 3–10 mm broad, convex to plano-convex, dry, glabrous to suedelike, white. Gills adnate, subdistant, narrow, often intervenose, white. Stem 3–10 x < 1 mm, cylindrical, solid, tough, pruinose to granulose, dark gray to black, arising from a dark gray velvety pad. Spore deposit white. Edibility: unknown.

Although small, clusters of *Tetrapyrgos nigripes* are easily spotted because of their white caps and recognized by their distinctly black stems. This litter-decomposing species has beautiful tetrapod-shaped spores and densely knobby cystidia. It is common on fallen braches of ohi'a. Is: HA.

Tetrapyrgos nigripes in Bird Park within the Volcanoes National Park.

Mycena spinosissima (Singer) Desjardin

Cap 3–12 mm broad, hemispherical, and covered with tall, white, conical spines in primordia, convex to campanulate at maturity, spines readily falling off or remaining only on the center, striate, glabrous or minutely granulose, white. Gills adnexed, close, narrow, white. Stem 5–15 x 0.5–1 mm, cylindrical, fragile, pruinose to hispid overall, white; lacking a basal disc. Spore deposit white. Edibility: unknown.

Mycena spinossisima is certainly one of the most striking *Mycena* species. The primordia are covered with white, conical spines that eventually fall off as the fruiting body matures. *M. spinosissima* is widespread in Central and South America and was probably introduced to Hawai'i from these areas. Is: HA, KA.

Mycena spinossisima in all its glory. This fruiting body is approximately 10 millimeters tall.

WET WINWARD ALIEN FORESTS

Porpoloma bambusarum
Desjardin & Hemmes

Cap 25–60 mm broad, obtusely conical to campanulate, expanding to plano-convex often with a broad umbo, dry, granulose to fibrillose, brown to grayish brown in the center, tan to nearly white on the margin. Gills adnate to notched, crowded, forked near the cap margin, narrow, white discoloring pink where bruised, drying reddish brown. Stem 40–70 x 2–4 mm, narrowed downward to a rooting base, fibrous, white, base discoloring reddish brown. Spore deposit white. Edibility: unknown.

This newly described species of *Porpoloma* grows singly, scattered in bamboo groves. It shows some features similar to the genus *Cantharellula*, in particular *C. humicola* from Malaysia, but differs in microanatomy. The forked gills that easily separate from the cap tissue, long rooting stem base, and reddish discoloring reaction are characteristic. Is: MA, OA.

Note the rooting extension on the stems of these *Porpoloma bambusarum* fruiting bodies found in bamboo thickets along the Hana Highway on Maui.

Entoloma aff. *placidum* (Fr.: Fr.) Noordel.

Cap 10–30 mm broad, convex to obtusely conical, expanding to plano-convex in age, finely squamulose in the center, becoming glabrous towards the striate margin, dark brown to grayish brown. Gills adnexed to adnate, subdistant, broad, white becoming pinkish brown in age. Stem 25–50 x 1–2 mm, cylindrical, hollow, glabrous above a white-tomentose base, bluish gray to purplish gray. Spore deposit pink. Edibility: unknown.

There are several blue-stemmed *Entoloma* species in Hawai'i and we are uncertain of their identification. *Entoloma* aff. *placidum* can be found scattered on the ground in wet alien forests often in association with bamboo and guava. The cap of this species is dark brown to grayish brown and has small squamules on the disc, and the stem is bluish to purplish brown. Is: HA, KA.

Note the bluish cast to the stems of these specimens of *Entoloma* aff. *placidum*. This species can be found scattered on the alien forest floor during wet periods.

Entoloma purum from Pala'au State Park on Moloka'i.

Entoloma purum E. Horak & Desjardin

Cap 4–10 mm broad, convex to plano-convex, dry, smooth to wrinkled, suedelike, white to pale pink. Gills adnate, distant, moderately broad, white becoming deep pink in age. Stem 3–10 x 1.5–7 mm, cylindrical, dry, solid, pruinose to hispid, white. Spore deposit pink. Edibility: unknown.

Entoloma purum is a relatively small species with fruiting bodies only about 4–10 millimeters broad and tall. It was described originally from bamboo thickets at Akaka Falls State Park on the Big Island. We have since collected it on ironwood, guava, and ohi'a from Maui and Moloka'i. Is: HA, MA, MO.

Entoloma stylophorum (Berk. & Broome) Sacc.

Cap 10–15 mm broad, conical with a tall papilla, dry, glabrous, nonstriate, white to pale yellowish white. Gills adnate, subdistant, narrow, pinkish white becoming dark pink in age. Stem 30–45 x 1–1.5 mm, cylindrical, hollow, dry, glabrous, pale yellowish white. Spore deposit pink. Edibility: unknown.

The fruiting bodies of *E. stylophorum* are pure white to light yellow and can be recognized by the pointed projection at the apex of the cap. This species is often found in mosses covering wet piles of woody debris. Is: HA, MA.

Several specimens of *Entoloma stylophorum* from the forests around Honua Hawai'i on the Big Island.

The petiole of a *Cecropia* leaf (left) is lined with the tiny fruiting bodies of *Marasmius exustoides*, shown also with a close-up of their gills (right).

Marasmius exustoides Desjardin & E. Horak

Cap 1–4 mm broad, convex, sulcate, minutely granulose, at first brown to pale reddish brown overall, remaining so in age or with brown center and light yellowish brown to cream-colored margin. Gills adnexed, distant, moderately broad, white. Stem 5–10 x 0.1 mm, wiry, glabrous, dark brown to black; rhizomorphs lacking. Spore deposit white. Edibility: unknown.

Another tiny litter decomposing species, *Marasmius exustoides* is commonly found on petioles of *Cecropia* and *Macaranga* as well as on other tree leaves in Hawai'i. It was first described from New Zealand, where it occurs on *Cordyline* leaves. The cap has tiny brown granules on it, as if it were sprinkled with pepper. Is: HA.

Marasmius anisocystidiatus Antonin, Desjardin & Gsell

Cap 5–15 mm broad, convex, shallowly umbilicate, sulcate, minutely granulose, at first pale reddish tan, in age pale rusty tan to cream-colored. Gills adnate, distant, broad, white with yellowish edges. Stem 20–30 x 0.5–1 mm, cylindrical, dry, glabrous, tough, apex golden yellow, base dark brown. Spore deposit white. Edibility: unknown.

Until we discovered specimens of *Marasmius anisocystidiatus* in Hawai'i, the species was known only to grow on South American plants in a greenhouse in Zürich, Switzerland! The species was probably introduced to Hawai'i via South American plants that are present in our wet windward alien forests. Is: HA.

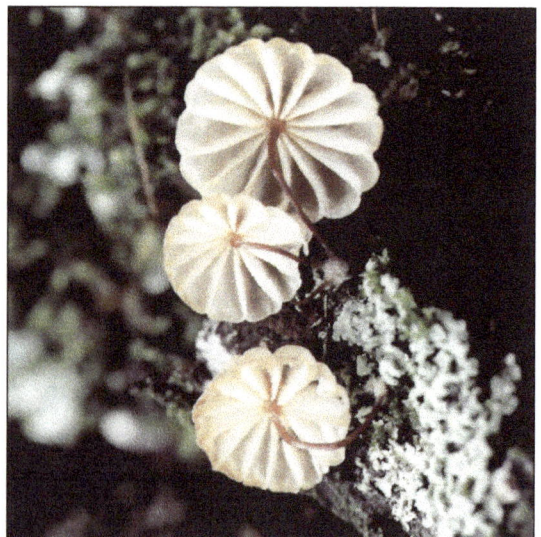

Marasmius anisocystidiatus fruiting on a stump in Hilo.

Marasmius pseudobambusinus var. *hawaiiensis* on banana leaves.

Marasmius pseudobambusinus var. *hawaiiensis* Desjardin

Cap 2–5 mm broad, convex, sulcate, wrinkled in the center, reddish orange to orange or pale rusty cinnamon. Gills adnexed, distant, narrow, white, often with pale orange edges. Stem 10–18 x <0.2 mm, wiry, tough, glabrous, apex white, base brownish orange to brown. Spore deposit white. Edibility: unknown.

Described from Hawai'i, this small orange-capped variety of *Marasmius pseudobambusinus* grows singly or in clusters on the leaf blades and petioles of monocotyledonous plants such as banana, ginger, heliconia, and various grasses. Is: HA.

Marasmius thwaitesii Berk. & Broome

Cap 1–3 mm broad, obtusely conical expanding to broadly campanulate, covered overall when young with brown tufted conical spines, these soon fall off leaving a glabrous surface, deeply radially grooved, dark brown fading in the grooves and on the margin to pale yellowish brown. Gills adnexed, distant, narrow, white. Stem 5–15 x 0.5 mm, wiry, solid, tough, glabrous, dark brown to black. Spore deposit white. Edibility: unknown.

The tiny fruiting bodies of *Marasmius thwaitesii* must be observed under a hand lens to appreciate their delicate beauty. The caps are decorated in the center with brown conical spines. This little *Marasmius* grows on the woody capsules of *Bombax* trees. Is: HA.

Marsmius thwaitesii fruiting on capsules of the *Bombax* tree on the University of Hawai'i at Hilo campus.

Crepidotus roseus var. *boninensis* on a log in Kamakou Forest Preserve on Moloka'i.

Crepidotus roseus var. *boninensis* Hongo

Cap 10–50 mm broad, sessile, rounded chordate or fan-shaped to plano-convex, nonstriate, glabrous to minutely felted, hygrophanous, deep pink or pinkish brown fading to pale grayish red or nearly white in age. Gills adnexed to point of cap attachment, close to subdistant, broad, pink. Stem absent. Spore deposit brown. Edibility: unknown.

Crepidotus roseus var. *boninensis* produces lovely pink fruiting bodies that grow as overlapping clusters on logs in wet environments. Although the gills are a beautiful pink, they actually drop a brown spore deposit. Is: HA, MO, OA.

Crepidotus stromaticus (Cooke & Massee) Sacc.

Cap 5–15 mm broad, sessile, chordate to convex becoming plano-convex, nonstriate, suedelike to felted, deep sulfur yellow to pale brownish yellow fading to yellowish white in age. Gills adnexed to point of cap attachment, close to subdistant, moderately broad, yellow. Stem absent. Spore deposit brown. Edibility: unknown.

In wet alien forests the undersides of logs may become covered with dozens of small, deep sulfur yellow, shelving fruiting bodies of *Crepidotus stromaticus*. Because of its bright yellow colors, this species is not likely to be confused with other gilled mushrooms that lack a stem. Is: HA, KA.

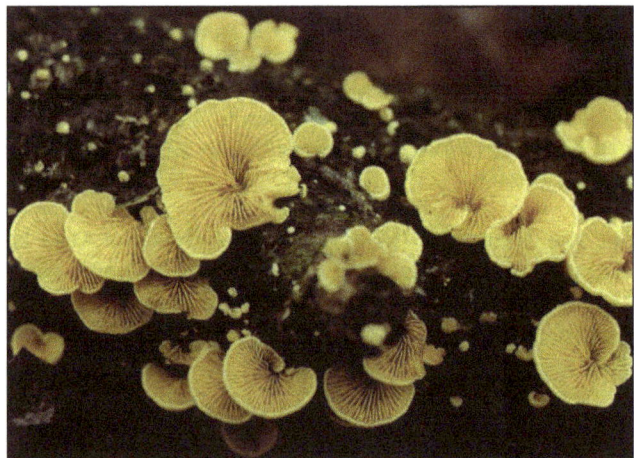

A beautiful cluster of *Crepidotus stromaticus* on the bottom of a rotting log. Because of its deep yellow color, this species has also been known as *C. citrinus* and *C. sulphurinus*.

Crepidotus uber (Berk. & M. A. Curtis) Sacc.

Cap 5–30 mm broad, sessile, fan-shaped to plano-convex, translucent-striate, margin wavy, white tomentose at point of attachment, glabrous elsewhere, hygrophanous, pale grayish to brownish white to flesh-colored, fading to dingy buff. Gills adnexed to point of cap attachment, close to subdistant, moderately broad, pale grayish brown. Stem absent. Spore deposit brown. Edibility: unknown.

Crepidotus uber is the most common *Crepidotus* in wet alien forests. The fruiting bodies get soggy in wet weather and become plastered to the side of the log on which they are growing. Is: HA.

Crepidotus uber on a dead tree in an alien forest near Hilo. Pink-colored millipedes are feeding on the fruiting bodies.

Chaetocalathus liliputianus (Mont.) Singer

Cap 2–6 mm broad, conical to campanulate, attached by the center of the cap to the woody substrate, radially silky-fibrillose, dry, nonstriate, white. Gills convex, subdistant, moderately broad, white. Stem absent. Spore deposit white. Edibility: unknown.

Even though the fruiting bodies of this species are tiny, they are readily spotted in the dark, damp forest because they line twigs and branches on the forest floor. The caps are conical with radiating silky hairs; they lack a stem, and instead they are attached by the center of the cap to woody substrates. Is: HA.

A close-up of *Chaetocalathus liliputianus* clinging to the bottom of a stick.

Lentinus ciliatus Lev.

Cap 20–85 mm broad, convex with inrolled margin when young, soon funnel-shaped, velvety or densely covered with short, brown erect hairs, remaining hairy in the center and becoming glabrous and slightly striate on the margin in age, leathery, cinnamon brown to brown with darker concentric zones. Gills decurrent, densely crowded, very narrow, cream-colored, drying brown. Stem 20–60 x 3–10 mm, cylindrical above a swollen base, velvety, tough, cinnamon brown to brown. Spore deposit white. Edibility: edible but too tough to eat.

Lentinus ciliatus has tough, long-lasting fruiting bodies that grow on the stumps and logs of introduced trees in the wet lowland forests. The surface of the brown cap is characterized by concentric zones of fibrils and a funnel-shaped depression in the center. The light-colored gills are crowded and decurrent. Although the descriptions of *L. ciliatus* and *L. bertieri* are nearly identical, the two species are easy to distinguish in the field. Mature fruit bodies of *L. ciliatus* have a nearly glabrous cap, whereas the cap of *L. bertieri* remains densely hairy at maturity. Is: HA, KA, MA, MO, OA.

Lentinus ciliatus frequents trails in Halawa Valley on Moloka'i (top). It forms crowded and very narrow decurrent gills (bottom).

Lentinus bertieri (Fr.) Fr.

Cap 20–60 mm broad, convex with inrolled margin when young, soon funnel-shaped, densely covered with long, white to pale brown erect hairs, remaining hairy on the margin and becoming glabrous and slightly striate on the margin in age, leathery, cinnamon brown to brown with darker concentric zones. Gills decurrent, densely crowded, narrow, white to yellowish brown. Stem 15–30 x 3–6 mm, cylindrical with flared apex, with small tufts of hairs, tough, white above, dark brown below. Spore deposit white. Edibility: edible but too tough to eat.

Lentinus bertieri resembles the Spring Polypore, *Polyporus arcularius*, with a brown, funnel-shaped cap, but a quick look under the cap shows crowded, decurrent gills instead of angular pores. Is: HA.

The fruiting bodies of *Lentinus bertieri* are tough and leathery. (For an additional photo, see page xii.)

Spring Polypores, *Polyporus arcularius,* grow in large clusters on logs in the alien forest during the wet spring months. Look for the funnel-shaped caps and elongated pores underneath.

Polyporus arcularius Batsch: Fr.

Cap 20–40 mm broad, convex-umbilicate but soon funnel-shaped, with appressed-fibrillose scales and a hairy margin, glabrous in age, tough and leathery, yellowish brown to brown. Pores radially arranged, large and angular with ragged edges, white to off-white. Stem 20–40 x 2–3 mm, cylindrical, solid, tough, glabrous, yellowish brown to brown. Spore deposit white. Edibility: edible but too tough to eat.

The Spring Polypore, *Polyporus arcularius,* is indeed most common in Hawai'i in the spring, growing from sticks and logs from January through July. This polypore has a stalked fruiting body and looks like a gilled mushroom until you turn it over and see the network of pores forming the hymenial surface. Tiny hairs stick out of the edges of the cap, giving this polypore another common name, the Fringed Polypore. Is: HA, KA, MA, MO, OA.

Rigidoporus microporus (Fr.) Overeem

Cap 50–150 mm broad x 25–75 mm radius x 5–10 mm thick, semicircular to fan-shaped, often imbricate, tough and woody, glabrous, dull to shiny, orange to reddish orange or orangish brown with concentric zones. Pores round, 6–9 per mm, yellowish brown to cream-colored; tubes in a single layer, 1–5 mm long. Stem absent. Spore deposit white. Edibility: edible but too tough to eat.

Rigidoporus microporus forms dark-orange, overlapping woody brackets on stumps and logs. The species name is in recognition of the tiny pores on the hymenial surface. Is: HA, OA.

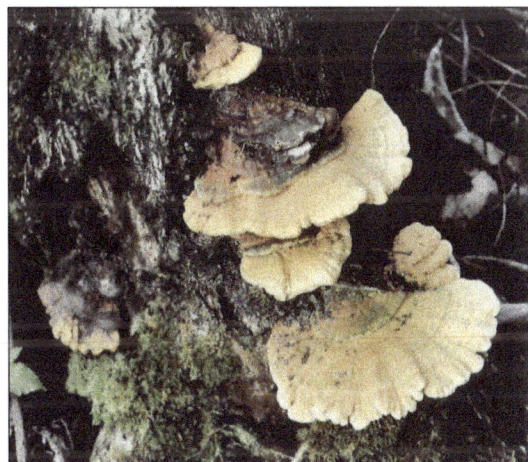

The wood-rotting polypore, *Rigidoporus microporus,* on a stump in the Panaewa Forest near Hilo.

Earliella scabrosa
(Pers.) Gilb. & Ryvarden

Fruiting body resupinate to shelflike, sometimes imbricate, 20–80 mm broad x 4–8 mm thick, tough and leathery, at first white to cream-colored overall but soon red to burgundy with a white margin. Pores angular to irregularly elongated, 2–3 per mm, burgundy; tubes in a single layer, 1–5 mm long. Stem absent. Spore deposit white. Edibility: edible but too tough to eat.

This reddish to burgundy-colored polypore is largely resupinate but also forms overlapping layers of brackets on the fallen branches and logs of mango and kukui nut trees in windward valleys. The young, growing edges are white. Is: HA, KA, MA, MO, OA.

Earliella scabrosa on mango in Halawa Valley on Moloka'i.

Pycnoporus sanguineus
(L.: Fr.) Murrill

Cap 50–80 mm broad x 2–4 mm thick, semicircular to fan-shaped or irregular in outline, sometimes resupinate to shelflike, tough and woody, finely tomentose to glabrous, radially wrinkled, deep orangish red to deep red, sometimes with white concentric zones, fading slowly to salmon-colored in weathered specimens. Pores round, 5–6 per mm, deep red; tubes in a single layer, 1–2 mm long. Stem absent. Spore deposit white. Edibility: edible but too tough to eat.

Deep red brackets of *Pycnoporus sanguineus* on a fallen *Pandanus* log.

Pycnoporus sanguineus is one of the more common shelving polypores in Hawai'i. The tough, bright-red bracts can be spotted on stumps, fallen logs, and branches. Weavers are familiar with the yellow dye that can be extracted from these fruiting bodies. A less common look-alike species, *Pycnoporus cinnabarinus,* also occurs in Hawai'i but differs in forming thicker fruiting bodies that fade rapidly to pale orangish white. Is: HA, KA, MA, MO, OA.

Phellinus gilvus (Schwein.) Pat.

Cap 100–150 mm broad x 70–100 mm radius x 10–30 mm thick, irregularly semicircular to shelflike, wrinkled to lumpy, tomentose to glabrous, dark brown to dark yellowish brown with a yellow margin; flesh tough and leathery, yellowish brown. Pores round, 6–8 per mm, purplish brown to purplish yellowish brown; tubes in a single layer, 5–10 mm long. Stem absent. Spore deposit white. Edibility: edible but too tough to eat.

Phellinus gilvus lining a log in Waipio Valley on the Big Island.

Phellinus gilvus is probably the most commonly seen large conk-forming polypore in Hawai'i. The dark-brown fruiting bodies form series of shelves on standing dead trees and fallen logs. The pore surface is brown or yellow-brown with a purplish tint. Is: HA, KA, MA, MO, OA.

Microporus flabelliformis (Fr.) Kuntze

Cap 30–80 mm broad x 15–60 mm radius x 1–2 mm thick, fan-shaped, margin often wavy or lobed, radially ridged, tough and leathery, with concentric zones of brown, reddish brown, yellowish brown, orange, green gray, black, and a white margin. Pores round, extremely tiny, 9–11 per mm, white to straw-colored; tubes in a single layer 0.25 mm deep. Stem lateral, 5–15 x 3–5 mm, solid, black. Spore deposit white. Edibility: edible but too tough to eat.

Microporus flabelliformis is common in Moloka'i's Halawa Valley.

Microporus flabelliformis is characterized by colorful reddish, greenish, yellowish, and black concentric growth lines. The pore surface is white. Artists in Hawai'i dry and press specimens and incorporate them into earrings, necklaces, and other jewelry. Is: HA, MO, OA.

Auricularia cornea
(Ehrenb.: Fr.) Ehrenb. ex Enkdl.

Fruiting body 50–120 mm broad x 1–2 mm thick, ear-shaped to convex-fan-shaped, texture rubbery, upper surface smooth to wrinkled, tomentose to velvety, lower surface smooth to veined, glabrous to pruinose, grayish brown, brown to purplish brown over-all with white to tan tomentum. Spore deposit white. Edibility: edible and choice.

Pepeiao, the Ear Fungus or Wood Ear, is easily the best known of the jelly fungi in Hawai'i. Pepeiao occurs as clusters of rubbery, purple-gray bracket-type fruiting bodies on fallen logs all year when the forest is wet. These fruiting bodies are collected, dried, and added to soups or meat and vegetable dishes, where they add a crispy texture to the meal and soak up the flavors of other foods (see section on Edible Mushrooms). Is: HA, KA, MA, MO, OA.

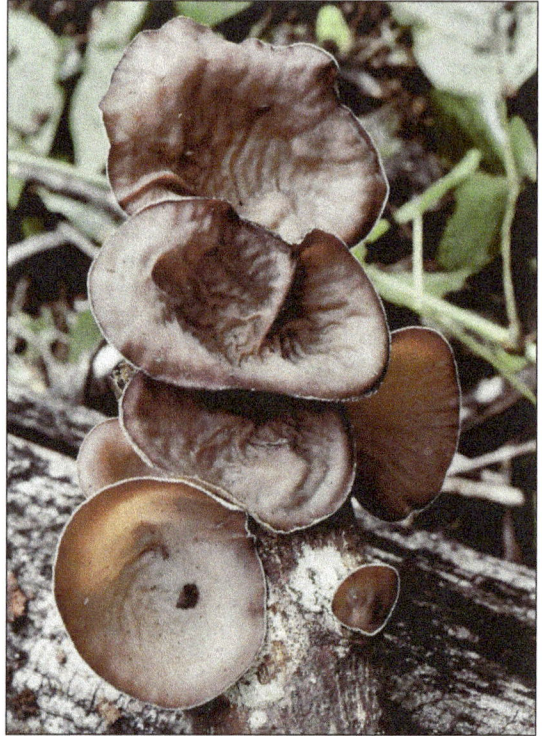

This jelly fungus is called the Ear Fungus or Wood Ear. Can you see why? It is known to be an edible species, and in Hawai'i it is known as Pepeiao.

Tremella boraborensis Olive

Fruiting body 20–40 mm broad x 10–15 mm tall, brain-like, irregularly lumpy and convoluted, texture rubbery and gelatinous, glabrous, black. Spore deposit white. Edibility: edible.

This black jelly fungus, originally described from Tahiti, proliferates on fallen branches in the wet windward valleys of Moloka'i, Hawai'i, and O'ahu. Is: HA, MO, OA.

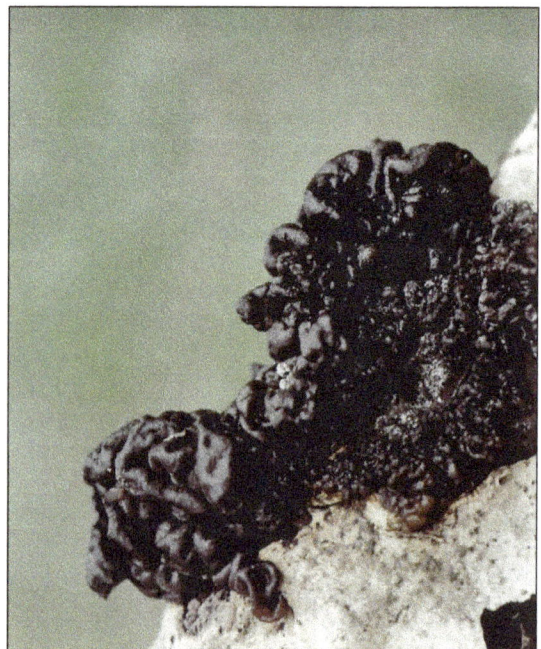

A typical fruiting of *Tremella boraborensis* as seen on a fallen branch in Waipio Valley.

Tremella fuciformis Berk.

Fruiting body 30–80 mm broad x 10–20 mm tall, foliose to irregularly branched or coralloid, texture rubbery and gelatinous, glabrous, translucent, white. Spore deposit white. Edibility: edible and choice.

Tremella fuciformis is a large, white jelly fungus that can be spotted from a distance in the dark, wet alien forest. The foliose fruiting body has a typical gelatinous, jellylike texture. This species is also collected, dried, and added to soups and vegetable dishes (see section on Edible Mushrooms). Is: HA, MO, OA.

Tremella fuciformis is often seen at Kolekole Park along the Hamakua Coast on the Big Island. This jelly fungus is another highly sought-after edible species that actually has a crunchy texture.

Dacryopinax spathularia (Schwein.) Martin

Fruiting body 4–8 mm broad x 5–10 mm tall, horn-shaped to spatula-shaped, margin often lobed or branched, flattened, texture rubbery, tough, orange to yellowish orange. Stem 2–4 x 1–2 mm, lateral, cylindrical, pruinose, orange. Spore deposit white. Edibility: edible.

This tiny jelly fungus appears as clusters of slightly branched orange horns or spatulas extending out of cracks in logs and branches. The jellylike fruiting bodies become tough upon drying. Is: HA, KA, OA.

Dacryopinax also loves plywood, two-by-fours, lanai railings, or any other wood that is wet. It has even been seen fruiting on polyester rugs.

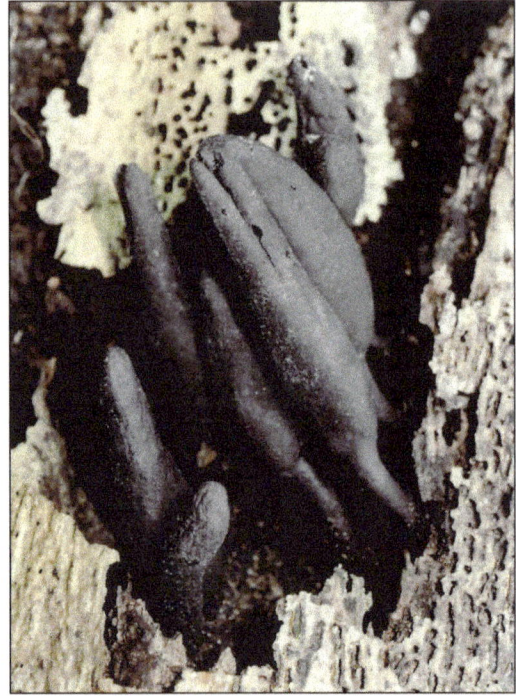

The beautifully branched anamorph or asexual stage (left) and teleomorph or sexual stage (right) of *Xylaria moelleroclavis*.

Xylaria moelleroclavis J. D. Rogers, Y. M. Ju & Hemmes

Fruiting bodies when young (anamorphic stage) 50–80 mm tall x 3–5 mm broad, cylindrical or tapered towards the tip with numerous short side branches terminated by a globose head, upper branched portion white to grayish white, base black; fruiting bodies in age (teleomorphic stage) 10–30 mm broad, irregularly clavate to fusoid, flattened, wrinkled, with or without spiny remnants of the side branches, tough and woody, black. Spore deposit black. Edibility: unknown.

The white anamorphic or asexual stage of *Xylaria moelleroclavis* is highly branched with small heads at the end of the branches. As the teleomorph or sexual stage develops, the branches dehisce and the fruiting body grows into a large, black, club-shaped structure. This interesting wood-decaying species was described from material collected in Hawai'i. Is: HA.

Xylaria apiculata Cooke

Fruiting bodies when young (anamorphic stage) 10–20 mm tall x 2–3 mm broad, cylindrical or tapered to a narrow tip, apex white and smooth, base black and velvety; fruiting bodies in age (teleomorphic stage) 4–8 mm broad, bullet-shaped on a narrower stem, often with a pointed tip, warted, tough and woody, black. Spore deposit black. Edibility: unknown.

One of the more commonly seen *Xylaria* in the Hawaiian Islands, the sharply pointed fruiting bodies of *Xylaria apiculata* inhabit twigs and sticks. This species is commonly referred to as Mouse Feces on a Stick. Is: HA.

A typical grouping of *Xylaria apiculata* on a stick.

ADDITIONAL SPECIES IN WET WINDWARD ALIEN FORESTS

Entoloma umbiliciforme

This small yellowish brown to pinkish capped *Entoloma* with pink gills and pale yellow stem has been collected commonly in windward wet alien forests, as well as in coconut groves and in lawns (see Lawns for full description).

Marasmius radiatus

A beautiful litter-decomposing species with a rusty brown pleated cap, *Marasmius radiatus* likes to grow on leaves and small twigs of monkey pod and African tulip trees(see Montane *Casuarina* Forests for a full description).

Geastrum aff. welwitschii

The Hawaiian material of this interesting earthstar probably represents a previously undescribed species closely allied with *Geastrum welwitschii*. It is the most common earthstar in coastal *Casuarina* forests (see Coastal *Casuarina* Forests for a full description).

COASTAL *CASUARINA*

Casuarina equisetifolia, the Australian pine or ironwood, was introduced to Hawai'i in the late 1800s and planted along coastlines on all islands to cut down on wind and salt spray. The trees grow well on barren basaltic benches and drop branchlets that choke out all competing vegetation and produce a thick layer of duff ideal for fungal growth. After heavy coastal rains, especially during the fall and winter months, these coastal *Casuarina* groves support a large number of mushrooms, earthstars, and stinkhorns.

Coastal *Casuarina* groves line the windward coast of the Big Island from Pololu Valley to Kalapana. MacKenzie Park near Kalapana, shown above, is typical. *Casuarina* or Australian pine is not a true pine, but an angiosperm or flowering plant.

Lepiota besseyi
H. V. Smith & N. S. Weber

Cap 50–80 mm broad, subcylindrical to campanulate when young, expanding to broadly convex or plane with a broad umbo, dry, minutely velvety in the center, breaking up into flattened squamules towards the nonstriate margin, white with reddish brown to grayish brown center and squamules. Gills free, close, broad, white. Stem 30–75 x 8–12 mm, cylindrical or enlarged towards the subbulbous base, fibrous, white, with a small persistent annulus near the apex. Flesh and surface of cap, gills, and stem quickly turn yellow then red when cut; fruiting bodies dry dark reddish brown. Spore deposit white. Edibility: unknown.

Note the blushing reaction on the gills in these specimens of *Lepiota besseyi*.

Lepiota besseyi is readily identified by the orangish-red bruising reaction when you touch the gills. Fruiting bodies are common under coastal ironwoods and occasionally grow on lawns and in gardens. Since the edibility of this species is unknown it is best avoided for the table. Is: HA, KA.

Agaricus rotalis
K. R. Peterson, Desjardin & Hemmes

Cap 50–95 mm broad, convex to plano-convex, dry, appressed-fibrillose, radially cracked and split in age, at first black to dark grayish brown overall, in age black in the center and radially streaked black over a white background. Odor of phenol. Gills free, close, broad, white to reddish brown then dark brown. Stem 35–80 x 5–15 mm, cylindrical or enlarged downwards to a subbulbous or abruptly bulbous base, glabrous, white above, brown below, with a large, skirtlike annulus near the apex. Stem base stains bright yellow where bruised. Spore deposit dark brown. Edibility: unknown but probably poisonous.

Agaricus rotalis in ironwood duff at MacKenzie Park.

The black cuticle on this new species of *Agaricus* is at first solid but splits radially as the cap expands revealing the white tissue underneath. The base of the stem turns yellow when rubbed or sliced open. It is best to avoid eating all yellow-staining species of *Agaricus* that have a phenol odor. Most of them cause gastrointestinal upset when ingested. Is: HA, KA.

A fairy ring or menehune ring of *Gymnopus menehune* at MacKenzie Park on the Big Island.

Gymnopus menehune
Desjardin, Halling & Hemmes

Cap 8–30 mm broad, convex expanding to plano-convex or plane with a central umbilicus, striate, hygrophanous, thin-fleshed, glabrous, brown to reddish brown, fading to light brown or beige with moisture loss. Gills adnate, close, narrow, orangish white to pale grayish brown. Stem 15–60 x 1–3 mm, cylindrical, sometimes cleft, tough, pruinose to pubescent, tan to pale grayish brown above, base dark brown. Spore deposit white. Edibility: unknown.

Close-up of *Gymnopus menehune* showing the striate, umbilicate cap, close gills, and thin, pubescent stem.

This small, tough-stemmed *Gymnopus* forms circular fairy rings or arcs in *Casuarina* duff. (A *menehune* is a small, mischievous Hawaiian equivalent of a fairy, thus the species name.) The cap is thin and the gills bruise a reddish brown. *Gymnopus menehune* also grows in great clusters in wood-chip piles. Under these moist conditions, fruiting bodies tend to have more convex caps with an obvious indentation in the center, rather than the planar caps typical of specimens growing in coastal *Casuarina*. Is: HA.

The generic name *Gymnopus* (not *Gymnopilus*, which is altogether different) may sound unfamiliar to most mushroom collectors. Recently, most species historically accepted in the genus *Collybia* have been transferred to *Gymnopus*. For a discussion of the taxonomic and nomenclatural reasons behind these transfers, see Antonín, Halling, and Noordeloos (*Mycotaxon* 63: 359–368; 1997). Is: HA, MA.

Gymnopus luxurians
(Peck) Murrill

Cap 20–65 mm broad, convex expanding to plano-convex or plane with uplifted margin, short-striate when moist, sub-hygrophanous, thick-fleshed, glabrous to radially appressed-fibrillose, brown to dark brown at first, in age center brown and margin pale yellowish brown to orangish white. Gills adnate, subdistant, broad, white to pale grayish orange. Stem 20–60 mm, cylindrical to clavate, striate, twisted, tough pubescent, white to grayish orange. Spore deposit white. Edibility: unknown.

A typical fruiting of *Gymnopus luxurians* at MacKenzie Park. Sometimes the bases of the stems are dramatically thickened.

Gymnopus luxurians has a longitudinally ribbed stem that may be greatly enlarged at the base at maturity. This species usually appears in large groupings and forms arcs in *Casuarina* duff. It can be distinguished from *G. menehune*, which also forms arcs under ironwoods, in forming less striate and thicker-fleshed caps without an umbilicus, broader gills, and thicker stems. Is: HA.

Lactocollybia epia
(Berk. & Broome) Pegler

Cap 15–25 mm broad, convex expanding to plano-convex to plane, dry, nonstriate, glabrous, white to pale yellowish white. Gills adnexed, close to subdistant, narrow, white. Stem 25–45 x 1.5–3 mm, cylindrical, glabrous above a tomentose base, white. Spore deposit white. Edibility: unknown.

Lactocollybia epia is a pure white, porcelainlike mushroom that commonly grows on partially buried pieces of *Casuarina* wood and directly on *Casuarina* capsules. This species has also been found on the fallen twigs and branches of monkey pod trees along the Kona coastline and will also grow directly on fallen coconuts. Is: HA.

Lactocollybia epia, as shown from these specimens from MacKenzie Park, favor *Casuarina* sticks and capsules as substrates.

Geastrum pectinatum Pers.

Exoperidium separating from endoperidium and splitting into 6–9 rays, outer surface adhering debris, rays recurved, pale brown. Endoperidium 10–20 mm broad, elevated on a stem (pedicel) 3–5 mm long; base of endoperidium radially ridged where it meets the stem, surface smooth, dark gray to black; peristome well delimited, strongly plicate, with an annular ridge around base of plicae. Spores dark brown. Edibility: unknown.

The peridium is elevated on a short stalk in fruiting bodies of *Geastrum pectinatum*.

Geastrum pectinatum, the Beaked Earthstar, forms a smooth spore sac that is elevated by a short stem, has ridges radiating from the stem up the base of the spore sac, and has a whorl of ridges (plicae) surrounding the pore mouth (ostiole), giving the earthstar a beaked appearance. This species is similar to *G. berkeleyi*, which also grows in the same habitat, but the latter differs in forming a shorter stem and lacking radiating ridges at the base of the coarsely roughened spore sac. Is: HA, OA.

Geastrum aff. welwitschii Mont.

Exoperidium covered with pyramidal warts or tufts of hair, yellowish brown to dark grayish brown, not encrusting debris, epigeal, separating from endoperidium and splitting into 5–8 recurved rays, often saccate, fornicate. Endoperidium 15–35 mm broad, sessile or with a very short stalk, surface smooth, grayish brown with a dark grayish brown, poorly delimited, fibrillose peristome. Spores dark brown. Edibility: unknown.

The Hawaiian taxon appears closest to *G. welwitschii*, but differs in forming much coarser pyramidal warts on the exoperidial surface, a sessile and saccate endoperidial body, and smaller spores. It is one of the larger and more common earthstars in Hawai'i, proliferating in *Casuarina* duff. The roughened outer surface of the exoperidium resembles a lychee fruit. This fornicate species also appears in leaf mulch in wet alien forests. Is: HA.

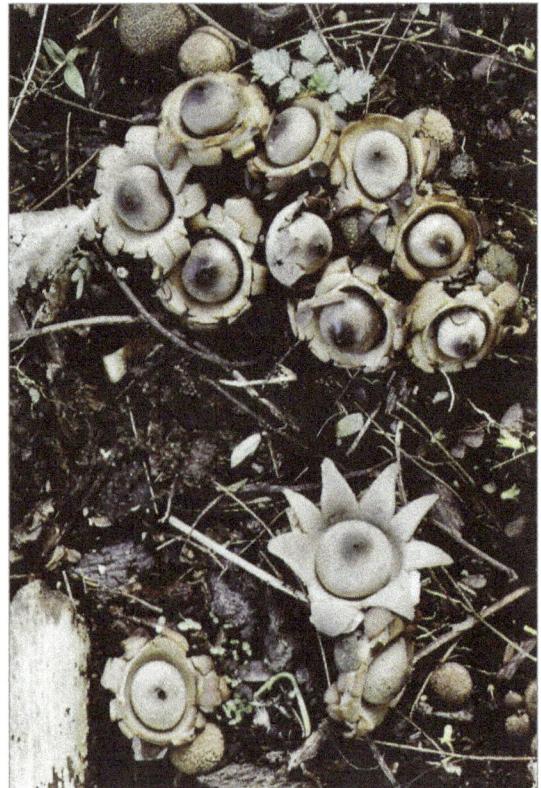

Note the coarse, warted outer surface, fleshy and cracked rays, and indistinct fibrillose peristome of *Geastrum* aff. *welwitschii*.

Geastrum berkeleyi Massee

Exoperidium separating from endoperidium and splitting into 7–10 rays, outer surface adhering debris, rays recurved, brown. Endoperidium 10–20 mm broad, sessile or with a short stalk, base of endoperidium even, not ridged, surface roughened like sandpaper, brown to dark brown; peristome well delimited, strongly plicate, lacking an annular ridge. Spores dark brown. Edibility: unknown.

Geastrum berkeleyi is very similar to *G. pectinatum*, which grows in the same habitat. However, the latter species forms a well-developed stalk

Geastrum berkeleyi, with its characteristic pointed, strongly plicate peristome, grows in small clusters in *Casuarina* duff.

that elevates a dark gray to black, smooth endoperidial body that typically has radial ridges at the base where it meets the stalk. In comparison, *G. berkeleyi* usually lacks a stalk, and has a roughened endoperidial body that lacks the radial ridges. Both species form strongly plicate peristomes and are not fornicate. Is: HA.

Geastrum fimbriatum Fr.

Exoperidium separating from endoperidium and splitting into 7–10 rays, outer surface adhering debris, rays recurved, sometimes saccate, pale brown. Endoperidium 8–15 mm broad, sessile, surface smooth, brown to dark grayish brown, with an indistinctly delimited, pale, fibrillose peristome. Spores brown. Edibility: unknown.

Like *Geastrum welwitschii* from the same habitat, *G. fimbriatum* has an indistinctly delimited fibrillose peristome. *Geastrum fimbriatum* differs in lacking the coarse pyramidal warts on the outer exoperidial surface when young, and it is usually much smaller. Is: HA, MO.

Clusters of *Geastrum fimbriatum* in *Casuarina* duff at MacKenzie Park on the Big Island. Note the smooth outer surface on young specimens and the fibrillose peristome on older ones.

Phellinus kawakamii
M. J. Larsen, Lombard & Hodges

Fruiting bodies perennial, imbricate, shelflike, 300–500 x 50–100 mm; cap pubescent to tomentose, nodulose, rusty brown with yellowish tan margin, becoming dull brown overall; flesh tough and corky, rusty brown. Pores round to slightly angular, 5–7 per mm, yellow to yellowish brown; tubes in 1–12 layers, 2–5 mm long. Stem absent. Spore deposit yellowish brown. Edibility: edible but too tough to eat.

Phellinus kawakamii, a wood-rotting polypore, causes a white pocket rot at the base of ironwoods. The large bracket-type fruiting bodies develop at the root collar and are often partially buried in duff. This species, described from Hawai'i, also causes heartwood decay of koa on Kaua'i. Is: HA, KA, OA.

Large conks of *Phellinus kawakamii* at the bases of ironwoods at MacKenzie Park.

Dictyophora multicolor Berk. & Broome

Unexpanded fruiting body ovoid, 25–35 mm broad, spiny, white to pale gray. Expanded fruiting body 100–120 mm tall. Head broadly conical or minaret-shaped with a small apical hole; surface yellow, netted and covered by an olive brown, gelatinous spore mass (gleba). Stem 20–30 mm broad, cylindrical or narrowed upward, netted and perforate, white to yellowish white. Indusium attached at base of cap, short and pendulous, yellowish orange. Volva spiny, white to pale gray. Odor strongly spermatic. Spores olive brown. Edibility: reported to be poisonous.

Dictyophora multicolor, which features a yellow head and short yellowish orange indusium, appears in *Casuarina* duff at MacKenzie Park on the Big Island. Like a good stinkhorn, it gives off a sickening, spermatic odor that attracts flies to aid in spore dispersal. Is: HA.

Dictyophora multicolor emerging from *Casuarina* duff at MacKenzie Park (above). Note that the indusium is shorter and paler orange than that of *Dictyophora cinnabarina*. A primordium or "egg" is cut in half to show the immature fruiting body inside (below).

ADDITIONAL SPECIES IN COASTAL *CASUARINA*

Amanita marmorata subsp. myrtacearum

This deadly poisonous species is common under coastal *Casuarina* during wet periods. Fruiting bodies under the forest canopy often display flattened grayish fibrils on top of the cap (see *Eucalyptus* Forests for full description).

Chlorophyllum molybdites

Fruiting bodies may appear right next to the ocean salt spray. This is also a poisonous species (see Lawns for full description).

Agaricus subrufescens

Along with *A. rotalis*, these are the two common *Agaricus* in Coastal *Casuarina* (see Compost Piles and Wood Chips for full description).

Gymnopilus subtropicus

The orange fruiting bodies can be spotted on *Casuarina* logs and buried sticks (see Wet Windward Alien Forests for full description).

Polyporus arcularius

Fruiting bodies peek through *Casuarina* duff from buried sticks (see Wet Windward Alien Forests for full description).

Pycnoporus sanguineus

This species forms deep red brackets on fallen *Casuarina* logs and branches (see Wet Windward Alien Forests for full description).

Mycena alphitophora

This small *Mycena* with sugary granules on the cap is common on *Casuarina* fruits and sticks (see Wet Windward Alien Forests for full description).

COASTAL COCONUT

Coconut palm fronds and coconut husks are excellent substrates for fungal growth. In dense groves with closed canopies the fronds and coconuts pile up and remain wet; these are great places to look for mushrooms and other fleshy fungi.

Coconut debris at the berm of the beach at MacKenzie Park (left). Waves during high tides sweep fronds and coconuts into piles. Wood-rotting fungi break down the coconut trunks (right) to provide a substrate for new plants to grow on the barren lava substrate.

Pycnoporus cinnabarinus (Jacq.: Fr.) P. Karst.

Cap 40–100 mm broad x 5–10 mm thick, semicircular to fan-shaped or irregular in outline, tough and woody, glabrous, wrinkled, deep orangish red, sometimes with white concentric zones, fading readily to orangish white in weathered specimens. Pores round, 3–4 per mm, deep red; tubes in a single layer, 1–2 mm long. Stem absent. Spore deposit white. Edibility: edible but too tough to eat.

Pycnoporus cinnabarinus appeared in incredible numbers in late 1991 and in subsequent years on coconut trees felled by lava flows at the famed black sand beach at Kalapana on the Big Island. *Pycnoporus cinnabarinus* has thicker fruiting bodies than its more common look-alike, *P. sanguineus*. These red polypores make a wonderful dye for weaving enthusiasts. Is: HA.

Pycnoporus cinnabarinus is shown growing on coconut trees felled by a recent lava flow at Kalapana black sand beach.

This large *Limacella* was found growing in the deep black sand surrounding coconut and *Casuarina* at MacKenzie Park on the Big Island.

Limacella species

Cap 50–70 mm broad, obtusely conical to convex becoming plano-umbonate, glabrous, dark brown to brown overall when young, surface soon radially split and cracked into brown appressed scales over white background. Lamellae free, close, broad, white. Stem 70–100 x 8–10 mm, cylindrical, white with brown appressed scales; annulus white, thin, ephemeral, soon disappearing. Spore deposit white. Edibility: unknown.

We have been unable to identify this interesting species of *Limacella* with certainty. It is a large, brown, conical-capped species that grows out of black sand around coconut leaf debris and in deep *Casuarina* duff along the Puna coastline. When mature it looks like a *Lepiota* or *Leucoagaricus* species. Is: HA.

Pleurotus djamor (Fr.) Boedijn

Cap 20–50 mm broad x 30–70 mm long, fan-shaped to spatula-shaped, dry, pubescent to fibrillose, ranging from white to gray. Lamellae decurrent, close, moderately broad, white. Stem absent or lateral, poorly developed, tomentose, white. Spore deposit pale yellowish white. Edibility: edible and choice.

The whitish to gray Hawaiian form of *Pleurotus djamor* commonly appears on fallen coconuts and petioles of palm fronds, but can also be found in native forests, especially at Koke'e, Kaua'i, on fallen ohi'a branches. This Oyster Mushroom is relatively thin fleshed and not the best candidate for culture. Is: HA, KA.

Pleurotus djamor will grow on a variety of substrates, but is often seen on coconuts and coconut fronds near the beach.

Psathyrella aff. *singeri* is one of the more common mushrooms growing on coconuts and coconut fronds at MacKenzie Park.

Psathyrella aff. *singeri* A. H. Smith

Cap 10–20 mm broad, convex to plano-convex, striate, glabrous, veil remnants absent, brown to dark grayish brown fading to pale brownish gray. Lamellae adnate, close, narrow, brownish gray to brown (not black). Stem 20–30 x 1–2 mm, cylindrical, dry, glabrous, white. Spore deposit brown. Edibility: unknown.

The fruiting bodies of this Hawaiian species of *Psathyrella* grow in great profusion on coconut and *Casuarina* debris during wet periods and are very similar to *Psathyrella singeri* described from Florida. The latter species differs from our material in forming smaller spores with a discernable germ pore. Is: HA.

Marasmiellus palmivorus Sharples

Cap 5–40 mm broad, convex to plano-convex, depressed, striate to wrinkled-sulcate, dry, glabrous, orange-white fading to white. Lamellae adnate, distant with numerous lamellulae, narrow, intervenose, white. Stem 5–20 x 1 mm, central to eccentric, cylindrical, solid, tough, glabrous, white overall or with the base becoming reddish brown in age. Spore deposit white. Edibility: unknown.

Marasmiellus palmivorus on coconut fronds at MacKenzie Park.

Marasmiellus palmivorus was first described as a pathogen of coconut palm from material collected in Malaysia. It is similar to *M. troyanus*, which is a pathogen on banana, ginger, and taro in Hawai'i, but the latter lacks the orange tones in the cap and lacks reddish brown tones on the stem base. Is: HA.

Pulveroboletus xylophilus (Petch) Pegler

Cap 5–40 mm broad, convex to plano-convex, dry, suede-like to felted or subvelutinous, brownish orange to yellowish brown or brown with red tones, staining dark brown to bluish brown where bruised; flesh white to pale yellow, staining grayish blue where cut. Tubes 3–5 mm long, olivaceous yellow. Pores 3–5 per mm, bright yellow to orangish yellow becoming olivaceous yellow in age and staining blue immediately when bruised. Stem 40–70 x 10–20 (–40) mm, cylindrical to subclavate, solid, dry, glabrous, not reticulate, apex yellow, base reddish brown, with bright yellow mycelium. Spore deposit olivaceous brown. Edibility: edible.

A grouping of *Pulveroboletus xylophilus* growing in black sand under coconut trees less than 20 yards from the ocean. Note the blue staining on the cut specimens.

Pulveroboletus xylophilus fruits out of black sand around coconut trees from June to August on the beach at MacKenzie Park on the Big Island. It is easily recognized by the brown felted cap, bright yellow pores, and blue staining reaction where bruised. It was first described from Sri Lanka, where it grows on rotten logs—hence the choice of species name (*xylo* = wood; *philus* = loving). This species is apparently a decomposer instead of a mycorrhizal species (root symbiont) as are most boletes. *Pulveroboletus xylophilus* has also been collected on coffee plantations in Kona. Is: HA.

ADDITIONAL SPECIES IN COASTAL COCONUT

Lactocollybia epia

This pure white mushroom fruits directly on fallen coconuts and on coconut leaf debris (see Coastal *Casuarina* for full description).

Chlorophyllum molybdites

Fruiting bodies of this poisonous species are scattered in the black sand surrounding coconut trees wherever there is a small amount of organic debris (see Lawns for full description).

Geastrum aff. *welwitschia*

This earthstar appears in large clusters in the black sand under coconut trees at MacKenzie Park on the Big Island (see Coastal *Casuarina* for full description).

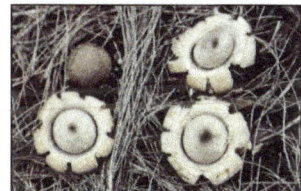

ARID LEEWARD COASTAL HABITATS

The high interior mountains on the major Hawaiian Islands block tradewind flow and moisture laden clouds from the northeast to create rain shadows–desertlike conditions on the leeward sides of the islands. The vegetation on these arid coasts is dominated by alien species: kiawe trees *(Prosopis pallida),* hoale koa *(Leucaena glauca),* and fountain grass *(Pennisetum setaceum).*

Pu'u Kohola National Historic Site in the Kawaihae region of the Big Island is typical of the arid leeward coasts. It is protected from the tradewind showers by Kohala Mountain and from Kona rains by Mauna Kea and Mauna Loa. The double rain shadow limits the annual rainfall to less than 10 inches per year.

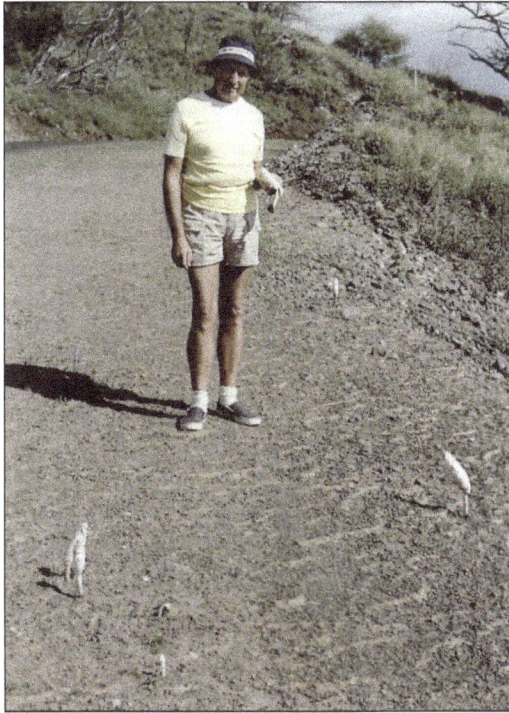

Podaxis pistillaris along roadways of a new subdivision in Kohala on the Big Island.

A disintegrating fruiting body of *Podaxis pistillaris.*

ARID LEEWARD COASTAL HABITATS

Podaxis pistillaris (L. ex Pers.) Morse

Cap 30–40 mm broad x 60–100 mm tall, ellipsoidal to obtusely conical, base of cap remains adhered to stem; surface dry, shiny, glabrous, fragile and papery, white to pale cream, breaking up into fibrous scales and sloughing in age. Gleba powdery or stringy-powdery, dark brown to black. Stem 60–80 x 6–10 mm, cylindrical with a basal bulb, dry, hard and woody, fibrous, striate, white to yellowish brown. Spores dark brown to black. Edibility: unknown.

The fruiting bodies of *Podaxis pistillaris* shown in the illustration are growing along roadways in a subdivision in Kohala on the Big Island. Watering of newly planted grass brought out the stalked puffball in profusion. This fungus is called an *agaricoid gasteromycete* since structural and molecular evidence show that the species has evolved from a gilled mushroom ancestor but now looks more like a stalked puffball. After maturing, the head disintegrates and the spores disperse in the wind. This fungus is known as the False Shaggy Mane because of its resemblance to *Coprinus comatus,* the true Shaggy Mane mushroom. Indeed, although *Podaxis* does not form true gills and does not autodigest, it is closely related to *C. comatus.* Is: HA, MA.

Battarraeoides digueti (Pat. & Har.) Heim & Herrera

Peridium 20–30 mm broad x 15–20 mm tall, hemispherical to cushion-shaped, resting on a concave base at the apex of the stem; surface glabrous, dry, persistent, white with scattered small holes through which the spores are released. Gleba powdery, rusty brown. Stem 100–200 x 8–10 mm, cylindrical, arising from a well-developed volva, dry, hard and woody, fibrous, sulcate, white to cream. Volva cup-shaped, tough, dingy white, often buried. Spores cinnamon brown. Edibility: unknown.

Battarraeoides digueti can be spotted among the fountain grass along the Kona Coast of the Big Island, especially where kiawe trees have been cut, because this fungus is a decomposer of buried roots. This stalked puffball may be mistaken for a *Tulostoma*, but the spore sac is covered with multiple pores or ostioles for spore release. Is: HA.

Battarraeoides is found around Spencer Beach Park and Pu'u Kohola Heiau at Kawaihae on the Big Island. Note that there are several openings in the peridium for spore release.

Gloeophyllum striatum (Sw.: Fr.) Murrill

Cap 30–60 mm broad and deep x 3–5 mm thick, fan-shaped with contracted stemlike base, single or with several fused; finely velvety to glabrous, wrinkled, dry, tough and leathery, with concentric zones of gray and brown. Spore surface of thin but tough gills that are forked and anastomosed, 1–4 mm deep, edges often toothed or eroded, dark grayish brown. Stem absent. Spore deposit white. Edibility: edible but too tough to eat.

Gloeophyllum striatum is the most common bracket fungus on the fallen logs and branches of kiawe trees along the dry coastlines in Hawai'i. The fruiting bodies become hard and brittle in this arid zone. Is: HA, KA, LA.

Gloeophyllum striatum on kiawe at Spencer Beach Park.

Tulostoma involucratum Long

Peridium 10–30 mm broad x 10–15 mm tall, ovoid, of two distinct layers: exoperidium membranous, fragile, dingy white, adhering sand and mostly sloughing off, remaining as a cup of sandy debris at the base of the spore sac; endoperidium tough, glabrous, white, with a single, central, apical elevated pore through which the spores are released. Gleba powdery, brown. Stem 20–100 x 3–7 mm, cylindrical with a basal bulb, tough and woody, fibrous, cinnamon brown. Spores brown. Edibility: unknown.

Collections of *Tulostoma involucratum* have been made at the berm of beaches in association with kiawe thickets at Kihei on Maui and at Kiholo on the Big Island. The species also occurs in association with mamane-naio habitats at high elevations on Mauna Kea on the Big Island. The genus *Tulostoma* is a commonly collected stalked puffball found in xeric habitats throughout the world. Is: HA, MA.

Tulostoma involucratum at the berm of Kiholo Beach on the Kona Coast of the Big Island.

Tulostoma dumeticola Long

Peridium 4–6 mm broad x 3–5 mm tall, ovoid, tough, glabrous, dingy white, with a single, central, apical pore through which the spores are released. Gleba powdery, brown. Stem 8–15 x 2–3 mm, buried in soil, cylindrical with a basal bulb, tough and woody, fibrous, pale grayish brown. Spores brown. Edibility: unknown.

This tiny stalked puffball was found growing in duff on lava boulders under kiawe trees at Spencer Beach Park at Kawaihae on the Big Island. The comparison with the size of a dime, in the illustration, shows why mycologists keep their noses to the ground. Is: HA.

You need to look closely and keep your eyes to the ground to spy this tiny dime-sized *Tulostoma*.

ARID LEEWARD MONTANE HABITATS

The higher elevations along the leeward coasts of Mauna Kea on the Big Island and Haleakala on Maui are also part of the rain shadow created by the blocking of the tradewinds by these high mountains. Even in these dry areas, fungi are at work breaking down old tree roots and other organic materials. Desert stalked puffballs and earthstars are characteristic of these areas; they spring up after rare all-island storms and remain in a dried condition for months.

The arid mamane-naio vegetation zone encircles Mauna Kea on the Big Island at the 1,800- to 2,900-meter elevation. Mamane *(Sophora chrysophylla)* is endemic to the Hawaiian Islands, whereas naio *(Myoporum sandwicense)* is found in Hawai'i and the Cook Islands. Agarics and gasteromycetes appear after infrequent Kona storms and seasonal afternoon rains.

Heliocybe sulcata
(Berk.) Redhead & Ginns

Cap 15–25 mm broad, convex to plano-convex, margin sulcate, disc with small raised scales, minutely fibrillose elsewhere, dry, tough, grayish orange with brown scales. Gills adnate to adnexed, subdistant, broad, thick, tough, pale grayish orange to tan. Stem 10–20 x 2–3 mm, cylindrical, dry, scaly towards the base, tough, brownish orange to brown. Spore deposit white. Edibility: edible.

The fruiting bodies of *Heliocybe sulcata* appear on fallen naio branches in the dry saddle area and slopes of Mauna Loa, Hualalai, and Mauna Kea. They dry out and harden, and may persist for weeks before deteriorating. Is: HA.

Fruiting body of *Heliocybe sulcata* on a fallen naio branch near Pu'u La'au on the slopes of Mauna Kea.

Onygena corvina
Alb. & Schwein.

Fruiting body a globose head elevated on a short stem; fertile head 1.5–2 mm broad, roughened, pale brown. Stem 2–4 x 1 mm, cylindrical, glabrous, white. Spores pale brown. Edibility: unknown.

These tiny, unusual ascomycetes form fruiting bodies resembling miniature stalked puffballs on keratin-rich substrates like owl dung and owl pellets. The spores are formed by asci embedded in the globose head, which cracks open at maturity to release the spores. Is: HA.

Onygena covina fruiting on an owl pellet regurgitated by an introduced barn owl, a species that lives in these dry montane habitats.

Myriostoma coliforme
(With.: Pers.) Corda

Exoperidium cracking into angular seg-ments (areolate), pale yellowish brown, not encrusting debris, epigeal, separat-ing from endoperidium and splitting into 7–12 recurved rays, not hygroscopic. Endoperidium 30–60 mm broad, elevated by numerous tiny stalks in dried material, surface roughened with small warts and ridges, grayish brown to brown, develop-ing numerous holes 1–3 mm in diameter through which the spores are released. Spores dark brown. Edibility: unknown.

The Salt-and-Pepper Shaker Earthstar, *Myriostoma coliforme*, is one of the more common gasteromycetes found under mamane-naio thickets on Mauna Kea.

This large earthstar is common in the mamane-naio vegetation zone of Mauna Kea. More than 50 fruiting bodies have been seen under a single mamane tree. Manuka State Park near South Point on the Big Island is another good place to see this interesting species. The genus *Myriostoma* is easy to distinguish from other earthstars in the genus *Geastrum* because numerous holes develop in the endoperidium, instead of only one, to facilitate spore release. Is: HA, OA.

Disciseda anomala
(Cooke & Massee) G. Cunn.

Fruiting body 15–30 mm broad, flattened-globose. Exoperidium brown, composed of hyphae mixed with dirt and sand, soon sloughing off and remaining as a sandy cup at the base of the endoperidium. Endoperidium glabrous, gray to pale grayish brown, developing a single (rarely several) beaked apical pore through which the spores are released. Spores dark purplish brown. Edibility: unknown.

Three partially buried fruiting bodies of *Disciseda anomala*.

Disciseda anomala is easily spotted where game birds have scratched the puffballs out of the dirt. Fruiting bodies of this species are usually found in large groupings. Look for the sand case at the base of each puffball, a characteristic that distinguishes *Disciseda* from *Lycoperdon*. A second species of *Disciseda, D. verrucosa*, also occurs in this habitat but differs in that it forms much larger spores. Without the aid of a microscope, you will not be able to distinguish these two species. Is: HA.

Geastrum fornicatum
(Huds.) Hook.

Fruiting body hypogeous, separating into three distinct layers. Mycelial layer encrusting debris, cuplike and buried in soil. Middle layer evaginating and splitting into 4–5 recurved arms resting at their tips on the mycelial cup (i.e., fornicate), brown to beige, inner surface sometimes cracked. Endoperidium 10–20 mm broad, subglobose to turbinate with an annular ridge at the base (apophysis), elevated on a short stem, surface minutely hairy, grayish brown; peristome indistinctly delimited, fibrillose. Spores brown. Edibility: unknown.

Geastrum fornicatum is one of seven different earthstars found within the mamane-naio vegetation zone. *Geastrum fornicatum* "stands" on its rays, a fornicate condition.

Geastrum fornicatum is the only earthstar in the arid mamane-naio habitat that is fornicate. The exoperidium separates into two layers, with the outer mycelial layer typically remaining as a cup-shaped structure buried in the soil, while the inner layer everts, splits into rays, and stands on its tip toes at the edge of the buried cup. If the star-shaped inner layer and its attached spore sac are broken off the mycelial cup, then it becomes difficult to distinguish the species from other nonfornicate earthstars that occur commonly in the arid montane habitats. This species has also been found under kiawe trees along the leeward coasts of the Big Island. Is: HA, MA.

Geastrum corollinum
(Batsch) Hollos

Exoperidium separating from endoperidium and splitting into 8–11 sharply pointed rays, outer surface not adhering debris, rays hygroscopic and curved over spore sac when dried, pale brownish white to nearly white. Endoperidium 7–13 mm broad, sessile, surface smooth, dark grayish brown, with a usually distinctly delimited, fibrillose peristome. Spores brown. Edibility: unknown.

A group of *Geastrum corollinum* on Mauna Kea. In this tiny species the rays of the star are curved back over the spore sac, a hygroscopic condition.

Geastrum corollinum, a hygroscopic earthstar, appears in large groups of 25–50 fruiting bodies in the mamane-naio vegetation zone. Basidiocarps of the Hawaiian populations are smaller than those in European or North American populations, with spore sacs averaging only about 10 millimeters in diameter. In this regard they are more reminiscent of *Geastrum hungaricum*, which differs in spore features. A second small hygroscopic earthstar from the mamane-naio habitat is *Geastrum campestre*, which differs in having a sulcate peristome. Is: HA, OA.

Battarraea phalloides (Dicks.: Pers.) Pers.

Peridium 30–45 mm broad x 15–30 mm tall, hemispherical to cushion-shaped, resting on a concave base at the apex of the stem; surface glabrous, dry, white, falling off as a cup revealing the spore mass (circumsessile dehiscence). Gleba powdery, rusty brown, exposed at maturity. Stem 150–350 x 10–15 mm, cylindrical, dry, hard and woody, fibrous to scaly, brown, arising from a well-developed buried volva. Volva cup-shaped, tough, dingy white. Spores cinnamon brown. Edibility: unknown.

These foot-tall stalked puffballs have no ostiole for spore release. Instead, the entire upper endoperidium dehisces to reveal the spore mass. These desert stalked puffballs are found in the dry, high elevation regions of the Big Island, including Manuka State Park, but a nice collection was also found at a bus stop in downtown Honolulu, so *B. phalloides* may be found in any dry, leeward location in Hawai'i. Is: HA, OA.

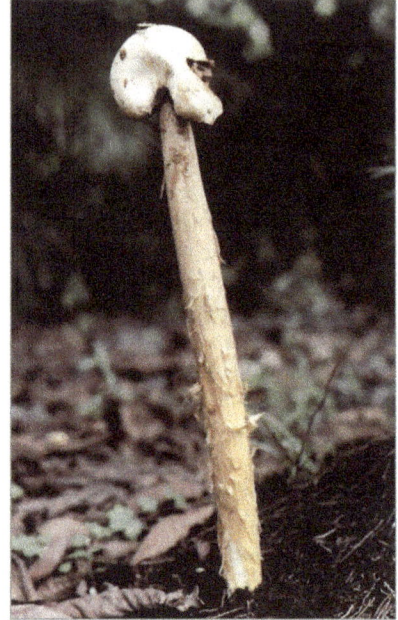

Battarraea phalloides found under mamane-naio trees.

Tulostoma fimbriata var. *campestre* (Morgan) G. Moreno

Peridium 10–18 mm broad x 8–10 mm tall, hemispherical to ovoid, tough, glabrous, dingy white, with a single, central, apical pore through which the spores are released; base of spore sac often with a thin layer of brown mycelium that adheres sandy soil. Gleba powdery, brown. Stem 20–40 x 2–4 mm, entirely buried in soil, cylindrical with a small basal bulb, tough and woody, scaly pale orangish brown. Spores brown. Edibility: unknown.

Tulostoma fimbriata is one of the more frequently encountered stalked puffballs in the high elevations of Mauna Kea. What looks like a small puffball about 1 centimeter in diameter actually has a thin stalk buried underneath in the soil. Is: HA.

Tulostoma fimbriata var. *campestre* growing among the silverswords on Mauna Kea at 3,000 meters elevation.

Phellinus robustus
(P. Karst.) Boudot & Galzin

Cap 200–300 mm broad x 70–100 radius x 40–60 mm thick, irregularly semicircular to shelflike, cracked, sulcate, glabrous, brown to dark brown; flesh tough and woody, yellowish brown, zonate. Pores round, 7–9 per mm, yellow to yellowish brown; tubes in several layers (perennial), each layer 2–3 mm thick. Stem absent. Spore deposit white. Edibility: too tough to eat.

Phellinus robustus is rarely found elsewhere in Hawai'i, but conks are scattered on the trunks of living naio trees on the slopes of Mauna Kea. *Phellinus robustus* differs from the more common *P. gilvus* in forming much larger basidiocarps with yellowish instead of purplish brown pores, and in forming much larger, dextrinoid spores. Is: HA, KA.

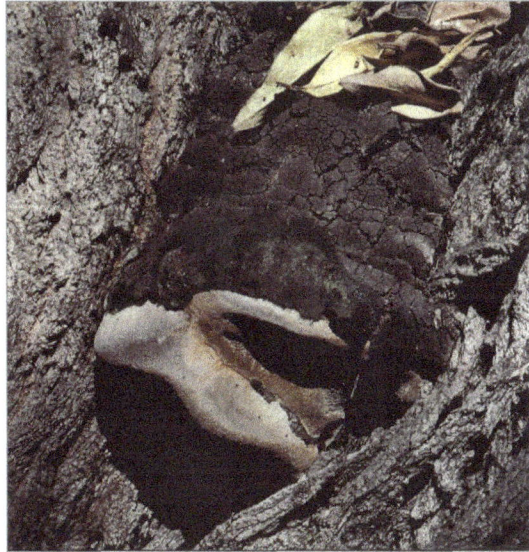

A large conk of *Phellinus robustus* nestled in the crotch of a naio tree.

Gloeophyllum trabeum (Fr.) Murrill

Cap 30–50 mm broad x 15–20 mm deep x 4–6 mm thick, fan-shaped, sometimes imbricate, single; surface knobby to radially undulate, finely tomentose becoming glabrous in age, tough and leathery, usually not zonate, brown to cinnamon brown with grayish margin. Spore surface of radially elongate pores (daedaleoid), 2–4 per mm, 1–4 mm deep, edges even, pale brown to brownish orange. Stem absent. Spore deposit white. Edibility: too tough to eat.

Basidiocarps of *Gloeophyllum trabeum* are the most commonly encountered bracket-forming fungi on fallen naio trunks and branches. It is similar to *G. striatum* from arid lowland coastal habitats, but that species has a more gill-like and less poroid spore-bearing surface. Is: HA.

Gloeophyllum trabeum forms rows of brackets on fallen naio branches.

ARID LEEWARD MONTANE HABITATS

CONIFER FORESTS

A number of pines (*Pinus* spp.), sugi pines *(Cryptomeria)*, cypress (*Cupressus* spp.), redwoods *(Sequoia),* and other conifers were planted on the high mountain slopes of the various Hawaiian Islands during the early 1900s. Dense stands can be seen at Koke'e State Park on Kaua'i, Polipoli Springs State Park on Maui, Kamakou Forest Reserve on Moloka'i, and along the Keanakolu Road on the Big Island. These forests support a number of mycorrhizal fungi, and saprotrophic species that decompose conifer needles.

Polipoli Springs State Park on the slopes of Haleakala on Maui encompasses 1,200 acres of pines, cypress, redwoods, and other conifers planted in multiacre groves. Literally thousands of *Suillus, Mycena,* and other mushrooms appear here in the winter months when storms and evening cloud banks dampen the forest floor.

Suillus brevipes (Peck) Kuntze

Cap 60–120 mm broad, convex to plano-convex, glabrous, shiny, glutinous, dark brown or olivaceous brown fading to cinnamon brown; flesh thick, soft, yellowish white. Tubes 4–10 mm long, yellow becoming olivaceous brown. Pores 1–2 per mm, bright yellow becoming olivaceous brown, not staining blue when bruised. Stem 30–70 x 15–20 mm, cylindrical, glabrous, lacking glandular dots, white to yellow. Spore deposit olivaceous brown. Edibility: edible with caution.

A cluster of Short-stemmed Slippery Jacks from under Monterey pines on Mauna Kea.

Short-stemmed Slippery Jacks are abundant under Monterey pine *(Pinus radiata)* on Mauna Kea on the Big Island, Polipoli Springs State Park on Maui, and Koke'e State Park on Kaua'i during the fall and winter months. The pore surface is bright yellow when young and turns dingy brown with age. Even though the caps are slimy and unattractive when wet, this species is edible. There are reports of gastric upsets from some individuals, however, so be forewarned before eating this species. Is: HA, KA, MA, MO.

Suillus granulatus (Fr.) Kuntze

Cap 60–100 mm broad, convex to plano-convex, glabrous, shiny, glutinous, brown or pale reddish brown with splotches of creamy brown, fading to cinnamon brown; flesh thick, soft, yellowish white. Tubes 5–10 mm long, yellow becoming olivaceous brown. Pores 1–2 per mm, bright yellow, becoming olivaceous brown, not staining blue when bruised. Stem 40–80 x 8–12 mm, cylindrical, white to yellow and covered with brown glandular dots. Spore deposit olivaceous brown. Edibility: edible.

Typical fruiting bodies of *Suillus granulatus* from along the Makaha Ridge Road at Koke'e, Kaua'i.

Suillus granulatus might be confused with *S. brevipes* but *S. granulatus* prefers slash pine *(Pinus elliotii)* to Monterey pine, and has a more reddish brown cap and a narrower stem covered with glandular dots. It grows symbiotically with slash pines along with *S. salmonicolor*, which also looks similar but is easily distinguished by the presence of a gelatinous partial veil. Is: HA, KA, MA, OA.

Suillus salmonicolor
(Frost) Halling

Cap 40–80 mm broad, convex to plano-convex, glabrous, shiny, glutinous, ochraceous salmon to pinkish brown becoming yellowish brown; flesh thick, soft, yellowish white. Tubes 6–10 mm long, olivaceous yellow. Pores 1–2 mm, yellow becoming olivaceous brown, not staining blue when bruised, covered at first by the gelatinous partial veil. Stem 40–70 x 10–15 mm, cylindrical, dingy salmon brown and covered with reddish brown glandular dots; partial veil persistent, gelatinous, grayish salmon with white margin. Spore deposit olivaceous brown. Edibility: edible.

A large grouping of *Suillus salmonicolor* under slash pines along Makaha Ridge Road at Koke'e, Kaua'i.

Suillus salmonicolor is found under slash pines *(Pinus elliotii)* at Koke'e on Kaua'i and on lawns wherever slash pines are planted in landscaping. A quick look under the cap shows a gray-colored partial veil covering the pore surface in young specimens and then peeling away to form a sheathlike annulus. Is: HA, KA.

Paxillus panuoides (Fr.: Fr.) Fr.

Cap 30–100 mm broad x 20–40 mm deep, fan-shaped with incurved, wavy and often lobed margin, several fruitbodies often fused, surface dry, downy or felted, yellowish brown to olivaceous brown. Gills radiating from base of cap, close, narrow, often intervenose, yellow to creamy brown. Stem absent. Spore deposit yellowish brown. Edibility: unknown but potentially poisonous.

Paxillus panuoides forms fan-shaped fruiting bodies with no stem. This species prefers conifer logs and stumps. Specimens have even been

These specimens of *Paxillus panuoides* are growing on pine logs at Polipoli Springs State Park on Maui.

found on wooden boxes, presumably made of pine, discarded in the wet forest. Although *P. panuoides* forms gills and lacks a stem, there are good micromorphological and molecular data that indicate the species is more closely related to the boletes than it is to the gill fungi. Is: HA, MA.

Laccaria proxima under conifers at the Kamakou Forest Reserve on Moloka'i. This species is very common under Monterey pines in the Saddle Area of the Big Island.

Laccaria proxima (Boud.) Pat.

Cap 15–45 mm broad, convex to plano-convex, centrally depressed, minutely scaly overall, translucent-striate, reddish brown or paler. Gills adnate, subdistant, broad, pinkish white becoming grayish red. Stem 40–75 x 2–6 mm, cylindrical, tough, fibrillose, striate, grayish red to reddish brown; basal mycelium white; basidiocarps lacking violet colors. Spore deposit white. Edibility: edible.

In Hawai'i, *Laccaria* species are mycorrhizal with pines and *Eucalyptus*. *Laccaria proxima* is common in pine plantations, especially on those edges of the forests facing the tradewind showers. This species is characterized by its ellipsoid spores. A second species, *Laccaria fraterna*, grows only in association with *Eucalyptus*. Is: HA, KA, MA, MO, OA.

Hemimycena tortuosa (P. D. Orton) Redhead

Cap 2–6 mm broad, convex to plano-convex, nonstriate, dry, pruinose overall, pure white. Gills adnate, close to subdistant, narrow, white. Stem 3–10 x 0.5–1 mm, eccentric, cylindrical, pruinose overall, pure white. Spore deposit white. Edibility: unknown.

This beautiful tiny agaric grows on rotting branches of sugi pine *(Cryptomaria japonica)* on the island of Kaua'i. It gets its specific epithet "tortuosa" from the helically twisted sterile cells that cover the stem surface (caulocystidia). Is: KA.

Hemimycena tortuosa on debris of sugi pines at Koke'e State Park on Kaua'i.

Mycena metata (Fr.) Kummer

Cap 10–20 mm broad, campanulate to convex-umbonate, striate when moist, glabrous, hygrophanous, brown to grayish brown fading to grayish white, tan or grayish orange; odor faintly like bleach. Gills adnexed to adnate, close to subdistant, narrow, grayish white to grayish orange. Stem 40–120 x 1–2 mm, cylindrical, pliant, hollow, glabrous, dry, grayish white to grayish brown. Spore deposit white. Edibility: unknown.

Mycena metata in loblolly pine (*Pinus taeda*) litter at Kamakou Forest Preserve on Moloka'i. This *Mycena* is the most abundant mushroom in pine forests throughout the islands during the wet winter months.

Mycena metata blankets pine needle litter by the thousands during the winter months at Polipoli on Maui, at Kamakou on Moloka'i, and in isolated pine groves on Mauna Kea on the Big Island. The species is hygrophanous, with caps initially brown and striate, then they fade with moisture loss to grayish white or tan and lose their striations. Is: HA, MA, MO.

Mycena pura (Pers.: Fr.) Kummer

Cap 15–35 mm broad, convex to plano-convex, with a small umbo or shallowly depressed, glabrous, hygrophanous, reddish brown to purplish brown fading to pinkish brown or grayish red; odor and taste strongly of radishes. Gills adnate, subdistant, moderately broad, grayish red to purplish gray. Stem 35–50 x 1.5–3 mm, cylindrical, glabrous, dry, hollow, brittle, reddish brown to purplish brown. Spore deposit white. Edibility: poisonous.

This deep violet variety of *Mycena pura* has been found in groves of Monterey cypress in the Kamakou Forest Preserve on Moloka'i.

There have been many forms of *Mycena pura* described from around the world, and the Hawaiian form is certainly not *M. pura* f. *pura,* but rather comes closest to *M. pura* f. *roseoviolacea.* Our material always has violet tones in the cap, gills, and stem and a rather strong radishlike odor. It occurs not only under cypress, but also in mesic montane native forests. Is: KA, MO.

Mycena sanguinolenta (Alb. & Schwein.: Fr.) Kummer

Cap 5–15 mm broad, obtusely conical to campanulate, striate, glabrous, dry, reddish brown. Gills ascending, narrowly adnate, close to subdistant, narrow, white with red edges. Stem 50–80 x 1–1.5 mm, cylindrical, fragile, hollow, glabrous above, tomentose below, reddish brown, exuding a brownish red latex when cut. Spore deposit white. Edibility: unknown.

Mycena sanguinolenta grows under redwoods at Koke'e, Kaua'i. The cap is reddish brown, the edges of the white gills are red, and the stem bleeds red droplets when broken or squeezed. Is: KA.

Mycena sanguinolenta is common under redwoods surrounding the lawns at the visitor's center at Koke'e State Park on Kaua'i.

Marasmius androsaceus (L.: Fr.) Fr.

Cap 5–10 mm broad, convex to plano-convex, rugulose-striate, glabrous, dry, brown to pale brown. Gills adnate, subdistant, narrow, buff. Stem 30–50 x <1 mm, wiry, glabrous, dark brown to black, with wiry black rhizomorphs. Spore deposit white. Edibility: unknown.

Marasmius androsaceus, the Horsehair Fungus, derives its name from its hair-thin, tough stem and rhizomorphs that measure less than a millimeter in diameter. Look for this species at Hosmer's Grove on Haleakala and in other high-elevation conifer groves, where it grows out of pine needles. Is: MA.

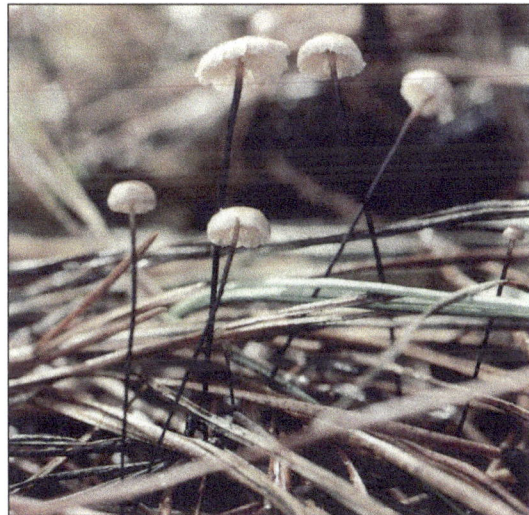

These fruiting bodies of *Marasmius androsaceus,* with their "horsehair" stems, are growing from pine needles at Waikamoi, Maui.

Hygrocybe conica (Schaeff.: Fr.) Kummer

Cap 8–25 mm broad, conical, striate, radially appressed-fibrillose to silky-streaked, greasy, red to orangish red fading to yellow or brownish yellow, staining black overall in age. Gills free, subdistant, broad, waxy, grayish yellowish white with red tones, blackening in age. Stem 25–60 x 2–4 mm, cylindrical, twisted-fibrous, glabrous, dry, yellow above, white below, staining black in age. Spore deposit white. Edibility: reported to be mildly poisonous.

The bright colored fruiting bodies of *Hygrocybe conica* have been found in mosses and needle duff under pines and cypress in Hawai'i. The Conical Waxy Cap stains black overall in age and dries entirely black. For a comparison with *H. conicoides*, see the section on Lawns. Is: MA, MO.

These *Hygrocybe conica* were growing under Monterey cypress *(Cupressus macrocarpa)* at Kamakou Forest Preserve on Moloka'i.

Amanita muscaria var. formosa (Pers.: Fr.) Bertillon

Cap 70–150 mm broad, subglobose to convex becoming plano-convex, subviscid, covered with scattered, white to pale yellowish white, pyramidal universal veil warts, surface orange to yellowish orange. Gills subfree, close, broad, white. Stem 80–200 x 10–20 mm, cylindrical or enlarged downward to a bulbous base, fibrillose to scaly, white; with a skirtlike, pendulous, white annulus; volva composed of several concentric rings of white tissue over the basal bulb. Spore deposit white. Edibility: poisonous and hallucinogenic.

Amanita muscaria is probably one of the most recognized mushrooms in the world because of its striking coloration and large size. This species is commonly depicted on postcards, cartoons, and ceramic figurines. The Fly Agaric is also well known because of its notoriety as being both poisonous and hallucinogenic (see sections on poisonous and hallucinogenic mushrooms). Juices of this mushroom added to milk will kill flies, thus the name Fly Agaric. The yellowish orange *formosa* variety of *Amanita muscaria* can be found under pines at Koke'e State Park on Kaua'i from December through February after heavy winter rains. Is: KA.

These spectacular, large fruiting bodies of *Amanita muscaria* are growing under pines along Makaha Ridge Road at Koke'e, Kaua'i.

Agaricus lanatorubescens
K. R. Peterson, Desjardin & Hemmes

Cap 40–60 mm broad, hemispherical to broadly convex, covered at first by a cottony, white universal veil, becoming appressed fibrillose to squamulose in age, white then finally reddish brown; flesh staining pink when cut; odor of almonds. Gills free, close, broad, reddish gray becoming dark brown. Stem 60–80 x 10–13 mm, cylindrical above a bulbous base, covered at first with white cottony veil, glabrous and white to pinkish brown above annulus, white then darkening to reddish brown at the base; with a pendulous, floccose annulus. Spore deposit dark brown. Edibility: unknown.

This newly described species of *Agaricus* is easily recognized by the white, cottony, fluffy universal veil tissue that initially covers the cap and stem. The universal veil tissue often disappears with age and the cap becomes reddish brown. In addition cut tissues stain pink to red and smell like almond extract. Although we suspect that the species is edible, we have not yet tried it. Is: HA.

Specimens of *Agaricus lanatorubescens* under pines on Mauna Kea on the Big Island.

Leucopaxillus gentianeus (Quél.) Kotl.

Cap 50–100 mm broad, convex becoming plane-depressed, glabrous, dry, reddish brown to cinnamon brown; flesh thick, white; taste bitter. Gills adnate, close, narrow, white. Stem 50–90 x 10–20 mm, cylindrical to clavate, dry, fibrillose, white; arising from a mat of copious white mycelium that binds the substrate. Spore deposit white. Edibility: inedible.

This large mushroom, also known as *Leucopaxillus amarus*, grows under conifers and *Eucalyptus* in Hawai'i. A large clump of mycelium and attached humus usually clings to the stem when you pick a fruiting body. This mushroom tastes bitter and is not good to eat. Is: HA, MA.

These specimens of *Leucopaxillus gentianeus* are growing under conifers at Hosmer's Grove on Haleakala on Maui.

Ramariopsis kunzei appears under cypress and redwoods at Polipoli Springs State Park on Maui.

Ramariopsis kunzei (Fr.) Donk

Fruiting bodies coralloid, 20–50 mm tall x 15–40 mm broad, with numerous erect branches arising dichotomously to polychotomously from a short rudimentary stem. Branches 1–2 mm thick, glabrous, white with white or yellowish tips in age. Stem 10–15 x 2–4 mm, tomentose, white. No bruising reactions. Spore deposit white. Edibility: edible.

This small white coral fungus is highly branched with almost no main stalk. The branch tips turn yellow with age. Is: MA.

Ramariopsis corniculata (Fr.) Petersen

Fruiting bodies coralloid, 20–40 mm tall x 15–30 mm broad, with few, erect, dichotomous branches arising from a short stem. Branches 1–2 mm thick, glabrous, bright yellow to yellowish orange. Stem 5–10 x 2 mm, glabrous, yellow. Spore deposit white. Edibility: edible.

Another small coral fungus, *Ramariopsis corniculata* (also known as *Clavulinopsis corniculata*) is readily located in the cypress duff because of its bright yellowish orange color. This species has been found under cypress at Waikamoi on Maui and Kamakou Forest Preserve on Moloka'i. Is: MA, MO.

Ramariopsis corniculata stands out in the dark, wet duff under cypress at Waikamoi on Maui.

Thelephora terrestris Fr.

Fruiting body fanlike, formed in confluent clusters 80–120 mm broad; margin hairy, pale grayish brown to brown, centrally lumpy and velvety, dark brown. Texture tough, leathery. Lower spore-bearing surface smooth to wrinkled, grayish brown on the margin, purplish brown to cinnamon brown elsewhere. Stem short, lateral to central, velvety, dark brown. Spore deposit purplish brown. Edibility: unknown, but too tough to eat.

The Earth Fan grows up small stems of living plants or over sticks fallen in pine needles to form fan-shaped fruiting bodies. It is symbiotic (mycorrhizal) with the roots of pine trees and helps maintain the health of the forest. The fertile surface lacks gills or pores, but instead is smooth or coarsely wrinkled. Is: HA, KA.

Thelephora terrestris often covers fallen branches in the duff of pine groves on the Big Island.

Bovista pila
Berk. & M. A. Curtis

Fruiting body 20–45 mm broad, globose. Exoperidium thin, furfuraceous, white to gray or gray brown, becoming areolate in age and readily sloughing. Endoperidium thin, glabrous, shiny, bronze to yellowish brown, opening by a large irregular central pore (seldom more than one pore) through which the spores are dispersed. Gleba white and chambered when young, becoming brown, powdery, and cottony at maturity. Spores brown. Edibility: edible when young with white gleba.

With age these puffballs develop a yellowish metallic luster. The fruiting bodies are lightweight and often detach from the substrate and blow with the wind, hence their common name Tumbling Puffball. Is: HA, MA, OA.

Bronzed fruiting bodies of *Bovista pila* under pines at Polipoli Springs State Park on Maui.

EUCALYPTUS FORESTS

As were conifers, a large number of *Eucalyptus* species were planted on the various Hawaiian Islands in the early 1900s. Large groves of *Eucalyptus* can be seen along the roads to Koke'e State Park and in Kukuiolono Park on Kaua'i, in Kamakou Forest Preserve and Pala'au State Park on Moloka'i, along the Waihe'e Ridge Trail and Kaumahina Wayside Park on Maui, and at Kalopa State Park and Honokaia on the Big Island.

This forest of *Eucalyptus* at Kamakou Forest Preserve on Moloka'i supports an incredible crop of mycorrhizal and saprophytic fungi during rainy fall and winter months.

Amanita marmorata under *Eucalyptus* along the Waihe'e Ridge Trail on Maui. This deadly poisonous species is common on all islands under *Eucalyptus* (gums), *Melaleuca* (bottle-brush or paperbark), and *Casuarina* (ironwoods or Australian pines).

Amanita marmorata subsp. *myrtacearum* O. K. Miller, Hemmes & G. Wong

Cap 50–70 mm broad, convex to plano-convex, often shallowly depressed, glabrous, subviscid, evenly colored white to grayish white or more often radially marbled (marmorate) gray to pale grayish brown. Gills free, close, broad, white. Stem 40–80 x 5–12 mm, gradually enlarged downward to a bulbous base, dry, fibrillose, white, with a large, pendulous, membranous white annulus near the apex. Volva saccate, thin to thick, white, persistent. Spore deposit white. Edibility: deadly poisonous.

Amanita marmorata is mycorrhizal with *Eucalyptus* and other members of the myrtle family introduced to Hawai'i from Australia, including *Melaleuca*, the bottlebrush or paper-bark trees so popular in landscaping. This fact was made apparent when hundreds of fruiting bodies of this species appeared in a section of the National Botanical Garden on Kaua'i featuring various myrtle trees native to Australia. *Amanita marmorata* is deadly poisonous if ingested. As little as one bite of a cap could be fatal to an adult (see section on Poisonous Mushrooms). Is: HA, KA, LA, MA, MO, OA.

Occasionally, the dark fibrils on the cap of *Amanita marmorata* are thick and give it an overall gray, marbled appearance, hence its scientific name.

Dermocybe clelandii
(A. H. Smith) Grgurinovic

Cap 40–60 mm broad, convex to plano-convex, often depressed, minutely appressed-fibrillose, dry, brown (umber) to orangish brown, darker in the center; flesh yellow. Gills adnate, close, broad, mustard yellow. Stem 40–60 x 5–8 mm, cylindrical, dry, fibrillose, yellowish white above, yellowish brown at the base; with yellow partial veil remnants (cortina) near the apex. Spore deposit rusty brown. Edibility: unknown and best to avoid.

Dermocybe clelandii is one of the few Cortinari found in Hawai'i. It is characterized by its brownish cap

A cluster of *Dermocybe clelandii* from Waihou Springs State Park on Maui.

and bright mustard-yellow gills that drop a rusty brown spore print. We have collected this species a number of times under *Eucalyptus* at Waihou Springs State Park on Maui, near Kamakou Forest Preserve on Moloka'i, and along the Munro Trail on Lana'i. Is: LA, MO, MA.

Setchelliogaster tenuipes
(Setch.) Pouzar

Cap 10–20 mm broad, hemispherical to obtusely conical, disc flattened, margin incurved and nearly touching the stem, ragged; surface glabrous, wrinkled, dry, dark reddish brown; odor strong, reminiscent of fresh green corn. Gills contorted, strongly anastomosed, sub-poroid, bright rusty brown. Stem 10–25 x 2–3 mm, cylindrical or narrowed downward, fibrillose, brownish orange to brown, with a thin zone of fibrils near the apex from the cortinate partial veil. Spores rusty brown. Edibility: unknown.

This species is of particular interest to mycologists because it has char-acteristics of both an agaric and a

Setchelliogaster tenuipes from a *Eucalyptus* forest along the Munro Trail on Lana'i.

Gasteromycete. The cap never fully expands, the gills are contorted and fused together, and the spores are not forcibly discharged. This condition is called *secotioid*. *Setchelliogaster* is closely related to the agaric genus *Descolea* and to the truffle genus *Descomyces*. Fruiting bodies from Maui and Lana'i give off a strong green-corn odor that can be detected in the forest from a long distance. Is: LA, MA.

Laccaria fraterna
(Cooke & Massee: Sacc.) Pegler

Cap 5–30 mm broad, convex to plano-convex with a central depression, transparent-striate, glabrous or with a granulose to scruffy disc, hygrophanous, reddish brown to rusty brown fading to grayish orange. Gills adnate, subdistant to distant, broad, grayish red. Stem 15–70 x 2–5 mm, cylindrical, fibrous, pliant, silky-striate, glabrous, reddish brown with white downy mycelium at the base. Spore deposit white. Edibility: unknown.

Laccaria fraterna is a reddish brown mycorrhizal species that can be abundant on the ground among fallen branches and leaves in wet *Eucalyptus* forests and will appear in the root system of *Eucalyptus* used for landscaping. *Laccaria fraterna* looks similar to *L. proxima* (see Conifer Forests), but the latter species is larger, grows associated with pines, and has four-spored basidia, whereas L. *fraterna* is always associated with *Eucalyptus* and has two-spored basidia. Is: HA, KA, LA, MA, MO, OA.

Laccaria fraterna growing under *Eucalyptus* trees at Koke'e, Kaua'i.

Sarcodon atroviridis
(Morgan) Banker

Cap 40–80 mm broad, convex to plano-convex, centrally depressed, dull, dry, felted, grayish brown becoming black where rubbed or in wet weather; flesh grayish white, bitter. Spore-bearing surface composed of narrowly conical spines up to 10 mm long, grayish brown. Stem 40–70 x 8–10 mm, cylindrical or with a flared apex, dry, glabrous, dark grayish brown but soon blackening overall. Spore deposit brown. Edibility: unknown.

Fruiting bodies of *Sarcodon atroviridis* resemble typical agarics or gilled mushrooms, but a look under the cap shows neither gills nor pores, but pointed teeth that represent iciclelike spore-bearing appendages. Is: HA.

Sarcodon atroviridis grows in wet *Eucalyptus* forests in the Hilo Forest Reserve near Hilo and all along the Hamakua coast on the Big Island, wherever there is *Eucalyptus*.

Fruiting bodies of *Pisolithus arhizus* from Kukuiolono Park on Kaua'i, cut open to show the colorful pseudoperidioles inside.

Pisolithus arhizus (Scop.: Pers.) Rauschert

Fruiting body clavate to turbinate, 50–80 mm broad x 80–120 mm tall, basal portion buried in and adhering soil. Peridium thin, dry, brittle, glabrous, yellowish brown. Gleba when young divided into small ovoid chambers (pseudoperidioles), these yellowish white to olivaceous black, becoming powdery at maturity, olivaceous brown to reddish brown. Spores brown. Edibility: not recommended.

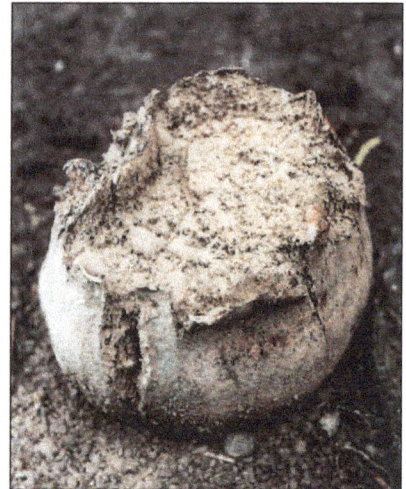

A mature, football-sized fruiting body of *Pisolithus arhizus* releasing millions of powdery spores to be spread by the wind.

Pisolithus arhizus, also known as *Pisolithus tinctorius*, forms club-shaped fruiting bodies and is found around *Eucalyptus*. When cut open small chambers called pseudoperidioles are revealed. This fungus is sometimes referred to as Dead Man's Foot or Dye-maker's False Puffball for the dyes that can be extracted from the fruiting body. *Pisolithus arhizus* forms a mutualistic mycorrhizal relationship with the roots of many different tree species, including both hardwoods and conifers. In reforestation projects, the roots of pine seedlings are often inoculated with mycelium (or spores) of *P. arhizus* before transplanting. The mycorrhizal fungus aids the plant in water and mineral uptake, especially those nutrients required for plant growth such as nitrogen, potassium, and phosphates. It is interesting that in the Hawaiian Islands we have encountered *P. arhizus* only in association with *Eucalyptus*, even though there are extensive pine plantations on many islands. Is: HA, KA, LA, MO, OA.

Scleroderma verrucosum (Bull.: Pers.) Pers.

Fruiting body 15–30 mm broad, globose to pear-shaped, with or without a sterile base. Peridium less than 1 mm thick, when young covered with appressed, tiny (0.5–1 mm dia.) angular scales, yellow to yellowish brown with brown scales; peridium flesh white but quickly staining pink to red. Gleba at first dark purplish black with white streaks, becoming dark grayish brown. Spores dark brown. Edibility: poisonous.

Note the pink staining on the cut peridial walls of *Scleroderma verrucosum*.

There are several species of Earth-balls that grow associated with *Eucalyptus* in Hawai'i. When young, the peridium of *Scleroderma verrucosum* is covered with small brown scales and when cut open, the very thin peridium flesh quickly stains pink to red. *Scleroderma cepa,* often collected at the same sites, is usually larger, has a thicker peridium that is initially smooth and then develops deep cracks in age and stains purple, not pink, when cut. Is: HA, KA, MA, MO, OA.

Scleroderma cepa Pers.: Pers.

Fruiting body 30–50 mm broad, globose to cushion-shaped. Peridium more than 1 mm thick, smooth when young, developing large cracks and scales (1–4 mm dia.) and becoming areolate in age, yellow to yellowish brown; peridium flesh white to yellow, staining purple when cut. Gleba at first dark purplish black with white streaks becoming dark grayish brown. Spores dark brown. Edibility: poisonous.

One mature fruiting body of *Scleroderma cepa* in this photo shows the boxlike structure with veins characteristic of the species; another is split open like an earthstar to release the spores.

The peridium of *Scleroderma cepa* is at first smooth and quite thick, but eventually cracks into large scales (areolae) and eventually splits open, sometimes in a star-shaped fashion, to expose the spore mass. Is: HA, KA, MA, MO, OA.

Laetiporus sulphureus (Bull.: Fr.) Murrill

Cap 100–300 mm broad x 80–140 mm thick, fan-shaped, in overlapping clusters, margin wavy, sulcate, surface dry, tomentose to velvety, zonate, sulfur yellow to orange or orangish red with white margin, becoming dingy brownish orange in age. Spore-bearing surface poroid, sulfur yellow. Tubes 2–4 mm long, yellow. Pores 3–4 per mm. Stem absent. Spore deposit white. Edibility: edible but read cautions below.

Laetiporus is commonly seen on fallen *Eucalyptus*. Although *Laetiporus sulphureus* is known as the Chicken-of-the Woods or Sulfur Shelves (see section on Edible Mushrooms) and considered a premium edible species, there are reports of gastric upsets resulting from eating fruiting bodies growing on *Eucalyptus*. *Laetiporus* is also found on koa and ohi'a in mesic montane habitats, and collections from these sites make excellent eating. Is: HA, KA, MA, MO, OA.

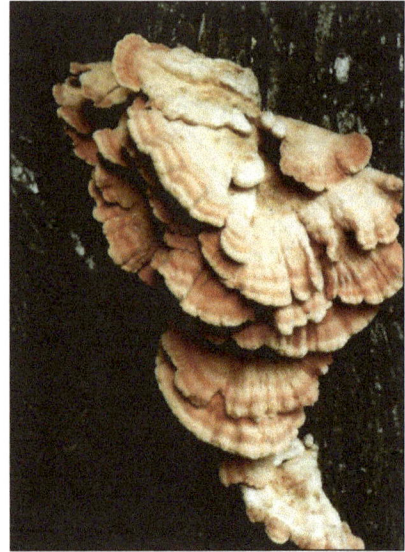

A *Eucalyptus* log in Kalopa State Park with Sulfur Shelves. This is a delicious edible species, but it is better to select them from koa trees instead of *Eucalyptus*.

Stereum hirsutum (Willd.) Pers.

Fruiting body effused-reflexed with broad resupinate base and pileate margins. Margins fan-shaped, lobed, wavy, in fused and overlapping clusters, surface coarsely hairy (hirsute), dry, zonate, with rings of gray, brown, yellowish brown, and rusty brown. Spore-bearing surface smooth to wrinkled, brown to orangish brown or grayish brown. Spore deposit white. Edibility: edible but too tough to eat.

Stereum hirsutum consists of yellowish brown to orange overlapping brackets, especially common on *Eucalyptus* in Hawai'i. The hymenial or spore-forming surface is smooth. Is: HA, KA, MO.

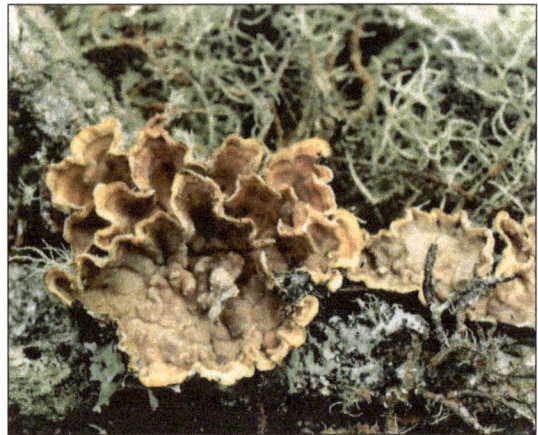

The fertile hymenial surface of *Stereum hirsutum* is shown in this photo.

Additional Species in *Eucalyptus* Forests

Crepidotus roseus var. boninensis

This beautiful pink mushroom that lacks a stem commonly grows on fallen *Eucalyptus* branches (see Wet Windward Alien Forests for full description).

Descomyces albus and Descomyces albellus

Small, spherical puffball-like fruiting bodies can be exposed in road cuts and hillsides in *Eucalyptus* forests (see Montane *Casuarina* for full description).

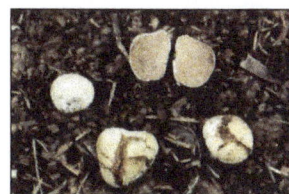

Gymnopilus subtropicus

This lignicolous agaric with bright rusty yellow gills occurs occasionally on rotting *Eucalyptus* logs (see Wet Windward Alien Forests for full description).

Leucopaxillus gentianeus

Although more commonly associated with conifers, this species is also mycorrhizal with *Eucalyptus* in Hawai'i (see Conifer Forests for full description).

MONTANE *CASUARINA* FORESTS

High elevation ironwood forests on the windward sides of the islands do not dry out as fast as their coastal counterparts and harbor somewhat different fungi. Dense ironwood stands at Kalopa State Park on the Big Island and Pala'au State Park on Moloka'i are good examples. *Leucocoprinus* and *Mycena* can be spotted on standing trees, *Amanita marmorata* grows along trails, and large shelving polypores can be seen on fallen logs.

This montane ironwood grove surrounds the famous phallic rock at Pala'au State Park on Moloka'i.

Leucocoprinus species

Cap 15–40 mm broad, obtusely conical becoming plano-conical or campanulate, margin short-striate, center glabrous to velvety grading towards the margin into small squamules, dry; center and squamules dark gray to black, white elsewhere. Gills free, close, broad, white. Stem 20–50 (–75) x 2–5 mm, cylindrical or with an enlarged base, dry, pruinose to granulose, white overall when young, in age apex white, base grayish brown to dark gray, with a small, membranous, persistent, white to gray annulus near the apex; tissue not staining or staining pale orangish red in stem base. Spore deposit white. Edibility: unknown.

This elegant *Leucocoprinus* with gray to black squamules over the white cap fruits out of the bark of living ironwood trees at Pala'au State Park on Moloka'i and Honokaia Boy Scout camp on the Big Island.

This delicate, apparently undescribed species of *Leucocoprinus* is unusual in its habit of forming fruiting bodies from ground level to 20 to 30 feet up the trunks of living ironwood trees. Although the typical substrate is *Casuarina* wood, we have also collected this species on the ground under *Casuarina*, black-wattle acacia *(Acacia mearnsii)*, Formosa koa *(Acacia confusa)*, or tropical ash *(Fraxinus uhdei)*. Is: HA, MA, MO.

Mycena papyracea Desjardin & Hemmes

Cap 15–35 mm broad, bullet-shaped expanding to broadly conical or campanulate, sulcate to the disc; disc furfuraceous, light brown to pale brownish orange; margin radially fibrillose to silky, white. Gills free, close to subdistant, broad, white. Stem 15–35 x 1.5–4 mm, cylindrical, curved, dry, glabrous to pubescent, white overall or with a reddish brown base in age. Spore deposit white. Edibility: unknown.

This newly described species of *Mycena*, closely related to *Mycena radiata*, is one of the more unusual species in the genus. With their pleated caps and free gills, fruiting bodies look more like a *Leucocoprinus* than a *Mycena*. They are difficult to collect because the cap tissue is very thin and silky and has a texture like damp tissue paper. This species grows on the bark of *Casuarina*, *Eucalyptus*, and *Acacia*. Is: HA, MO.

Mycena papyracea also grows on the bark of ironwoods at Pala'au State Park, Moloka'i.

Marasmius radiatus Desjardin

Cap 8–15 mm broad, obtusely conical becoming broadly campanulate, sulcate, dry, subvelutinous, disc rugulose, orange, pinkish orange or brownish orange in the center and pale orange to pale pinkish orange on the margin. Gills adnexed, distant, broad, with white to pale orange interlamellar spaces. Stem 20–40 x <1 mm, cylindrical, tough, pliant, glabrous, brown to dark brown. Spore deposit white. Edibility: unknown.

This beautiful little *Marasmius* with its pinkish orange, umbrella-shaped cap can be found in large clusters on *Casuarina* "needles" on the wet upland forest floor. This species was described from Hawai'i, although we suspect that it is a native of Australasia. Is: HA.

These fruiting bodies of *Marasmius radiatus*, with their beautiful orangish pink caps, were collected from ironwood "needles" at Kalopa State Park.

Descomyces albellus (Klotszsch) Bougher & Castellano

Fruiting body hypogeous to subhypogeous, 8–30 mm broad, globose to ovoid. Peridium suedelike to felted, thin, dry, white when young, soon becoming golden yellow to brownish yellow. Gleba of irregular, tiny, empty chambers, white becoming cinnamon brown. Spores cinnamon brown. Edibility: unknown.

Descomyces albellus is a hypogeous species that barely reaches the surface of the soil and leaf litter under *Casuarina* and *Eucalyptus*. It is usually spotted along road cuts or paths through the forest. A second species, *Descomyces albus*, also occurs in the same habitats but differs in subtle microscopic features. Is: HA, KA, MA, MO, OA.

These tiny fruiting bodies of *Descomyces albellus* were dug out of a road cut in the ironwood grove around the phallic rock on Moloka'i.

ADDITIONAL SPECIES IN MONTANE *CASUARINA* FORESTS

Amanita marmorata var. *myrtacearum*

Amanita marmorata is associated with *Casuarina* or myrtaceous plants wherever they grow (see *Eucalyptus* Forests for full description).

Ganoderma australe

Large, thick conks of *Ganoderma australe* grow on fallen *Casuarina* logs (see Mesic Montane Native Forests for full description).

Phellinus gilvus

Woody brackets of *Phellinus gilvus* line decaying *Casuarina* logs in these montane habitats (see Wet Windward Alien Forests for full description).

Rhodocybe hawaiiensis

This rare pink-spored species has been collected several times in mixed *Casuarina-Eucalyptus* forests at Pala'au State Park (see Mesic Montane Native Forests for a full description).

MESIC MONTANE NATIVE FORESTS

Giant koa and ohi'a trees dominate the mesic, native mountain forests of Hawai'i. These forests are generally on the higher slopes of the leeward sides of the islands where rain is less frequent than on the tradewind, windward slopes. The understory consists of hapu'u tree ferns (*Cibotium* spp.) and a number of smaller native trees. Gilled mushrooms are not as prevalent as in wetter areas, but the large conks of polypore fungi can be spotted easily. Thick shelves of the Artist's Conk *(Ganoderma australe)* form on fallen koa logs, Sulfur Shelves *(Laetiporus sulphureus)* appear on both koa and ohi'a, and the Turkey-tail Polypore *(Trametes versicolor)* lines smaller branches with concentric rings of color.

Kipuka Ki in Volcanoes National Park on the Big Island is typical of a mesic mountain native forest. The plants and fungi are quite different from the native rainforest just a few miles away on the windward side of the mountain.

Coprinus truncorum on manele trees in Bird Park within Volcanoes National Park (above).
Coprinus micaceus on standing, dead koa stump along the Nuʻalolo Trail at Kokeʻe, Kauaʻi (below).

Coprinus truncorum (Schaeff.) Fr. and *Coprinus micaceus* (Bull.: Fr.) Fr.

Cap 10–35 mm broad x 10–20 mm tall, ovoid to sub-cylindrical becoming obtusely conical, striate, dry, covered with tiny, white to silvery glistening granules when young, glabrous in age, light brown to yellowish brown when young, becoming grayish brown to cream or tan, finally black when deliquescing. Gills free, crowded, broad, white becoming black. Stem 30–70 x 2–4 mm, cylindrical above a clavate base, hollow, brittle, glabrous above, tomentose below, white with a grayish brown base. Spore deposit black. Edibility: edible.

Coprinus truncorum and C. *micaceus* (known as the Mica Cap mushroom) are indistinguishable in the field and both are easily recognized by the sugarlike, glistening granules that cover young caps. They differ only subtly in spore shape, with C. *truncorum* forming ellipsoid spores with a rounded germ pore and C. *micaceus* forming shield-shaped (mitriform) spores with truncated germ pores. Within hours of developing, the caps of both species deliquesce into black, inky masses. *Coprinus truncorum* grows in large clusters on fallen *Sapindus* trees in Kipuka Puaulu and Kipuka Ki on the Big Island, whereas C. *micaceus* prefers native koa and alien karakanut at Kokeʻe, Kauaʻi. Is: HA, KA.

A cluster of *Agrocybe parasitica* on Manele trees in Bird Park in Volcanoes National Park on the Big Island. Notice the large, drooping, skirt-like annulus with brown striations from deposited spores.

Agrocybe parasitica Stevenson

Cap 35–120 mm broad, hemispheric to convex becoming plano-convex, not striate, dry, glabrous, sometimes wrinkled or crackled at the center, cream to pale brownish cream. Flesh thick; odor buttery. Gills adnate, close, broad, pale grayish brown to brown. Stem 50–140 x 5–15 mm, cylindrical or enlarged below, solid, tough, fibrillose-striate, white to dingy tan; with a persistent, membranous, pendulous, white annulus near the apex. Spore deposit brown. Edibility: edible and choice.

Agrocybe parasitica, a species common to Australasia, is closely related to the north temperate *A. cylindrica*, differing only at the microscopic level. The Hawaiian species appears on standing and fallen manele *(Sapindus saponaria)* trees in Kipuka Puaulu (Bird Park) and Kipuka Ki within the Volcanoes National Park. The fruiting bodies form large caps up to 4 to 5 inches in diameter and have a large drooping annulus on the stem. Like its cousin *A. cylindrica*, *A. parasitica* is an excellent edible species, and it is easily cultivated on hardwood chips. In Europe, *A. cylindrica*, known there as *A. aegerita* or the Black Poplar Mushroom, is commercially cultivated. Is: HA.

Armillaria sinapina Berube & Dessur.

Cap 40–150 mm broad, broadly campanulate becoming plano-convex with a broad umbo, dry, covered with brown to yellowish brown squamules and small, yellow, scalelike universal veil remnants, margin with white partial veil remnants, light brown to yellowish brown or orangish brown. Gills subdecurrent, close, broad, grayish orange to grayish brown. Stem 50–90 x 10–25 mm, cylindrical to clavate, fibrous, white above, brown below, covered with white to yellow veil remnants; with a membranous, white to yellow, persistent annulus; with coarse, cylindrical, black rhizomorphs. Spore deposit white. Edibility: edible.

This large *Armillaria* grows singly or in pairs out of soil or from rotten logs under karakanut, a native tree of New Zealand seeded in the Koke'e area in the late 1800s. *Armillaria sinapina* is characterized by the yellow veil remnants on the cap and stem surfaces and noncespitose habit. *Armillaria* species are of interest to foresters and mycologists because many are pathogenic to some trees. They are at the same time edible and known to mycophagists as the Honey Mushroom (because of their color, not their flavor). Is: KA.

A cluster of *Armillaria sinapina* along the Nu'alolo Trail at Koke'e, Kaua'i (top). This species is usually found along this trail under karakanut trees, trees from New Zealand seeded in the Koke'e forests. Rhizomorphs of *Armillaria* on logs along the Nu'alolo Trail (bottom).

Gymnopus subpruinosus (Murrill) Desjardin, Halling & Hemmes

Cap 12–30 mm broad, convex to campanulate becoming plano-convex and often with a small papilla, rugulose-striate, dry, hygrophanous, glabrous or subpruinose, brown fading to grayish brown or grayish orange. Gills adnate, subdistant, narrow, pale grayish orange. Stem 15–40 x 1.5–3 mm, cylindrical, tough, hollow, pubescent to tomentose overall, grayish orange above, brown to dark brown below, lignicolous. Spore deposit white. Edibility: unknown.

Gymnopus subpruinosus, once known as *Collybia subpruinosa,* is one of the most common agarics along the Nu'alolo Trail, Koke'e, Kaua'i, during wet periods. It can be so common on fallen sticks and logs that you can barely walk in the forest without stepping on them. This *Gymnopus* is recognized by its thin flesh, the translucent striate cap, and its habit of growing on fallen sticks and branches. Is: HA, KA, MA.

Gymnopus subpruinosus along the Nu'alolo Trail at Koke'e, Kaua'i.

Lepista subalpina
(H. E. Bigelow & A. H. Smith)
Harmaja

Cap 25–75 (–115) mm broad, convex to plano-convex, irregularly undulate, margin wavy, nonstriate, glabrous, hygrophanous, brown to reddish brown fading to light brown, cinnamon brown, or grayish orange. Gills adnate, close to crowded, broad, pinkish buff. Stem 20–80 x 5–15 mm, cylindrical, fibrous, striate, glabrous, white, with or without white rhizoids. Odor strongly fungal; taste sour to bitter. Spore deposit white to pale pinkish buff. Edibility: unknown.

Lepista subalpina grows in clusters along the Nu'alolo Trail at Koke'e on Kaua'i.

This rather large, brown to cinnamon brown *Lepista* superficially looks like Hawai'i's native *Rhodocollybia laulaha*. However, *Lepista subalpina* has slightly more distant lamellae that are broader and not labyrinthine as in *R. laulaha*, and of course the microscopic features are quite different. The Hawaiian populations of *L. subalpina* differ from the mainland Washington-state populations only in lacking clamp connections. Is: HA, KA, MO.

Rhodocybe hawaiiensis Singer

Cap 15–30 mm broad, broadly convex becoming plano-convex and depressed, often funnel-shaped, margin even or slightly rugulose-striate, dry, glabrous, canescent, hygrophanous, dark grayish brown to dark brown fading to brown or pale brownish gray. Gills decurrent, distant to subdistant, narrow, pale grayish orange to brownish gray. Stem 10–25 x 1–3 mm, cylindrical, solid, glabrous, brown to dark brown with matted white mycelium at base, with coarse white rhizomorphs. Spore deposit pinkish brown. Edibility: unknown.

A nice grouping of *Rhodocybe hawaiiensis* from along the Ohelo Berry Flats Trail at Koke'e.

This poorly known species was originally described by Rolf Singer from a single collection made at the Hanapepe Canyon Outlook on Kaua'i. We have collected it several times on the Ohelo Berry Flats Trail at Koke'e State Park on Kaua'i and at Pala'au State Park on Moloka'i. The brown fruiting bodies have a funnel-shaped cap at maturity, decurrent gills, and a pinkish brown spore print. *Rhodocybe hawaiiensis* is known at present only from the Hawaiian Islands. Is: KA, MO.

Descolea alienata
Horak & Desjardin

Cap 20–30 mm broad, campanulate becoming plano-umbonate, surface radially corrugated-wrinkled, dry, hygrophanous, glabrous, dark brown to dark reddish brown fading to light brown or brownish yellow. Gills adnate to adnexed, distant, broad, brown. Stem 15–30 x 2–3 mm, cylindrical, silky, apex buff, base grayish orange to brown; with a membranous, persistent, grayish orange to brownish gray annulus in the middle or near the base of the stem. Spore deposit dark rusty brown. Edibility: unknown.

Descolia alienata from under black wattle, *Acacia mearnsii,* along the Ohelo Berry Flats Trail within Koke'e State Park, Kaua'i.

Descolea alienata is currently known from a single population associated with black wattle *Acacia* thickets on Ohelo Berry Flats Trail at Koke'e State Park on Kaua'i. As the specific epithet suggests, we recognize the species as an alien to the Hawaiian Islands, probably introduced from Australia along with *Acacia mearnsii.* Is: KA.

Callistosporium luteoolivaceum
(Berk. & M. A. Curtis) Singer

Cap 20–45 mm broad, convex to plano-convex, sometimes with a broad, centrally depressed, flattened umbo, translucent-striate, greasy, glabrous, yellowish brown to yellowish when young, often darkening to olive brown or reddish brown with age. Gills notched, close, narrow, grayish yellow. Stem 25–50 x 2–5 mm, cylindrical, pliant, hollow, glabrous, yellowish brown to yellowish olive. Spore deposit white. Edibility: unknown.

Callistosporium luteoolivaceum on a log at Pala'au State Park on Moloka'i. These are old specimens that have turned reddish brown with age.

Callistosporium luteoolivaceum looks like a lignicolous (wood-loving) *Collybia,* and indeed the species was once placed in that genus. It is such a morphologically variable species that it has been formally described eleven different times as eleven different species! In Hawai'i, the species grows on rotting logs of koa and *Eucalyptus,* and can be seen commonly along the Nu'alolo Trail at Koke'e on Kaua'i. A second, burgundy-colored species of *Callistosporium,* presently undescribed, grows in native forest on ohi'a logs. Is: HA, KA, MO.

Psathyrella hydrophila
(Bull.: Fr.) Maire

Cap 15–40 mm broad, convex becoming plano-convex, strongly rugulose to corrugated overall, glabrous, hygrophanous, dark brown to brownish gray fading to grayish orange; margin with hanging, submembranous to fibrillose, white remains of a partial veil. Gills adnexed, close to crowded, broad, brown to dark brown. Stem 30–55 x 3–6 mm, cylindrical, glabrous, white to beige; with a submembranous to fibrillose partial veil when young that ruptures and remains on the cap margin. Spore deposit dark brown. Edibility: unknown, not recommended.

Psathyrella hydrophila growing from a cut koa log along the Nu'alolo Trail at Koke'e State Park, Kaua'i.

The Hawaiian specimens are microscopically indistinguishable from the common north temperate *Psathyrella hydrophila*, but differ significantly in macroscopic features. Our taxon has a strongly wrinkled-corrugated cap and generally grows singly in gregarious troops instead of in cespitose clusters. It is common on stumps and logs of koa, an endemic tree, especially at Koke'e on Kaua'i. Is: KA.

Psathyrella fuscofolia
(Peck) A. H. Smith

Cap 15–40 mm broad, obtusely conical or convex becoming plano-convex, short translucent-striate, smooth or finely wrinkled, glabrous, dark brown fading to light brown, brownish gray or grayish orange, lacking conspicuous hanging partial veil fibrils on the margin. Gills adnexed, close to crowded, broad, brown to dark brown. Stem 20–50 x 2–3 mm, cylindrical, glabrous, shiny, white to beige; with a very thin, cobweblike partial veil (cortina) that disappears soon after cap expansion. Spore deposit dark brown. Edibility: unknown, not recommended.

Psathyrella fuscofolia on fallen logs along the Nu'alolo Trail.

Psathyrella fuscofolia grows in the same habitats as *P. hydrophila* and looks similar, and even has very similar micromorphology. However, the two species can be easily distinguished by the lack of a conspicuous, submembranous partial veil in *P. fuscofolia* and its presence as a tattered margin in *P. hydrophila*. We have collected the species on koa, ohi'a, and black wattle (*Acacia mearnsii*) wood. Is: KA.

Conocybe gracilenta Watling & Taylor

Cap 5–10 mm broad, obtusely conical becoming broadly campanulate, striate, disc sometimes rugulose, moist, hygrophanous, brown fading to brownish yellow or light brown, finally yellowish tan. Gills adnexed, subdistant, narrow, brownish yellow. Stem 20–40 x 0.5–1 mm, cylindrical with a slightly enlarged base, pliant, shiny, pruinose above, silky to furfuraceous below, pale brownish yellow to brown; with a well-developed, persistent, membranous, striate annulus near the apex. Spore deposit rusty brown. Edibility: unknown, but probably deadly poisonous.

This small, annulate, rusty brown-spored mushroom grows in muddy soil along trail edges under ohiʻa and koa. We have seen it only in the Kokeʻe State Park area on Kauaʻi. It is very similar to the north temperate *Conocybe filaris*, but differs in forming much larger spores with a prominent germ pore. Although the edibility of *C. gracilenta* is unknown, its close similarity to the deadly *C. filaris* provides sufficient evidence to advise against eating it. Is: KA.

Conocybe gracilenta growing under ohiʻa along Kaluapuhi Trail at Kokeʻe State Park on Kauaʻi. This tiny *Conocybe* has deadly poisonous relatives.

Pyrrhoglossum pyrrhum (Berk. & M. A. Curtis) Singer

Cap 5–15 mm broad, convex to fan-shaped, margin wavy, nonstriate, surface suedelike to glabrous, pale brownish orange; odor strong and pleasant; taste very bitter. Gills adnexed, close to crowded, narrow, deep brownish orange. Stem rudimentary, lateral, 1–2.5 x 1 mm, minutely pubescent, brownish orange, arising from copious coarse white rhizomorphs. Spore deposit rusty brown. Edibility: unknown.

Pyrrhoglossum pyrrhum is a rare species in the Hawaiian Islands, known at present from a single population on the Kaluapuhi Trail at Kokeʻe State Park on Kauaʻi. The fan-shaped caps with deep rusty brown gills and a rudimentary lateral stem, which arises from coarse white rhizomorphs, are diagnostic features. It grows on very rotten logs of native ohiʻa trees. Is: KA.

Notice the coarse white rhizomorphs from which the tiny rusty brown caps of *Pyrroglossum* arise.

Paxillus curtisii
Berk. & M. A. Curtis

Cap 20–50 mm broad, sessile, shelving, effused-reflexed to fan-shaped, margin incurved and lobed, surface suedelike to felted, dry, brownish orange to brownish yellow. Gills crowded, strongly corrugated, sometimes forked and intervenose, narrow, dark brownish orange near the base and bright yellow to yellowish orange with a hint of green near the margin. Stem absent. Odor very strong, spicy, nauseating. Spore deposit olivaceous yellow. Edibility: unknown, not recommended.

Paxillus curtisii, with its beautiful corrugated gills, growing on ohi'a logs along Devastation Trail in Volcanoes National Park on the Big Island.

This beautiful *Paxillus* was once known as *P. corrugatus,* named after the strongly wavy-corrugated, bright yellowish orange gills. The fruiting bodies are sessile and shelving, and grow from the sides or bottoms of rotting logs. We have collected it on ohi'a wood in montane native forests and on the wood of Monterey cypress in montane alien forests. Is: HA, MO.

Schizophyllum commune Fr.

Cap 10–35 mm broad, sessile, fan-shaped, margin incurved and lobed, surface densely hairy, dry, grayish brown to gray when fresh, drying white; texture tough, leathery. Gills split lengthwise, radiating from point of cap attachment, subdistant, narrow, tough, grayish brown with white edges. Stem absent. Spore deposit white. Edibility: edible but too tough to eat.

Schizophyllum commune is commonly found on fallen koa logs and branches in mesic montane forests. It grows in dense, often shelving clusters and is known as the Split-gill Mushroom because of the longitudinally divided nature of the gills. Is: HA, KA, MA.

Schizophyllum commune on a koa log along the Nu'alolo Trail at Koke'e on Kaua'i.

Geastrum aff. morganii Lloyd

Fruiting bodies globose and beaked when young. Exoperidium separating from endoperidium and splitting into 7–9 rays, 40–50 mm broad, outer surface not adhering debris, coarsely tomentose to felted-scaly, brown to yellowish brown, attached basally to the soil by coarse white rhizomorphs, rays recurved, inner surface fleshy, cracked grayish brown. Endoperidium 15–20 mm broad, sessile, glabrous, brownish gray to dark grayish brown; peristome well delimited, plicate to sulcate. Spores dark grayish brown. Edibility: unknown.

Geastrum aff. *morganii* is one of the larger earthstars in Hawai'i. These specimens are growing along the Nu'alolo Trail at Koke'e on Kaua'i.

The Hawaiian taxon is very similar to *Geastrum morganii*, but differs in forming a truly sulcate to plicate peristome instead of fimbriate-folded, and has a more coarsely tomentose-scaly exoperidium. Our species grows under karakanut, koa, and ohi'a along the Nu'alolo Trail at Koke'e on Kaua'i. Among the Hawaiian plicate earthstars, *Geastrum* aff. *morganii* is similar to *G. berkeleyi*, but the latter is easily distinguished by an exoperidium that adheres soil and debris and by a roughened endoperidium. Is: KA.

Geastrum velutinum (Morgan) Fischer

Fruiting bodies ovoid to pyriform when young. Exoperidium separating from endoperidium and splitting into 5–7 rays, 30–50 mm broad, outer surface not adhering debris, felted to scurfy, ornamentation brown over pink to cream, attached basally to the soil by coarse white rhizomorphs, rays recurved, inner surface orangish white to pinkish buff. Endoperidium 10–15 mm broad, sessile, glabrous, gray to grayish brown; peristome well delimited, fibrillose (never sulcate), surrounded by a dark ring. Spores dark grayish brown. Edibility: unknown.

The rays of *Geastrum velutinum* are a delicate pink and contrast nicely with the dark grayish brown endoperidium. These fruiting bodies were found along the Nu'alolo Trail at Koke'e.

Geastrum velutinum gets its name from the velvety or felted outer surface of the exoperidium. When opened, the folded-back rays have a distinct rose hue and the peristome is finely fibrillose. Although some authors accept the species as a synonym of *G. javanicum,* we accept these as two distinct species. Both *G. velutinum* and *G.* aff. *morganii* occur in the same habitat and share many similarities, but can be easily distinguished by their peristome features (see photos). We have also found *G. velutinum* under pines along the Makaha Ridge Road just outside of Koke'e State Park and in high-elevation kipukas on the Big Island. Is: HA, KA.

MESIC MONTANE NATIVE FORESTS

Fruiting bodies of the Starfish Stinkhorn (*Aseroe rubra*) from along the paths at Koke'e State Park on Kaua'i. The stinky, slimy gleba often washes off in the rain so that you might not detect the disgusting odor of fresh specimens. The gelatinous primordium or "egg" has been cut open to show the developing fruiting body inside (left).

Aseroe rubra Labill.: Fr.

Unexpanded fruiting body 25–30 mm broad, glabrous, white. Expanded fruiting body 50–60 mm tall, apex expanding into a flattened disc from which arises 5–7 pairs of starfishlike arms; arms 25–35 x 3–6 mm, hollow, brittle, rugulose, upper surface pink to bright red, lower surface pink to white. Spore mass mucilaginous, olivaceous, located centrally on the disc and at the base of arms. Stem 20–30 mm broad, cylindrical, hollow, rugulose, white. Volva thick, gelatinous, white. Odor strongly fetid. Spore olive brown. Edibility: edible when young and unexpanded.

This spectacular stinkhorn will easily catch your attention, partly because of its bright red, starfishlike arms, and partly because of its strong foul odor. Sometimes called the Starfish Stinkhorn, it is the most common stinkhorn in the Hawaiian Islands, often found associated with *Eucalyptus* in the fall. We have collected it on all the major islands. Is: HA, KA, LA, MA, MO, OA.

Ramaria aff. *myceliosa* has been spotted along the trails and in the forests surrounding Koke'e State Park.

Ramaria aff. *myceliosa* (Peck) Corner

Fruiting bodies coralloid, 70–110 mm x 50–70 mm broad, with numerous erect branches arising polychotomously to dichotomously from a single stem or from several fasciculate stems. Main branches 1.5–2 mm thick, narrow and delicate; secondary branches 0.5–1 mm thick, strict, apices needlelike, cream to light yellowish brown when young, becoming grayish orange, light brown, brownish yellow or brownish orange in age, tips concolorous. Stem 2–5 mm thick, white to yellowish brown, with copious white basal mycelium and rhizomorphs. Not discoloring blue-green but drying with olive tones. Flesh grayish orange to pale brownish orange; odor mild. Spore deposit rusty brown. Edibility: unknown.

The Hawaiian species is similar to but distinct from *Ramaria myceliosa*, first described from under conifers in California. Our species forms the narrowest and most delicate branches of any known spiny-spored *Ramaria*. It differs from *R. myceliosa* in forming larger spores, larger and more delicate fruiting bodies, and in growing in association with hardwoods. This beautiful coral fungus can be spied among leaf mulch under karakanut, koa, and ohi'a along trails at Koke'e State Park on Kaua'i. Is: KA.

Ganoderma australe (Fr.) Pat.

Fruiting bodies 80–400 mm broad x 70–150 mm radius x 30–60 mm thick, irregularly semicircular to shelflike, upper surface concentrically ridged, lumpy, dry, glabrous, dark brown to black with a paler brown, zonate margin; flesh hard, woody, chocolate brown. Pores round, 3–4 per mm, white, bruising reddish brown to dark brown; tubes in several layers (perennial), each layer 2–7 mm thick. Stem absent. Spore deposit yellowish brown. Edibility: edible but too tough to eat.

Ganoderma australe conks grow for years on fallen logs and often attain tabletop dimensions in Kipuka Puaulu

Mycologist Hope Miller checks out a huge conk of *Ganoderma australe* on a fallen koa tree in Kipuka Puaulu (Bird Park) within Volcanoes National Park.

in Volcanoes National Park on Hawai'i. The white hymenial (spore-producing) surface stains dark brown when touched. In the Pacific Northwest and other parts of the mainland, artists scratch or paint pictures on the pore surface of a related species, *G. applanatum,* and the fungus is referred to as the Artist's Conk. Is: HA, KA, MA, MO, OA.

Inonotus species

Fruiting bodies 100–180 mm broad x 100–140 mm radius x 30–40 mm thick, semicircular to shelflike, upper surface cracked, lumpy, dry, roughened, dark brown to grayish brown, often covered with a powdery golden yellow spore deposit; flesh fibrous, corky, brownish orange. Pores angular, 1–3 per mm, lavender-buff; tubes in one layer 7–10 mm thick, yellowish brown. Stem absent. Spore deposit golden yellow. Edibility: unknown.

This undetermined species of *Inonotus* grows commonly on dead manele or soapberry trees *(Sapindus saponaria)* at Kipuka Ki in Volcanoes National Park on Hawai'i. The large conks, with brownish orange, fibrous flesh, a pale lavender-buff spore surface, and golden yellow spores, are quite distinctive. Is: HA.

Inonotus on manele trees in Kipuka Ki in Volcanoes National Park. The golden color comes from spores that have been uplifted by breezes and deposited on top of the conks. Older dead conks are seen above.

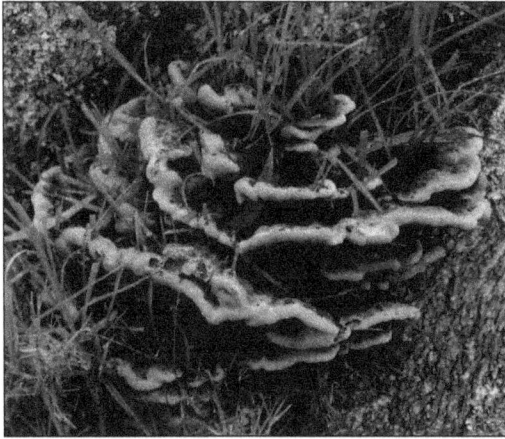

A fresh cluster of overlapping brackets of *Phaeolus schweinitzii* on a koa tree along the Mana Road on Mauna Kea (left) and an old, dried up conk (right).

Phaeolus schweinitzii (Fr.) Pat.

Cap 50–250 mm dia., circular and flattened to lobed, single or imbricate and arising from a central to lateral stem, tomentose to hirsute, yellowish brown to dark reddish brown, margin often yellow to greenish yellow; flesh tough and leathery, yellowish brown to dark rusty brown. Pores angular, 1–2 per mm, yellowish brown to greenish yellow; tubes in a single layer, up to 15 mm long. Stem short and stout, up to 50 mm diameter. Spore deposit white. Edibility: edible but too tough to eat.

Commonly seen on koa around Kipuka Puaulu and Kipuka Ki in the Volcanoes National Park and along the Keanokolu Road on Mauna Kea, *Phaeolus schweinitzii* produces overlapping clusters of reddish brown shelves that can be seen from a distance against the light colored bark of koa. The fresh hymenial surface has a greenish hue. Conks usually reach foot-wide dimensions and with age harden and become brittle. On the mainland it causes root rot and brown cubical rot that reaches to 8 feet on the living tree trunk. Is: HA.

Rigidoporus ulmarius (Sowerby: Fr.) Imazeki

Cap 200–300 mm broad x 40–90 mm radius x 40–60 mm thick, sessile or effused-reflexed, often hooflike, glabrous to finely tomentose, lumpy and often ridged in zones, buffy brown when young, typically covered with green algae or bryophytes in age. Pores angular, 5–6 per mm, pinkish buff; tubes in a single layer, up to 10 mm long. Stem absent. Spore deposit white. Edibility: edible but too tough to eat.

Rigidoporus ulmarius forms large, thick perennial conks that are usually green with algae or covered with bryophytes on the upper surface. The pore surface is pinkish. Specimens can be seen at Kipuka Puaulu (Bird Park) or Kalopa State Park on the Big Island, usually on large, old ohiʻa trees. Is: HA.

A large conk of *Rigidoporus ulmarius* on a living ohiʻa tree at Kalopa State Park on the Big Island.

MESIC MONTANE NATIVE FORESTS

Merulius tremellosus Fr.

Fruiting bodies resupinate to effused-reflexed, caps often imbricate, with a soft, elastic to gelatinous texture; cap portion 30–60 mm broad x 20–40 mm radius x 3–5 mm thick, upper surface hirsute to tomentose, white; margin wavy, often folded, white; spore-producing surface reticulate-folded to poroid, cream to pale yellowish orange or rusty. Spore deposit white. Edibility: unknown.

Merulius tremellosus, also known as *Phlebia tremellosus,* grows as overlapping layers of gelatinous brackets on hardwood logs and stumps. The hymenial surface is composed of mazelike ridges and folds and may appear almost poroid. Is: HA, KA.

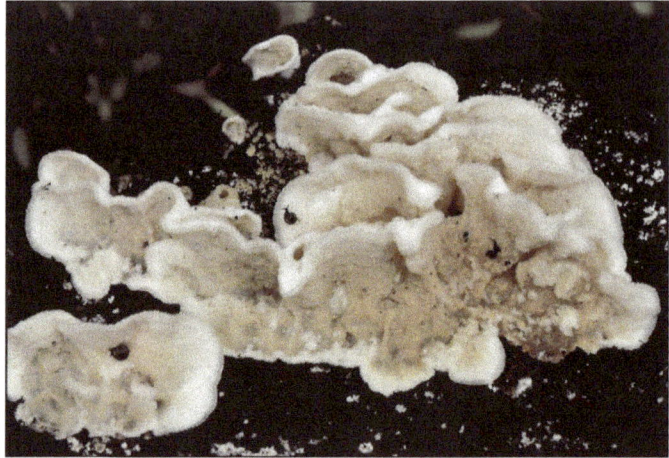

A cluster of *Merulius tremellosus* along the Nu'alolo Trail at Koke'e State Park. Tiny garlic snails are making a meal of the hymenial surface.

Trametes versicolor (L.: Fr.) Pilát

Cap 40–60 mm broad x 15–25 mm radius x 1 mm thick, sessile, fanlike, margin even to wavy, sometimes lobed, often in imbricate clusters; surface hirsute to tomentose, zonate, with concentric zones of buff, gray, bluish gray, brown, and reddish brown; texture tough and leathery. Pores round to angular, 4–5 per mm, cream-colored; tubes in a single layer, 1–3 mm long. Stem absent. Spore deposit white. Edibility: edible but too tough to eat.

Fallen hardwood logs and decaying saplings in Bird Park on the Big Island are often covered with brackets of the Turkey-tail Polypore. The fan-shaped brackets of this pantemperate wood-rotter feature concentric growth rings and come in a variety of colors ranging from tan to bluish gray. This species is an excellent addition to dried flower bouquets. *Trametes versicolor* is an immune system enhancer that has been used in China to treat various types of cancer. Dried and ground mushrooms are now available in tea form. Is: HA, KA, MA, MO, OA.

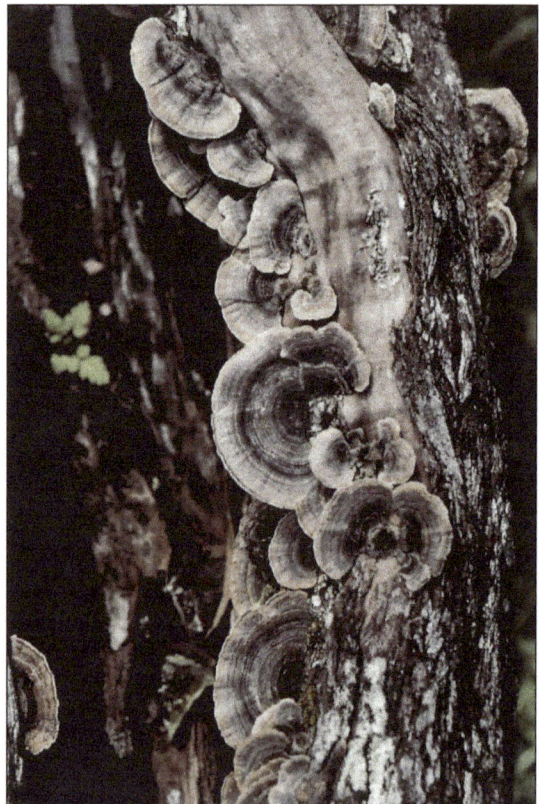

Colorful brackets of *Trametes versicolor* featuring concentric growth rings. Fruiting bodies come in a variety of colors from gray and brown to green and blue.

Gyrodontium versicolor
(Berk. & Broome) Maas Geest.

Cap 50–90 mm broad x 30–40 mm radius x 5–7 mm thick, sessile, fan- to kidney-shaped, often in imbricate clusters; surface felted to cottony, yellowish brown to brown; texture spongy to soft leathery. Hymenium of yellowish green spines 2–3 mm long, shorter and paler towards the white sterile margin. Spore deposit olivaceous brown. Edibility: unknown.

This beautiful wood-rotting fungus can be seen on fallen logs in the Koke'e region of Kaua'i. It forms huge yellow fruiting bodies that spread over woody debris. Is: KA.

Gyrodontium versicolor under black wattle along the Ohelo Berry Flats Trail. These massive fruiting bodies cover several square meters of the wood substrate.

Sarcoscypha mesocyatha F. A. Harr.

Fruiting bodies shallowly cupulate to flattened-discoid, 10–45 mm broad; upper (hymenial) surface glabrous, deep red; lower sterile surface felted, pinkish white to reddish white. Stem absent or small, 2–8 x 2–5 mm, eccentric to central, cylindrical to folded, white. Spore deposit white. Edibility: unknown.

The beautiful deep red cups of *Sarcoscypha mesocyatha* are easily spotted growing from dead koa logs or twigs at Koke'e State Park on Kaua'i. It will remind North American collectors of the Scarlet Cup Fungus (*S. coccinea* and *S. occidentalis*) to which it is related. This species was described from Hawai'i. Is: KA.

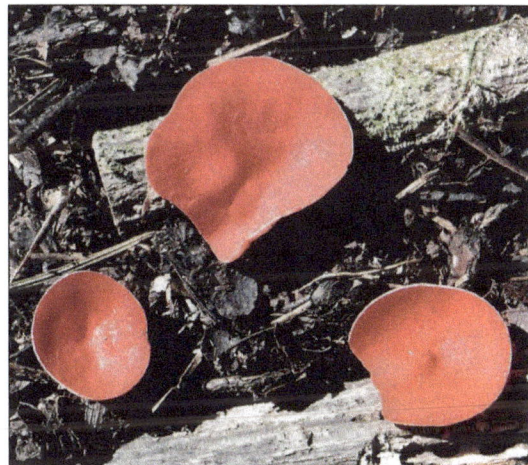

Brilliant red cups of the Hawaiian Scarlet Cup Fungus, *Sarcoscypha mesocyatha,* as they appear along the Nu'alolo Trail at Koke'e.

WET MONTANE NATIVE RAINFORESTS

Hawaiian native rainforests have long been recognized as living evolutionary laboratories with a high rate of endemism within the birds, insects, and vascular plants. The rainforests should now also be known for their unique fungi. Many of the species shown in this section have been recorded only in Hawaiian rainforests. Tiny *Marasmiellus, Mycena,* and resupinate wood-rotting fungi favor the tents of senescent petioles surrounding the *Cibotium* tree ferns, while colorful *Hygrocybe, Galerina,* and *Pholiota* peek out from moss-covered substrates.

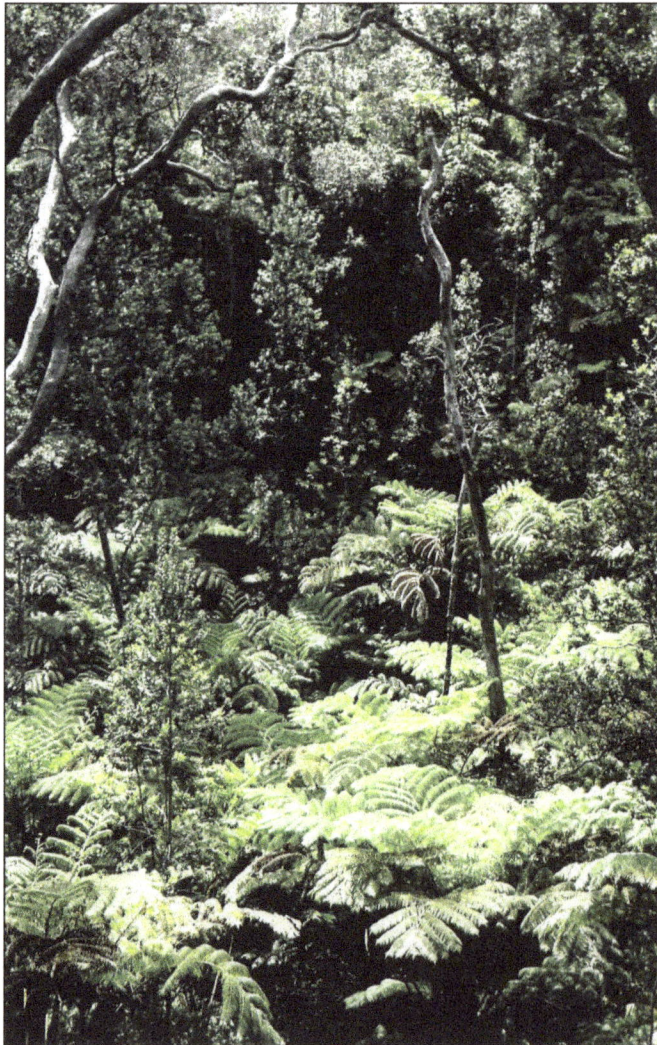

Native rainforest scene near Thurston Lava Tube in Hawai'i Volcanoes National Park. The forest is dominated by ohi'a trees *(Metrosideros polymorpha)* with a tree-fern *(Cibotium* spp.) understory.

Rhodocollybia laulaha on hapu'u logs in Pu'u Makaala Natural Area reserve. Fruiting bodies are long-lived and may remain on a log for several weeks before rotting away.

Rhodocollybia laulaha Desjardin, Halling & Hemmes

Cap 30–80 mm broad, campanulate to convex with a broad umbo, nonstriate, glabrous, hygrophanous, light brown to brown fading to grayish orange or orangish white in age. Gills adnexed to notched, extremely crowded, narrow, mazelike and constricted near stem, orange white, spotted reddish brown in age. Stem 30–80 x 5–7 mm, equal or clavate, striate, pruinose to felted, orange white to pale brownish gray. Bitter taste. Spore deposit cream-colored. Edibility: unknown.

The largest of the mushrooms in the native rainforest, this *Rhodocollybia* fruits in groups on fallen hapu'u tree ferns and in leaf mulch on the forest floor. The extremely crowded and narrow gills form a raised, collarlike region near the stem where they are forked and mazelike. This mushroom also grows directly out of cinder along Devastation Trail near Kilauea Iki in Hawai'i Volcanoes National Park. Biweekly collecting over four years in several native forests on Hawai'i indicate that *R. laulaha* has a very predictable cycle for fruitbody production. Mushrooms first appear profusely in July and continue abundant production through December. Throughout the remainder of the year mushrooms are rarely formed even if the environmental conditions appear optimal. We have observed some mushrooms remaining in fairly good, unputrefied condition for 3 to 4 weeks. Current data suggest that *R. laulaha* is a Hawaiian endemic species. Is: HA, KA, MA.

Close-up of the mazelike configuration of the gills of *Rhodocollybia laulaha*.

Pholiota peleae
E. Horak & Desjardin

Cap 12–40 mm broad, convex to campanulate expanding to plano-convex with a
small umbo, smooth, glutinous to viscid,
disc squamulose, margin glabrous or
with a few veil fibrils, reddish brown to
brown when young, becoming brownish
orange to grayish yellow in age. Gills
adnate, close, broad, yellowish brown to
brown. Stem 15–30 x 2–3 mm, cylindrical,
equal, curved, pubescent to furfuraceous,
yellowish white to yellowish brown. Spore
deposit brown. Edibility: unknown.

Fruiting bodies of *Pholiota peleae*
grow from the moss-covered branches
of ohiʻa or on the moss-covered bases
of hapuʻu tree ferns in most wet

Pholiota peleae as found in kipukas along the Saddle Road on the Big Island.
This is one of the more common mushroom species of the rainforest.

montane rainforests in Hawaiʻi. The surface of the cap is sticky and has reddish brown
squamules in the center of an otherwise orangish brown to brown cap. In addition, the mushrooms form yellowish brown gills and drop a brown spore deposit. Described from Hawaiʻi, the
species name honors Pele, the Hawaiian goddess of volcanoes. Is: HA, KA, MA, MO.

Galerina decipiens A. H. Smith & Singer

Cap 3–10 mm broad, conical, striate, glabrous, hygrophanous, brown fading to brownish orange or yellowish
brown or paler. Gills adnexed, subdistant to distant, moderately broad, brownish orange. Stem 12–30 x 0.2–1 mm,
cylindrical, equal, apex minutely pruinose, glabrous elsewhere, grayish orange to pale brownish yellow. Spore
deposit rusty brown. Edibility: not recommended.

Galerina decipiens also grows on moss-covered
branches and trunks of native forest trees or
directly from mosses over soil. Described originally from Michigan, *G. decipiens* is similar to the
pantemperate *G. hynorum* but differs in spore
features. A look-alike species, *G. atkinsoniana*
(next page), grows in the same habitats; it is very
difficult to distinguish these two taxa in the field.
Galerina atkinsoniana differs subtly in forming a
stem that becomes dark reddish brown at the base
at maturity and is densely pruinose overall. The
two species are easily differentiated microscopically. Is: HA, KA, MA, MO.

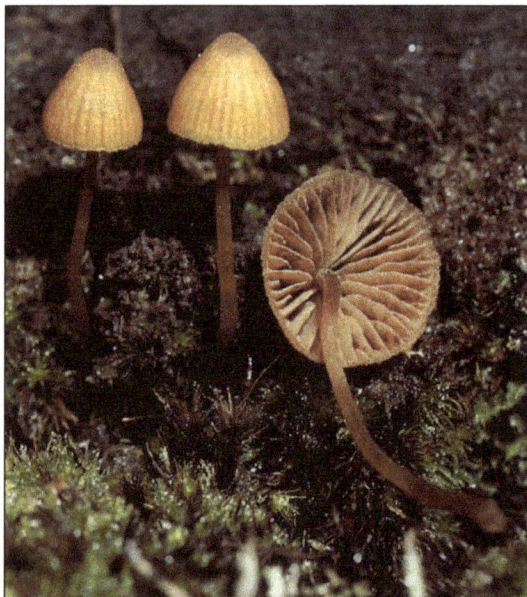

Galerina decipiens is tiny but contrasts with the dark green
moss and is easily spotted by a careful observer.

Galerina atkinsoniana A. H. Smith

Cap 5–10 mm broad, conical, striate, glabrous, hygrophanous, brown fading to brownish orange or brownish yellow or paler. Gills narrowly adnate, subdistant, moderately broad, brownish orange. Stem 15–35 x 0.5–1 mm, cylindrical, equal, pruinose to hispidulous overall, brownish orange, base becoming reddish brown in age. Spore deposit rusty brown. Edibility: not recommended.

Galerina atkinsoniana is another small, nondescript mushroom growing from mosses in montane native rainforests. This pantemperate species looks similar to *G. decipiens* in the field, but is distinguished by forming much larger spores on two-spored basidia, has numerous pleurocystidia, and differently shaped caulocystidia. Is: HA, KA, MO.

Galerina atkinsoniana can be distinguished by the dark coloring on the lower half of the stem.

Galerina nana (Petri) Kühner

Cap 5–15 mm broad, conical to convex with a small umbo, striate, glabrous, hygrophanous, disc and striations reddish brown, elsewhere pale brownish yellow, fading in age. Gills adnexed to adnate, distant, broad, brownish orange. Stem 10–25 x 1–2 mm, cylindrical, equal, apex pruinose, brown, base dark brown and covered with white tomentum. Spore deposit rusty brown. Edibility: not recommended.

The diminutive *G. nana* has a circum-Pacific distribution in the west and is common in the Hawaiian Islands where it grows in small groups on rotting logs of koa and ohi'a in native rainforests. It is easily distinguished from other Hawaiian *Galerina* species by its hairy white stem base and by its thick-walled, crystal-incrusted hymenial cystidia. Is: HA, KA, MA, MO.

Galerina nana growing at the Kuia Natural Area Reserve at Koke'e, Kaua'i.

Hygrocybe lamalama
Desjardin & Hemmes

Cap 10–20 (–40) mm broad, hemispherical to convex, nonstriate, dry, glabrous, disc deep orange and margin deep yellow when young, becoming yellow overall in age. Gills adnate, subdistant, broad, thick, pale yellow or yellowish white becoming deep yellow to orangish yellow in age. Stem 15–45 x 1.5–3 mm, cylindrical, equal, hollow, dry, glabrous above, base with white to pale yellow tomentum, deep orange to deep yellow overall. Red tones absent from fruiting bodies. Spore deposit white. Edibility: unknown.

This group of *Hygrocybe lamalama* is among dozens growing out of moss on the ground in the Kamakou Forest Preserve on Moloka'i.

Fruiting bodies of *Hygrocybe lamalama* are easily recognized by their nonviscid, orange to yellow cap, gills, and stem. The species, described from Hawai'i, shares many features with *H. constrictospora* (described later), which grows in the same habitats; the latter differs in forming a deep red cap and reddish orange stem. *Hygrocybe lamalama* typically grows in moss-covered areas on the ground. In Hawaiian, *lamalama* means "to glow as if touched by the sun." Is: HA, KA, MA, MO.

Hygrocybe pakelo Desjardin & Hemmes

Cap 10–15 mm broad, convex to plano-convex, striate, glabrous, glutinous, disc olive, olivaceous brown or orange, often lacking olive tones, margin orange to yellowish orange, in age fading to grayish orange, grayish yellow, or light orange. Gills narrowly adnate, distant, moderately broad, light orange. Stem 15–30 x 2–3 mm, cylindrical, equal, glabrous, glutinous to viscid, yellowish white to light orange. Spore deposit white. Edibility: unknown.

Hygrocybe pakelo, described recently from Hawai'i, forms olive and orange caps, light orange gills and stem, and is covered by a glutinous layer. It is allied with the pantemperate *H. psittacina* (Parrot Waxy Cap), which differs in forming fruiting bodies with bright green, blue, wine red, and flesh tones, and has subtly different micromorphology. The Hawaiian name *pakelo* means "slippery like a fish," referring to the viscid or glutinous nature of its cap and stem. Is: HA, MO.

Hygrocybe pakelo grows from moss-covered fern logs in kipukas along the Saddle Road during prolonged soaking conditions.

Humidicutis peleae
Desjardin & Hemmes

Cap 8–25 mm broad, obtusely conical to campanulate expanding to plano-umbonate, nonstriate, dry, glabrous, hygrophanous, deep orange fading to light orange. Gills adnate with a decurrent tooth, subdistant to distant, broad, brilliant orange, Stem 15–45 x 1.5–3 mm, cylindrical, equal, dry, glabrous, hollow, apex orange, base orangish white. Spore deposit white. Edibility: unknown.

The genus *Humidicutis* is a relatively recent segregate out of *Hygrocybe*, differing in the types of pigments present, in the absence of clamp connections in all tissues except at the

Humidicutis peleae from the Ola'a native forest tract near Volcano on the Big Island.

base of basidia, and in the proliferation of basidia from basal clamps. *Humidicutis peleae* is easily recognized by its deep orange, dry cap and stem, and brilliant orange gills. It is allied with *H. marginata* (Orange-gilled Waxy Cap) from eastern North America. Like other native forest species, *H. peleae* grows from moss-covered logs or soil during the wettest months. Described from Hawai'i, the species name honors Pele, the Hawaiian goddess of volcanoes. Is: HA, KA, MA, MO.

Humidicutis poilena Desjardin & Hemmes

Cap 12–20 mm broad, obtusely conical expanding to broadly campanulate, nonstriate, dry, glabrous, subhygrophanous, deep yellow fading to yellow. Gills adnate, often with a short decurrent tooth, distant, moderately broad, yellow to light yellow. Stem 25–45 x 2–4 mm, cylindrical, equal or with tapered base, dry, glabrous, hollow, apex yellow, base light yellow to yellowish white. Spore deposit white. Edibility: unknown.

Humidicutis poilena is a yellow version of *H. peleae*, differing not only in pigmentation but in forming larger spores. At present it is known from a single kipuka along Saddle Road on the Big Island and is indeed a rare Hawaiian endemic species. In Hawaiian, *poilena* means "yellowish cap." Is: HA.

A grouping of *Humidicutis poilena* from a kipuka along the Saddle Road on the Big Island.

Hygrocybe noelokelani Desjardin & Hemmes

Cap 10–30 mm broad, convex expanding to plano-convex, striate, glutinous to viscid, glabrous, not hygrophanous, deep pink fading to pinkish white. Gills adnate to shallowly subdecurrent in age, distant, broad, pinkish white. Stem 25–40 x 2–5 mm, cylindrical, equal, glutinous to viscid, glabrous, yellow to yellowish white. Spore deposit white. Edibility: unknown.

This spectacularly pink *Hygrocybe*, described from Hawai'i, is initially covered by a thick jellylike layer in wet conditions that becomes a thin viscid (sticky) layer as the mush-

Note the jellylike coating on the stem of *Hygrocybe noelokelani*. These specimens were growing in a kipuka along the Saddle Road on the Big Island.

room matures. It grows on moss-covered substrates and is allied with *H. laeta* from the northern hemisphere and *H. graminicolor* from New Zealand. The stem is also covered with a thick jellylike coating. The species name refers to the pink rose of Maui. Is: HA, KA, MO.

Hygrocybe constrictospora Arnolds

Cap 15–25 mm broad, convex expanding to plano-convex, nonstriate, dry to greasy (not viscid), glabrous, hygrophanous, deep red overall or with a narrow orange ring at the margin, fading slightly in age but retaining red and orange tones. Gills adnate to emarginate, distant, moderately broad, deep orange to yellowish orange. Stem 15–45 x 3–5 mm, cylindrical, equal, dry, glabrous, apex red to reddish orange, base yellow to yellowish white. Spore deposit white. Edibility: unknown.

The bright red cap, contrasting with orange gills and yellow stem base, is easy to spot against a green mossy background. Originally described from Europe, the species gets its name because of its spores, which are pinched in the middle like a peanut. We have found this lovely species only on the island of Hawai'i. Is: HA.

Like the other Hawaiian *Hygrocybe*, *H. constrictospora* grows in the moss that blankets fallen tree ferns and other woody substrates on the forest floor.

Hygrocybe puaena Desjardin & Hemmes

Cap 10–25 mm broad, convex expanding to plano-convex with a depressed center, nonstriate, dry, glabrous, hygrophanous, deep yellow or sometimes with a hint of orange, fading to light yellow in age. Gills decurrent to deeply decurrent, distant, narrow, yellowish white to yellow. Stem 20–55 x 2–4 mm, cylindrical, equal, dry, glabrous, deep yellow overall. Spore deposit white. Edibility: unknown.

Hygrocybe puaena growing in moss within the Puʻu Makaʻala Natural Area Reserve on the Big Island.

The species name *puaena* means "radiance" in Hawaiian and refers to the brilliant yellow color of the fruiting bodies of this small mushroom. The presence of decurrent gills is one field characteristic that distinguishes *H. puaena* from other yellow *Hygrocybe* species in the native rainforests. The yellow Hawaiian species is allied with the red, north temperate, *Hygrocybe cantharellus.* Is: HA, MO.

Hygrocybe hapuuae Desjardin & Hemmes

Cap 5–12 mm broad, obtusely conical expanding to broadly convex, striate, viscid, glabrous, orange to light orange or light yellow fading to orangish white. Gills narrowly adnate, distant, narrow, white. Stem 15–25 x 1 mm, cylindrical, equal, viscid, glabrous, deep yellow overall. Spore deposit white. Edibility: unknown.

This is the smallest native forest *Hygrocybe* in the Hawaiian Islands. It has an orange to yellow cap, white gills, and yellow stem and is viscid overall. The stature reminds one of a *Mycena* species. *Hygrocybe hapuuae* can be found growing on hapuʻu (tree fern) fronds and trunks in the Puʻu Makaʻala Natural Area Reserve on the Big Island, the only known site for this rare endemic species. Is: HA.

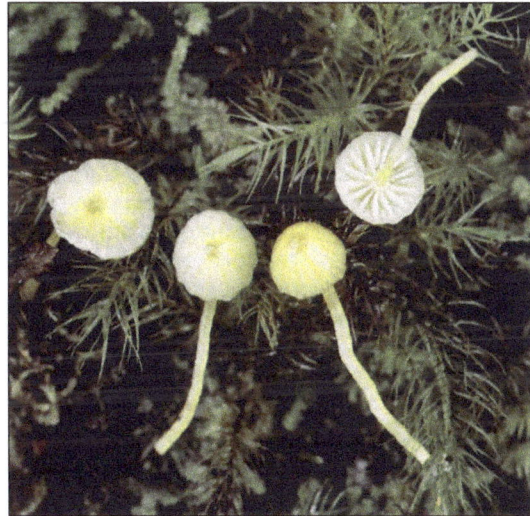

Hygrocybe hapuuae peeking out of hapuʻu fern fibrils and mosses.

Hygrocybe waolipo
Desjardin & Hemmes

Cap 20–35 mm broad, convex expanding to plano-convex with a depressed to umbilicate center that often becomes perforate, nonstriate, dry, radially appressed-fibrillose to streaked, dark gray to black overall. Gills adnate to emarginate, distant, broad, grayish white to gray. Stem 40–55 x 8–15 mm, cylindrical, equal, hollow, dry, glabrous, dark gray to black overall. Spore deposit white. Edibility: unknown.

A grouping of *Hygrocybe waolipo* from the Pu'u Maka'ala Natural Area Reserve on the Big Island.

The species name *waolipo* refers to its habit of growing in the dark shadows of the forest. Indeed the dark gray to black fruiting bodies grow from black mud underneath hapu'u logs and are very difficult to spot under the dense canopy of native rainforests. *Hygrocybe waolipo* is allied with the north temperate *H. ovinus* and *H. subovinus*, and with the New Zealand *H. squarrosa*. Is: HA.

Camarophyllopsis hymenocephala
(A. H. Smith & Hesler) Arnolds

Cap 8–17 mm broad, convex expanding to broadly convex, disc rugulose, margin short-striate, dry, glabrous, hygrophanous, pale brownish orange to grayish orange fading to orangish white. Gills adnate with a decurrent tooth, distant, broad, orangish white becoming grayish orange to pale brownish gray. Stem 25–40 x 2–4 mm, cylindrical, equal, hollow, dry, silky to glabrous, buff to pale yellowish white. Spore deposit white. Edibility: unknown.

Camarophyllopsis hymenocephala from the Na Pali Coast area of Kaua'i.

The micromorphology of the cap surface is quite distinctive in *Camarophyllopsis* and warrants acceptance as a genus distinct from *Hygrocybe*. The dull colors of the fruiting bodies will help to distinguish this small species from other orange native-forest *Hygrocybe* species, and of course, its microscopic features are clearly distinct. Is: HA, KA.

Marasmiellus hapuuae nom. prov.

Cap 2–8 mm broad, convex expanding to plano-convex, non-striate to rugulose-striate, dry, suedelike, buff to pale pinkish white overall. Gills adnate, distant, narrow, white, edges granulose. Stem 1–3 x 0.2–0.5 mm, lateral to strongly eccentric, cylindrical, equal, insititious, pruinose, white to pinkish buff. Spore deposit white. Edibility: unknown.

This undescribed, tiny white *Marasmiellus* attracts attention because it grows in great numbers on decaying fronds hanging down from hapu'u tree ferns. The fruiting bodies grow out horizontally from the fronds and have a white, lateral to strongly eccentric stem. It is allied with *M. segregabilis* from Bolivia. Is: HA, MA, MO.

A cluster of *Marasmiellus hapuuae* on hapu'u tree-fern fronds in Pu'u Maka'ala Natural Area Reserve.

Mycena marasmielloides nom. prov.

Cap 2–5 mm broad, convex to campanulate, sulcate, dry, glabrous to minutely suedelike, pale grayish orange with darker striations, sometimes with lavender tints. Gills shallowly adnexed, distant, moderately broad, pinkish buff. Stem 2–4 x 0.1 mm, strongly eccentric, cylindrical, equal, insititious, glabrous, brown. Spore deposit white. Edibility: unknown.

Mycena marasmielloides is a second tiny undescribed mushroom that lines drooping fronds of hapu'u tree ferns. In the field *Marasmiellus hapuuae* and *Mycena marasmielloides* are nearly indistinguishable but can be separated by careful observation of the brown, glabrous stem in *M. marasmielloides* versus the white, pruinose stipe of *M. hapuuae*. Under the microscope, however, they are as different as pineapple and guava. Is: HA.

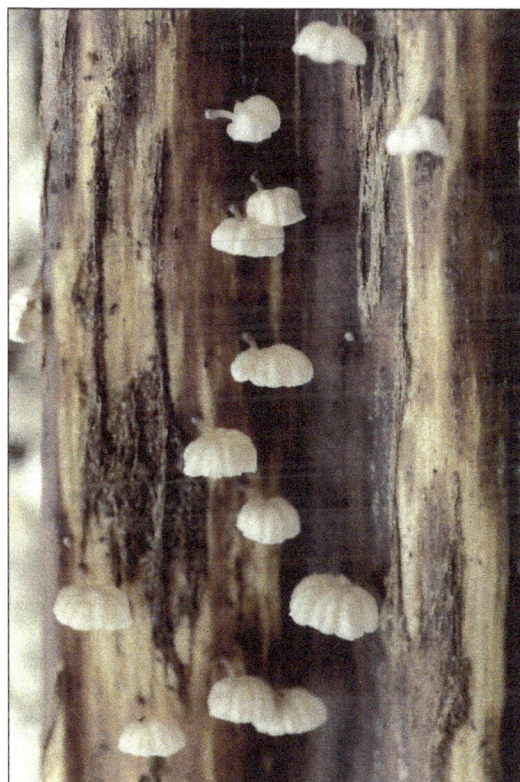

Mycena marasmielloides lining senescent tree-fern petioles in Pu'u Maka'ala Natural Area Reserve.

Mycena epipterygia (Scop.: Fr.) S. F. Gray

Cap 5–10 mm broad, convex, striate, viscid, smooth, glabrous, disc and striations yellowish brown, bright yellow to pale yellow elsewhere. Gills ascending-adnate with a short decurrent tooth, subdistant, narrow, white to pale yellowish white. Stem 15–30 x 1–1.5 mm, cylindrical, gradually enlarged downward to a bulbous base, apex pruinose, base glabrous, viscid, yellow to pale lemon yellow. Spore deposit white. Edibility: unknown.

Mycena epipterygia also grows in scattered clusters on old fronds drooping from native tree ferns in the understory of Hawaiian montane rainforests. It is easy to recognize by its yellow and viscid caps and stems. It grows in the same habitat and looks quite similar to *Hygrocybe hapuuae*, but the latter differs in forming a light orange to orangish yellow cap, a much paler yellow stem, and in having very different microanatomy. Is: HA, KA.

Mycena epipterygia grows in clusters on senescent hapu'u petioles.

Cystolepiota species

Cap 3–10 mm broad, obtusely conical to convex expanding to plano-convex, dry, covered overall by a thick layer of white powdery granules or flocculose-granulose, pure white, sometimes disc developing pale orange tones in age. Gills free, subdistant, narrow to moderately broad, white. Stem 5–15 x 0.5–1 mm, cylindrical, equal, pubescent to flocculose overall, white but developing red to reddish brown tones at the base in age; with a powdery-tomentose to flocculose partial veil when young, remaining as fibrils on cap margin. Spore deposit white. Edibility: unknown.

This is one of the more unusual mushrooms in native rainforests. Look on the moss-covered trunks of tree ferns for a splotch of white powder and you will probably find this undetermined *Cystolepiota*. The entire mushroom is covered by a thick layer of white powdery granules that are easily removed by touch or rainfall. Very few data are available on tropical *Cystolepiota* species so we hesitate to put a name on this Hawaiian native species. Is: HA.

A blotch of white powder on moss indicates *Cystolepiota* is developing underneath.

Armillaria aff. *ostoyae* (Romagn.) Henrik

Cap 15–50 mm broad, campanulate to plano-umbonate, umbo covered with tiny dark brown tufts, with scattered squamules towards the margin, dry, disc brown, margin pale creamy brown to beige. Gills adnate, subdistant, broad, grayish orange. Stem 25–40 x 4–5 mm, clavate, dry, pubescent, pale brown; partial veil forming a cottony, white annulus near stem apex when young, remaining as a white cottony ring or fibrillose zone in age. Spore deposit white. Edibility: unknown.

This Hawaiian *Armillaria* is found growing solitary or in scattered clusters on fallen tree ferns, or in large clusters on logs and decaying ohiʻa trees. It is closest to *A. ostoyae* from north temperate regions, but we have not yet confirmed this diagnosis with mating studies or DNA analysis. *Armillarin nabsnonia* has been reported recently from Hawaiʻi as growing on healthy koa and ohiʻa, and our material from native rainforests may represent that species. Is: HA.

This cluster of *Armillaria* aff. *ostoyae* is growing on an ohiʻa log in a kipuka along the Saddle Road on the Big Island.

Entoloma cibotiicola nom. prov.

Cap 10–25 mm broad, convex expanding to plano-convex with a depressed to umbilicate disc, strongly translucent-striate, disc scurfy to subsquamulose, glabrous on margin, dry, hygrophanous, disc and striations dark grayish brown to dark brown or nearly black, grayish brown elsewhere. Gills adnate, subdistant, broad, grayish white becoming pinkish brown. Stem 25–40 x 1.5–2.5 mm, cylindrical, equal, apex pruinose, base glabrous, dry, pale grayish brown. Spore deposit pinkish brown. Edibility: unknown.

Entoloma cibotiicola grows on the ground or on fallen tree ferns. Note the pink gills.

Entoloma cibotiicola is provisionally named after its predeliction for growing on hapuʻu tree ferns that belong to the endemic genus *Cibotium*. This is the most commonly encountered *Entoloma* species in native montane rainforests, among a number of small, darkly colored, difficult to identify species. It is similar to *E. mariae* from New Zcaland and *E. fibrosum* from eastern North America, but differs significantly in micromorphology. Is: HA.

Lycoperdon perlatum Pers.: Pers.

Fruiting bodies pear-shaped or subglobose with a tapered stem, 40–60 mm tall x 25–40 mm broad, white to creamy brown; peridium thin, membranous, opening by a single pore (ostiole) at fruiting body apex, covered with small, white to grayish brown conical spines, these fall off in age leaving a characteristic reticulate pattern of scars. Gleba white when young, becoming powdery and brown to olivaceous brown in age. Stem 20–30 x 10–15 mm, apex covered by spines, base glabrous. Spores brown. Edibility: edible when gleba is white.

Clusters of 30 or more fruiting bodies of *Lycoperdon perlatum* are often encountered on the ground or on fallen tree ferns on trails through the native Hawaiian rainforest. This puffball is perched on a sterile stalk, has a well-formed ostiole and is covered with tiny grayish brown spines, giving it the common name, the Gemmed Puffball. Is: HA, KA, MA, MO.

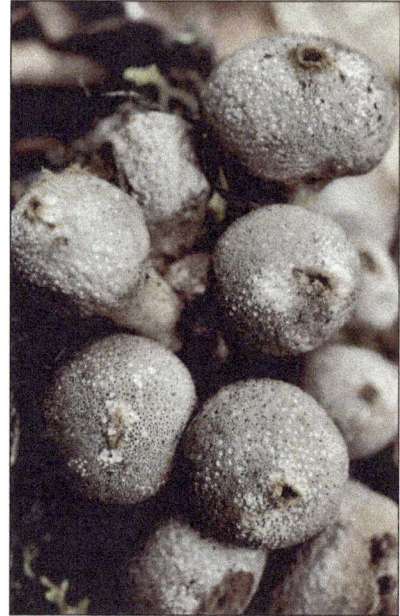

A cluster of *Lycoperdon perlatum* on a trail through Pu'u Maka'ala Natural Area Reserve on the Big Island. Pigs and humans may spread this puffball along trails in the native forest.

Morchella esculenta Pers. ex St.-Amans

Cap 30–70 mm tall x 20–30 mm broad, obtusely conical, composed of irregular vertical and horizontal ridges outlining angular to irregular pits, margin of cap attached to the stem, pale grayish brown to beige brown; interior hollow. Stem 10–40 x 8–15 mm, cylindrical or enlarged at the base, which is often folded, hollow, minutely granular, dry, off white to cream-colored. Spores creamy white. Edibility: edible and one of the most esculent.

Morel mushrooms (actually Ascomycetes) are occasionally found growing out of the fibrous trunks of living and fallen tree ferns in montane native rainforests. It is difficult to actually hunt for them in the rainforest. Mushroom collectors just happen to come upon a morel (if they are lucky), usually because the fruiting bodies are rare, usually found solitary, grow widely scattered, and are difficult to see in the dense undergowth and debris under tree ferns. Is: HA, KA, MA, OA.

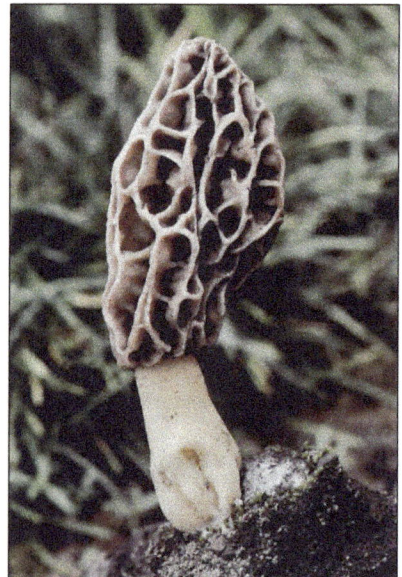

Morchella esculenta from the Kilauea Volcano area of the Big Island. This widely sought after edible species grows on tree ferns in the wet native rainforest.

Hobsonia mirabilis (Peck) Linder

Fruiting bodies (sporodochia) 3–7 mm broad, irregularly cushion-shaped to bloblike, gelatinous, soft, white to off-white; composed of a dense mass of helically coiled, multicellular filamentous conidia.

This imperfect fungus is ubiquitous in the native rainforest forming white jellylike blobs on the fallen petioles of tree ferns. The asexual spores are helical-shaped and multicellular. Is: HA, KA.

Hobsonia mirabilis is everywhere in the native Hawaiian rainforest, growing on decaying tree fern petioles.

Ascocoryne sarcoides
(Jacq. ex S. F. Gray) Groves and Wilson

Fruiting bodies 5–10 mm broad, shallowly cupulate to flattened disc-shaped, sessile, upper (hymenial) surface smooth or wrinkled, rosy pink; lower sterile surface glabrous to finely furfuraceous, rose pink. Stem absent. Spore deposit white. Edibility: unknown.

Clusters of small, rose pink, cuplike fruiting bodies of *Ascocoryne sarcoides* are often found on hapuʻu tree ferns that have fallen over the trail in native rainforests. Is: HA.

Fruiting bodies of *Ascocoryne sarcoides* on tree ferns in Puʻu Makaʻala forest on the Big Island.

SPHAGNUM BOGS

Sphagnum bogs are rare in the Hawaiian Islands, occurring naturally only at a few sites in the wettest areas of Maui and Hawai'i. In the Northern Hemisphere, the mushroom *Galerina paludosa* is commonly collected in sphagnum bogs dominated by *Sphagnum palustre*. Not surprisingly, we have found *G. paludosa* in several disjunct *S. palustre* bogs on the island of Hawai'i.

Sphagnum moss covers the banks of this bog on Mauna Loa on the Big Island.

Galerina paludosa (Fr.) Kühner

Cap 8–15 mm broad, conical to campanulate expanding to broadly campanulate with a prominent umbo, translucent-striate, dry, glabrous, hygrophanous, dark brown fading to brown or grayish orange. Gills ascending-adnate, subdistant, broad, grayish orange to rusty brown. Stem 50–90 x 1–2 mm, cylindrical, equal, dry, glabrous beneath partial veil fibrils, base tomentose, light orange to grayish orange, with a white, cobwebby to membranous, annular zone of fibrils near the apex. Spore deposit rusty brown. Edibility: not recommended.

Galerina paludosa, a species that is widespread in bogs in the Northern Hemisphere, grows directly from decaying *Sphagnum* moss. Currently it is known from only two sphagnum bogs on the island of Hawai'i. Is: HA.

Galerina paludosa peeking out from *Sphagnum* forming a small bog along the Saddle Road on the Big Island.

ADDITIONAL SPECIES IN SPHAGNUM BOGS

Humidicutis peleae

This bright-orange species also favors *Sphagnum* moss wherever the bog is covered by a canopy of forest trees (see Wet Montane Native Rain Forests for full description).

Hygrocybe lamalama

This deep-yellow species is commonly found in sphagnum bogs where there is a closed tree canopy above (see Wet Montane Native Rain Forests for full description).

CHAPTER 3
OTHER HAWAIIAN FUNGI

The bulk of this field guide has been devoted to the larger and fleshy fungi, often called the Macromycetes, that grow throughout the Hawaiian Islands. There are many other kinds of fungi that occur also in Hawai'i and a few of them are presented in this chapter.

Walk through the majestic koa-ohi'a forests on the windward side of the Big Island, Hawai'i, and look closely at the koa foliage. You might see some spotted and gnarled koa leaves, or compact clusters of abnormal branches called witches' broom. These diseased plant parts resulted from infections by pathogenic rust fungi. If you are lucky, you might spot one of the 13 species of rust fungi known only from the Hawaiian Islands. At first glance it might seem that these parasites are detrimental to the forest, but they are also beneficial in culling older trees to make room for new growth.

A walk over relatively recent lava flows between the high elevation kipukas (terrestrial islands of native vegetation) on Mauna Loa, Hawai'i, will reveal numerous lichen species. Lichens, a symbiotic association between an alga or a cyanobacterium and a fungus, are pioneer organisms on new lava flows. They are some of the first organisms to grow on this desolate landscape, preparing the site for the establishment of plants and other organisms. Many lichens are nitrogen-fixing organisms. They have the ability to convert atmospheric nitrogen into a usable form of nitrogen that is available to the lichen as well as to other organisms and needed for amino acid synthesis. In this way lichens play an important role in the nitrogen cycle.

Walk through any wet forest and look closely at decaying wet leaves or under the bark of a rotting log. You might see brightly colored, netlike veins of slimy plasmodium, one stage in the life cycle of a slime mold. Return in a couple of days and the plasmodium will have converted into its spore-producing stage, showing tiny, delicate but exquisitely beautiful sporangia. Slime mold plasmodia feed on bacteria, protozoa, algae, fungal cells, and other small creatures, and thereby serve a role in regulating the population size of these ubiquitous and prolific organisms.

We should never forget the important ecological roles that all of these fungi play in the environment.

RUST FUNGI

Rust fungi are obligate parasites noted for their virulence, which causes great losses to valuable economic crops worldwide. In Hawai'i, rusts are found on koa and many other endemic plants, as well as on agricultural crops. The rust fungi are famous for their complex life cycles, which may include as many as five different spore states, some of which may occur on two totally unrelated hosts. Obviously, the determination of life cycles presents substantial challenges for the investigator and requires a lot of time looking through a microscope. For a review of the characteristics of Hawaiian rust life cycles, see Gardner, 1997.

F. L. Stevens recorded 39 rust fungi in Hawai'i in his paper "Hawaiian Fungi" in 1925. Since then Donald Gardner of the Cooperative Studies Unit, National Biological Survey, Department of Botany, University of Hawai'i, and C. S. Hodges, working with the Pacific Southwest Forest and Range Experiment Station, Forest Service, U. S. Department of Agriculture, have described a number of endemic species and summarized the current status of rust fungi in Hawai'i (Gardner, 1988; Gardner and Hodges, 1989; Gardner, 1994; Gardner, 1997).

By 1989, a total of 74 rust species were recorded for Hawai'i. Twenty-two of these were recognized as native species, of which 13 are endemic and another 9 are indigenous (Gardner and Hodges, 1989). Recently, 16 more species have been added to the list, 4 of them endemic to the Hawaiian Islands (Gardner, 1997).

Atelocauda digitata (Wint.) Cumm. & Hirat., a rust infecting Hawaiian endemic *Acacia* hosts, is seen in this photo growing on phyllodes of *Acacia koa* on the Mauna Loa strip road on the Big Island. This particular rust, considered indigenous to Hawai'i, also occurs on a large number of *Acacia* species in Australia, New Zealand, and Java.

The endemic rust, *Atelocauda koae* Cumm. & Hirat. is shown growing on phyllodes of *Acacia koa* var. *latifolia*.

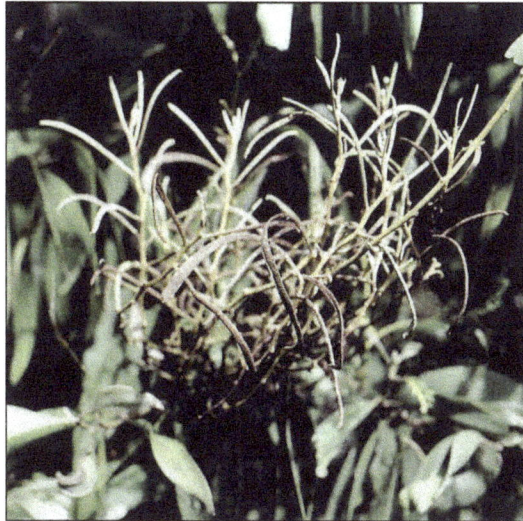

Atelocauda angustiphylloda Gardner, an endemic rust, produces brooms with narrow, linearly shaped phyllodes that may be almost circular in cross section. This species is limited in distribution to the variety of koa, *A. koa* var. *latifolia*, which occurs in upper-elevation forests of the Big Island. Older trees may have hundreds of witches' brooms, some as large as 1 m or more in length.

Endoraecium acaciae Hodges & Gardner is an endemic species and considered the most common rust on *Acacia* spp. in Hawai'i. The witches' broom is growing on koa at Kalaheo golf course on Kaua'i.

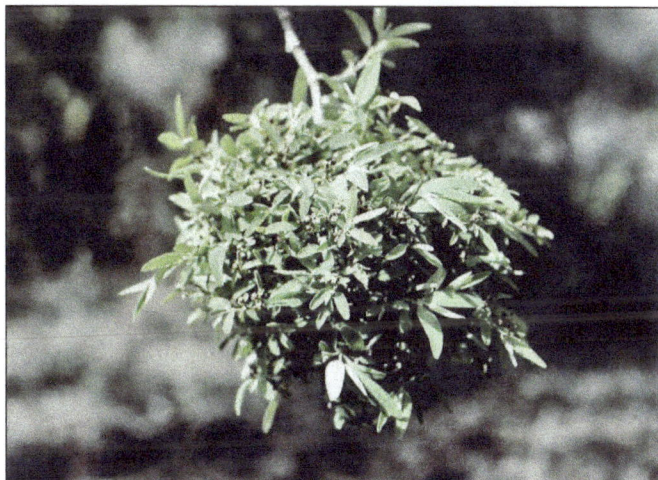

Puccinia vitata Hennen & Hodges is an endemic rust that causes witches' broom on endemic hosts such as *Euphorbia olowaluana* var. *gracilis*, shown here on the Saddle Road on the Big Island.

LICHENS

A lichen is a symbiotic relationship between a fungus (usually an Ascomycete) and a green alga, a blue green bacterium, or both. Lichens form crustose, foliose, or fruticose growths in diverse habitats in Hawai'i, including on the trunks of coconut trees along the ocean, on lava rocks in the full sun, and intertangled with bryophytes in the dense rainforest. Lichens are famous for their ability to dry out for long periods and then quickly resume growth when moisture is present. They are also important indicators of pollutants in the atmosphere (see a general botany textbook for a full discussion of lichens). Studies on lichens in Hawai'i have been carried out by C. W. Smith of the University of Hawai'i at Manoa (Smith, 1993). Some common species and those exhibiting fungal fruiting bodies (apothecia) are pictured here.

Within a few months after an eruption, the lichen *Stereocaulon vulcani* covers new lava flows and colors them gray on the wetter, windward sides of the Big Island. This species consists of a fungus and a cyanobacterium, nitrogen-fixing partner that add to the fertility of the flow and aid in the colonization of this new land by ferns and young ohi'a trees.

Usnea australis, a common lichen growing on limbs of koa trees in Bird Park within Hawai'i Volcanoes National Park (left), displays dime-sized apothecia (right), the cuplike sexual fruiting bodies of the Ascomycete fungal partner.

The reddish-brown apothecia contrast beautifully with the black and white thallus of
Parmeliella mariana, a lichen found on the bark of saplings in windward forests.

Apothecia are abundant on the thalli of *Xanthoparmelia coloradoensis* that grow on lava
boulders at the 6,000- to 8,000-foot level on Mauna Kea and Mauna Loa (left). The red fungal
fruiting body at the tips of the thalli of *Cladonia* sp. (right) looks like a red hat and gives this
lichen the common name British Soldier lichen.

MYCETOZOANS—THE SLIME MOLDS

The mycetazoans include the protostelids (subclass Protostelia), cellular slime molds (subclass Dictyostelia), and plasmodial slime molds or Myxomycetes (subclass Myxogastria: see Olive, 1975). Slime molds have historically been studied by mycologists because of their fungal-like characteristics, the presence of spores and sporangia, even though they are protists and significantly different from fungi, with amoeboid stages as part of their life cycles. Studies carried out in Hawai'i or that are in progress on each group include protosteliads, Spiegel and Hemmes, 1999a, 1999b; cellular slime molds, Landolt and Wong, 1998; and Myxomycetes, Eliasson, 1991. The fruiting bodies of myxomycetes are large enough to be seen with the naked eye in the field and a few species are illustrated here.

Plasmodial slime molds are quite common on fallen logs and leaves in the wet alien forests and in the wood-chip mulch used for landscaping. In their early stages slime molds first appear as golden-yellow, white, or red glistening masses of cytoplasm, the plasmodia (see photo below), and later as encrustations (aethalia) or clusters of tiny fruiting bodies (sporangia). Some of the diverse shapes and colors of the fruiting bodies are illustrated on the following pages. A recent review (Eliasson, 1991) listed over 100 species of plasmodial slime molds found in Hawai'i. For teachers and amateur scientists, these slime molds can be readily isolated from twigs, bark, and leaves onto water agar; when put into culture, they are ideal for observing cytoplasmic streaming and cellular development (see Stephenson, 1985, for isolation and culture methods, and Stephenson and Stempen, 1994, for a more in-depth review).

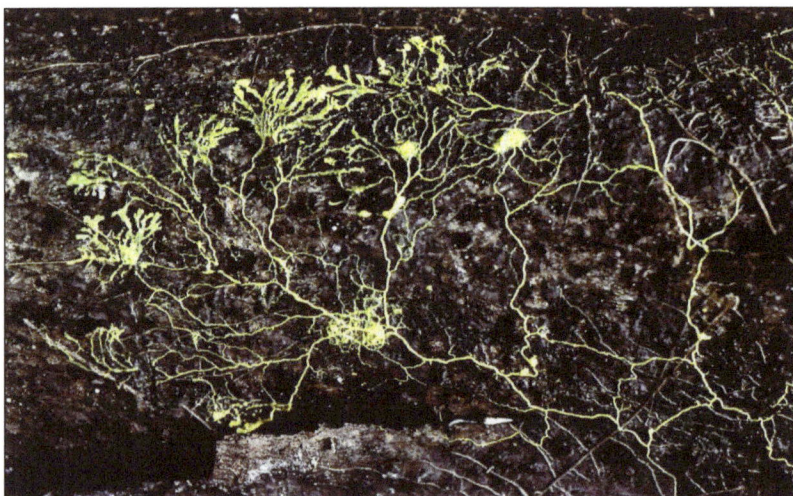

Look under logs in wet, shady places, especially under loose bark for the plasmodia. Plasmodia are interesting biologically in that they are large multinucleate masses of cytoplasm bounded by a single cell membrane. The plasmodia engulf bacteria and protozoa as food sources. A single plasmodium may cover several square feet of substrate. Even though mycologists have historically studied the plasmodial slime molds, biologists consider Myxomycetes as members of the kingdom Protista, and not as true fungi.

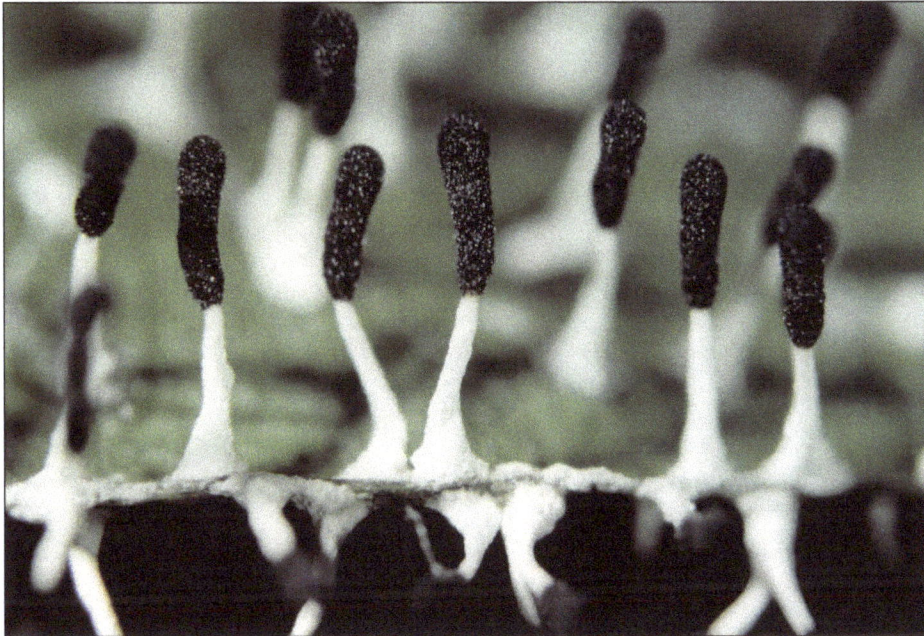

Diachea leucopodia, with black sporangia and white stalks, cover this leaf. These fruiting structures are about 2 millimeters tall and thus can be seen with the naked eye, but a hand lens helps reveal the details of these beautifully delicate structures.

The plasmodial slime mold, *Fuligo septica*, appears in grass, on wood-chip mulch, and on fallen logs as a yellow, encrusted mass called an *aethalium*. It is found in the wet, windward forests of Hawaiʻi. This particular specimen was photographed on a fallen *Eucalyptus* log at Palaʻau State Park on Molokaʻi. The entire mass is 150 mm or more in diameter.

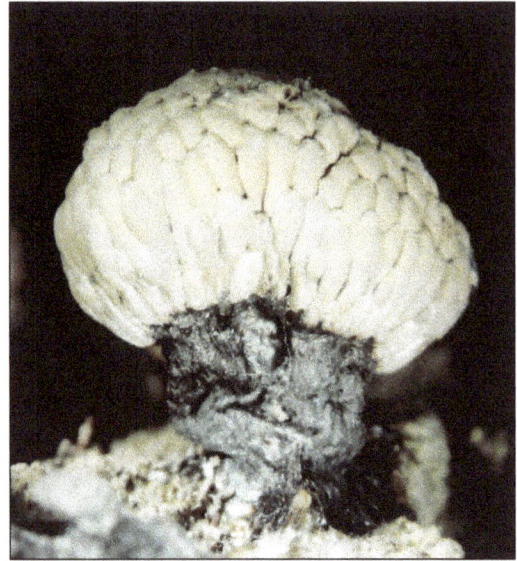

Physarum globuliferum (left) growing at Honua, Hawai'i, on the Big Island. The sporangium is 1 mm in diameter. *Tubifera microsperma* (right) in a University of Hawai'i at Hilo garden. It is 5 mm in diameter.

An elegant cluster of *Stemonitis fusca* growing on a rotting log in a backyard in Hilo; each one is about 7 mm tall.

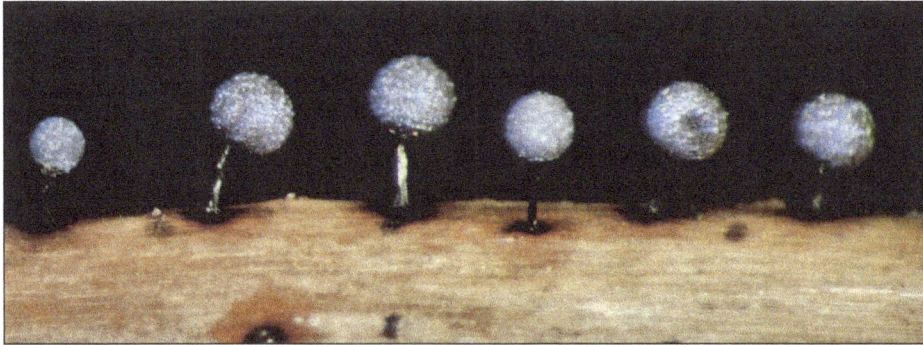

The spherical sporangia of *Lamproderma scintillins* reflect a bluish color. These fruiting bodies, about 2 mm tall, are found on twigs in the wet forest around Hilo.

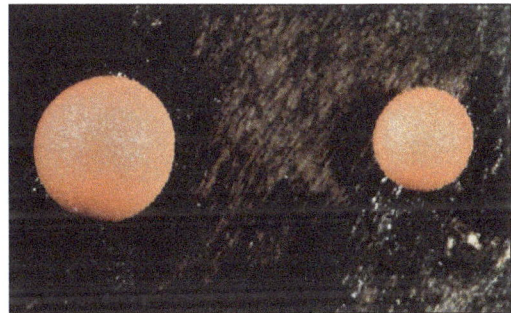

Ceratiomyxa fruticulosa (left), is a common species in alien Hawaiian forests and is occasionally found in the native rainforests. Fruiting bodies are pure white, about 1 mm tall. *Lycogala epidendrum* (right) is another common slime mold that appears on fallen logs in the wet alien forest. Sporangia appear as pink to orange spheres that change to a bronze-brown color when mature; it is 5–10 mm in diameter.

The fruiting bodies of *Hemitrichia serpula* resemble a pretzel-like maze. This species is common on branches and logs at the Boy Scout camp at Honua, Hawaiʻi, near Hilo. The entire mass is 40 mm in diameter.

When sporangia of *Arcyria denudata* shed their spores, they leave these pink, cotton-candylike fibers, the *capillitium,* behind. The sporangia are 8 mm tall.

These sporangia of *Hemitrichia calyculata* (left) also show capillitia after spore release; they are 6 mm tall. Sporangia of *Physarum nutans* (right) found on rotten wood at Koke'e, Kaua'i; are about 1 mm tall.

A few of these tiny sporangia of *Trichia favoginea* have ruptured open to release spores. The sporangia are 0.5 mm in diameter.

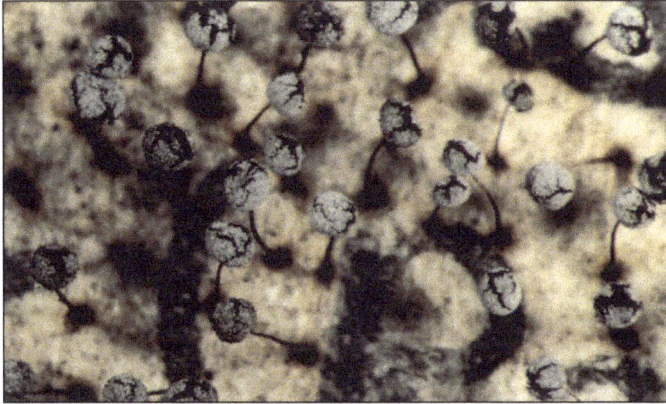

Sporangia of *Didymium verrucosporum* growing on a labelling tag in a misting house for plant propagation. Size: 1mm tall.

These sporangia of *Physarum bogoriense* (left), found at the UH-Hilo agriculture farm, have split open to release spores. Size: 1mm in diameter. Sporangia of *Lamproderma arcyrionema* (right) growing on a fallen kopiko tree at the Boy Scout camp at Honokaia on the Big Island. Size: 1.5 mm tall.

Orange sporangia of *Physarum melleum* cover these dried leaves of the "charcoal tree," *Trema orientalis*. Size: 1 mm tall.

ANIMALS THAT FEED ON FUNGI

Mushrooms and other fungi serve as food sources for native insects, as well as alien insects, slugs, snails, and millipedes in Hawai'i. For humans who collect mushrooms to eat, it is a race to see who gets to dine on these gourmet items first.

A mushroom lover, this pink-colored millipede covers and devours *Crepidotus* and other fungi growing on logs and stumps.

Even deep in the native rainforest, the alien spotted garden slug *(Limax maximus)* has found a cluster of puffballs to feed upon (top). This garlic snail *(Oxychilus alliarius)* is systematically rooting out the spore-bearing surface of *Merulius tremellosus* (bottom).

A number of Hawaiian fruit flies (*Drosophila* spp.) feed on mushrooms and bracket fungi in the native forest (above). In fact, entomologists capture these insects for study by baiting sponges with a mixture of mushrooms, banana, and yeast. Stand back and watch a Sulfur Shelf or any large fleshy mushroom in the Hawaiian rainforest and native *Drosophila* will be seen feeding on the fungal tissue.

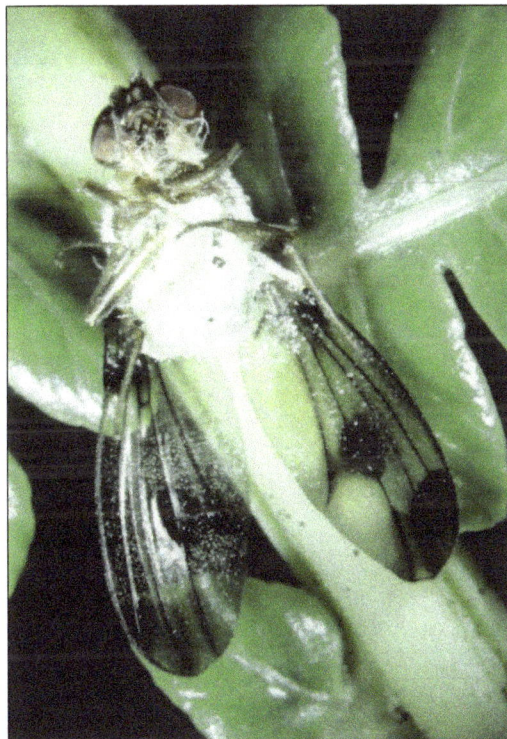

Insects beware, however. The fungi can turn the tables on the mycophagist. Here a native picture-wing fly is infected with *Entomophthora*, a fungus that grows on the chitin covering the insect's body.

This Western yellowjacket, *Vespula pensylvanica*, a fairly recent introduction into the drier native forests of Hawai'i, has also met its match with a fungal infection. These photos remind us of the important role fungi play in the dynamics of any ecosystem.

CHAPTER 4
MEDICINAL MUSHROOMS

Kombucha, also widely known as the Manchurian mushroom, undergoes cycles of popularity in Hawaiʻi. The concoction is not really a mushroom but a soft gelatinous mixture of several yeast species and several bacteria that form a curd (see Hobbs, 1996, for a detailed analysis of the yeasts and bacteria involved, and the step-by-step preparation of Kombucha). A small portion of the curd is added to a jar of tea with sugar or honey and allowed to grow to the edges of the jar. Health benefits supposedly derived from drinking the broth include everything from detoxification of the blood, prevention of cancer, to prevention of the common cold. Unfortunately, there is little or no scientific evidence to back up these claims. A word of caution: It may not be beneficial to consume daily the antibiotics produced in Kombucha broth. The practice of using Kombucha tea has been handed down from generation to generation by the Chinese for over 2,000 years.

Reishi (Japanese) or Ling Zhi (Chinese) is a wood-rotting polypore fungus, *Ganoderma lucidum,* that is widely used as a tea or powder to strengthen the immune system, protect the user from disease, and generally promote long life. This fungus is not naturally found in Hawaiʻi, but can be found by the bushel basket in herbal shops in Honolulu's Chinatown. In contrast to Kombucha, there is good scientific evidence that Reishi has antitumor activity and does stimulate macrophage

Jar of Kombucha broth.

Reishi.

production (see Hobbs, 1996 for experimental studies). Reishi or Ling Zhi has been utilized as an herbal medicine for over 4,000 years in Japan and China.

Mycomedicinals are exploding on the herbal scene to take their place alongside *Echinacea, Ginkgo,* and kava. *Cordyceps sinensis,* the Caterpillar Fungus, *Trametes versicolor,* the Turkey-tail Fungus, and *Grifola frondosa,* the Hen-of-the-Woods, have demonstrated antitumor properties and modulate blood pressure. *Lentinula edodes* (Shiitake) lowers cholesterol, has antiviral properties, and enhances the immune system. *Ganoderma lucidum* (Ling Zhi) has antiflammatory properties, as well as an ability to enhance the immune system and act as an antitumor agent. The study of mycomedicinals is still in its infancy and many other species need to be examined for their medicinal properties.

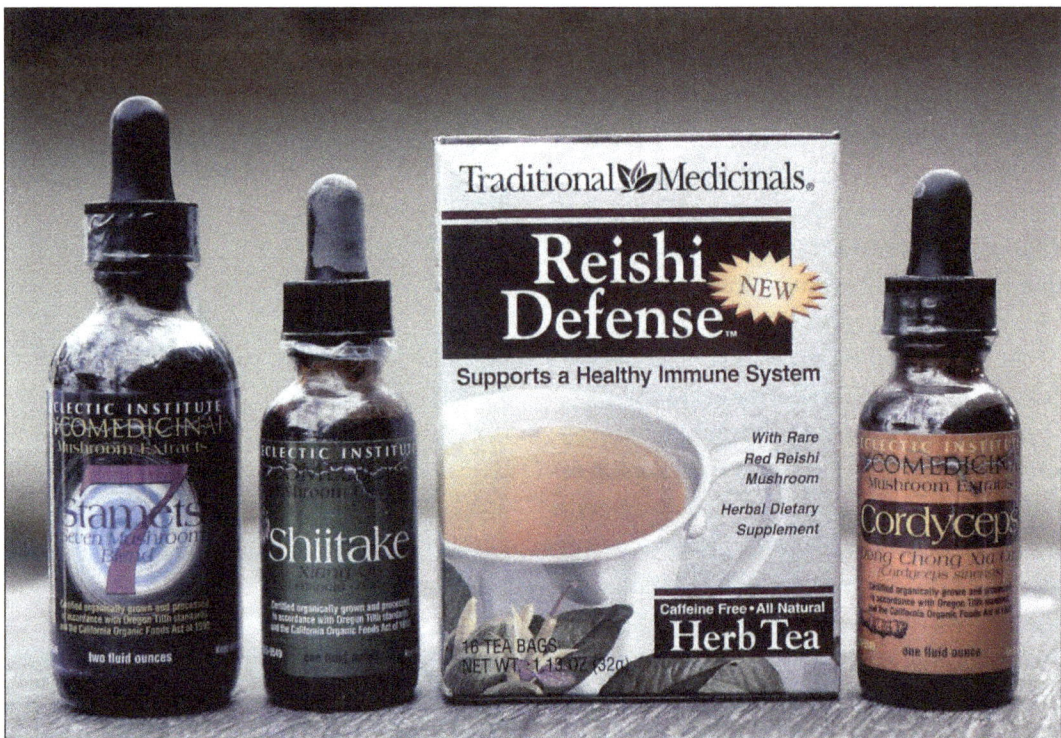

Mycomedicinals, such as these mushroom extracts and tea, are now available from a number of sources. For more information concerning medicinal mushrooms, consult Stamets, *Growing Gourmet & Medicinal Mushrooms,* Ten Speed Press, 2000.

CHAPTER 5
POISONOUS HAWAIIAN MUSHROOMS

A small percentage of Hawaiian mushrooms are poisonous. Unfortunately, several of these species are common in lawns and pastures around households and playgrounds and are frequently encountered. One, *Amanita marmorata,* which belongs to the "destroying angel" group, is potentially fatal if eaten. The general public, especially youngsters, should be alerted to the poisonous nature of some mushrooms, and they should be taken to the hospital emergency room immediately if a questionable mushroom has been ingested. If possible, take along a specimen of the mushroom in question for proper diagnosis and treatment.

This is *Amanita marmorata* var. *myrtacearum,* undoubtedly the most poisonous mushroom in Hawai'i (see *Eucalyptus* Forests for a full description). Eating a portion of one cap could be fatal to a full-grown adult. This *Amanita,* 3–4 inches tall with a cap about 2–2-1/2 inches wide, is white with some flattened gray fibrils on the cap, a skirtlike annulus on the stem, and a characteristic, cup-shaped volva at the base of the stem. *A. marmorata* var. *myrtacearum* is often found on lawns, but must be in close proximity to introduced myrtle trees such as the paperbark or bottlebrush trees (*Melaleuca* spp.) used in landscaping or various *Eucalyptus* species. This *Amanita* is also found under *Casuarina,* the ironwood or Australian pine, that is so common along the shorelines in Hawai'i. *Amanita marmorata* was first described from Australia and was probably introduced to Hawai'i with nursery plants.

The toxins involved with *Amanita marmorata* are the amatoxins, cyclic peptides that inhibit cellular enzymes that synthesize messenger RNA. Symptoms, including vomiting, diarrhea, and intense abdominal pain, appear 6 to 24 hours after ingestion. Severe liver and kidney damage follow after a few days. Death usually ensues. Detailed information about poisonous mushrooms and their toxins can be found in *Toxic and Hallucinogenic Mushroom Poisoning* by Lincoff and Mitchel (1977), *Poisonous Mushrooms of the Northern United States and Canada* by Ammirati, Traquair, and Horgen (1985), *A Colour Atlas of Poisonous Fungi* by Bresinsky and Besl (1990), and *Mushrooms: Poisons and Panaceas* by Benjamin (1995).

The toxins in *A. muscaria* include muscimol, ibotenic acid, and muscazone. The concentrations vary with the specific location and time of the year, and the severity of the poisoning depends on the amount of mushroom ingested. Symptoms of delirium and hallucination appear 30 to 90 minutes after ingestion and usually disappear after 12 hours.

Another *Amanita* species, *A. muscaria* var. *formosa,* the Fly Agaric, is common under loblolly and slash pines in the Koke'e region of Kaua'i in the fall and winter months. This large, spectacular species (cap may reach the size of a frisbee, up to 200 mm in diameter) can be recognized by its orange to yellow cap with white patches of universal veil scattered over the surface (see Conifer Forests for a full description). Although not as poisonous as *A. marmorata,* if ingested this species usually makes most people seriously ill.

Chlorophyllum molybdites (below) is a medium-sized to large mushroom (cap from 3 to 5 inches wide) found in pastures, on lawns, along golf-course fairways, around compost, and under coastal ironwood trees. At maturity the gills show a distinct green tone. Also, look for the corn flake–like squamules on top of the cap and a thick annulus or ring that usually slips up and down the stalk. The toxins are not deactivated or destroyed by cooking.

Reports show that *Leucoagaricus leucothites* causes gastrointestinal upset when ingested by some people, even though it is listed as an edible species in many mushroom manuals *(Leucoagaricus naucinus;* see Pastures for a full description). The primary concern is that this pure white species may be confused with the deadly *Amanita marmorata,* which may also be nearly pure white. Compare the two photos and note that *L. naucina* does not have a volva at the base of the stalk and the annulus is more like a ring on your finger that will slip up and down the stem, in contrast to the thin, skirtlike annulus of *Amanita marmorata.*

Chorophyllum molybdites, the Green-spored Parasol mushroom, sends more people to the hospital emergency room than any other mushroom in Hawai'i (see Lawns for a full description). These mushrooms smell good, look good, and even taste good, according to reports. Confounding the problem is that some people can eat this species with impunity and recommend it to their best friends. However, most people become violently ill within 1 to 2 hours with stomach cramps, vomiting, hypothermia, diarrhea, and a general feeling that they wished they had not eaten this particular mushroom. These acute symptoms may continue for 4 to 5 hours. The victim will usually recover completely in a day or two.

The bright yellow Flowerpot Parasol, *Leucocoprinus birnbaumii,* so common in the potting mixes of nursery pots and hanging baskets, is another species that causes gastrointestinal upsets if eaten. There are reports of pets becoming ill after playfully devouring these obvious additions to the interior decorating. *Leucocoprinus birnbaumii* also often grows in wood-chip mulch (see Flowerpots for a full description).

Hypholoma fasciculare, also known as *Naemataloma fasciculare,* is a yellow-capped mushroom that grows in clusters on wood-chip piles (see Compost Piles and Wood Chips for a full description). We have collected the species a number of times near Haleakala National Park on Maui. This Sulfur Tuft or Sulfur Cap is reported to cause liver and kidney damage, and even death. The toxins in this species have not been fully elucidated.

Reports show that the Earthballs, *Scleroderma* species, are extremely unacceptable to the human system and will be regurgitated almost immediately after consumption (see *Eucalyptus* Forests for a full description). *Scleroderma* fruiting bodies resemble puffballs but have a mustard-yellow, cracked outer surface, and purple-gray spore mass inside. Do not ingest any puffballs when the spore mass is colored.

EDIBLE VS. POISONOUS

The question is often asked: "How can you tell if a mushroom is edible or poisonous?" There is only one safe way. You must accurately identify the specimen to species, and you must have information available concerning the edibility of that particular species. There are no short cuts other than eating the mushroom and waiting to find out what happens to your system–and we strongly recommend against such frivolous and potentially dangerous actions. Many myths abound purporting methods for determining edibility. For example, one myth suggests that if you add a silver coin in with cooking mushrooms and the coin tarnishes black, then the mushrooms are poisonous. Another myth suggests that if you cook the mushrooms with rice and the rice turns red, then the mushrooms are poisonous. These diagnostic techniques fail miserably when used with a number of very poisonous mushrooms, so we recommend against using any of these procedures. The only way to know if a mushroom species is edible or poisonous is to learn how to identify the species accurately. Once you have identified your specimen to species, you must consult the literature, such as a field guide or a scientific monograph, to find information on its edibility. Often, data on the edibility of a particular species is nonexistent, and hence it is listed as "unknown." Although it is true that most of our edibility data comes from records of people ingesting the species, we recommend against eating any species of unknown edibility. There are plenty of good edible fungi in the Hawaiian Islands that are not difficult to identify and we suggest that you stick to eating these.

CHAPTER 6
HALLUCINOGENIC HAWAIIAN MUSHROOMS

The most common hallucinogenic or Magic Mushroom in Hawai'i, *Copelandia cyanescens*, can be found growing directly in cow dung in the lowland pastures of Hawai'i. This species contains psilocybin, a psychoactive chemical that mimics the normal neural transmitter serotonin. Psilocybin causes increased visual effects, including enhanced color perception, impaired distance perception, and euphoria. These psilocybin-containing mushrooms typically bruise blue-black when handled. Magic Mushrooms are dangerous for consumption and may have serious side effects including vomiting and paralysis. In addition, they are illegal to possess. Long term usage or ingestion of large quantities of these mushrooms may cause a chronic feeling of illness, decreased concentration, and poor judgment (see Stamets, 1996, for an excellent discussion of the historical use of hallucinogenic mushrooms).

Other psychoactive, coprophilous species reported for Hawai'i include *Copelandia tropicalis*, *Copelandia bispora*, and *Copelandia cambodginiensis*. See Merlin and Allen (1993) for a summary of the identification and chemical analysis of psychoactive fungi in Hawai'i.

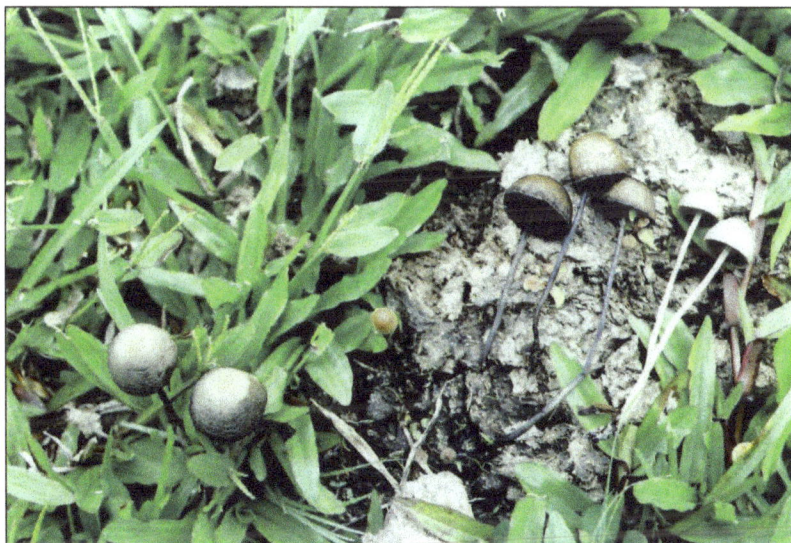

A cluster of *Copelandia cyanescens* in cow dung in a pasture near Maluhia, Maui. The cap often darkens and cracks when exposed to the direct sun (see Pastures for a full description).

The blue staining of the stalk of dung-inhabiting mushrooms is a sign that they contain psychoactive compounds. There are a number of other look-alike, dung-loving mushrooms that are not hallucinogenic, some of which may cause serious gastrointestinal irritation. Shown above is *Copelandia cyanescens,* the most common Magic Mushroom of the Hawaiian Islands.

Amanita muscaria var. *formosa,* seen here under pines near Koke'e, Kaua'i, is another species with hallucinogenic properties. Hallucinations and feelings of grandeur may occur within 30 minutes to 2 hours after ingestion, but these feelings are often accompanied by nausea and vomiting, hypothermia, and profuse sweating (see the Poisonous Mushrooms section for the toxins involved; see Conifer Forests for a full description).

CHAPTER 7

CULTURING MUSHROOMS AT HOME

Culturing mushrooms on a small scale at home or on a larger scale commercially requires hard work and considerable care to avoid contamination from other fungi and bacteria. The step-by-step procedures and the equipment and supplies required are described and illustrated in *The Mushroom Cultivator* by Paul Stamets and J. S. Chilton (1983), and *Growing Gourmet & Medicinal Mushrooms* by Paul Stamets (2000). The accompanying photos show the basic steps involved. Oyster Mushrooms, *Pleurotus* spp., are probably the easiest to grow and the best genus with which to begin. Oyster Mushrooms grow readily on wood chips and outgrow almost any type of competitive contaminants. Other mushroom species often have more stringent growth requirements and are more difficult to cultivate.

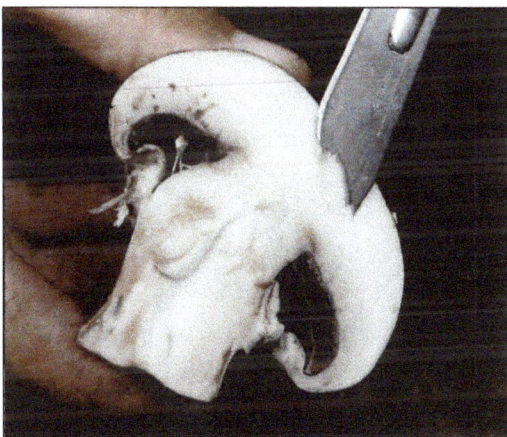

Sterile tissue is cut from the context or stalk with a sharp, heat sterilized blade and placed on culture media (malt extract or potato dextrose agar). Make several inoculations, because the chance of contamination from the surface of the mushroom is quite high.

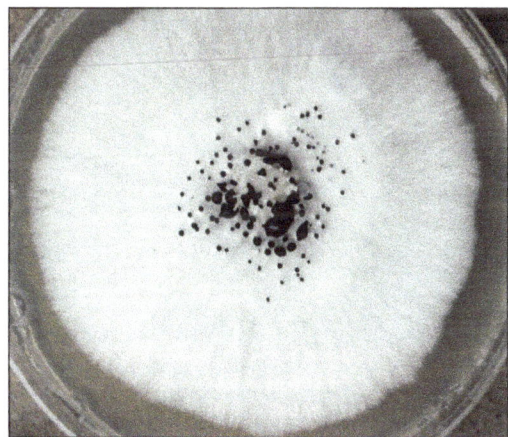

The hyphae are growing out radially from this clean piece of tissue isolated from the Oyster Mushroom, *Pleurotus cystidiosus*. The mycelium will grow to the edge of the plate in a few days.

A half dozen pieces of the mycelium cut from the agar plate were used to inoculate these quart fruit jars containing sterilized rye grains (bags of rye grains can be obtained from health food stores). When colonized by the fungal mycelium, the rye grains serve as points of inoculum for the bags of wood-chip substrate.

A good clean substrate for Oyster Mushrooms is four parts wood chips (chips from weedy trees such as *Trema, Melochia,* and guava all work well) and one part wheat or rice bran (obtained from health food or animal feed stores). Plastic, autoclavable bags are filled with the wood chip–bran substrate, sterilized in a pressure cooker, and inoculated with one-fourth a jar of mycelium-covered rye grains.

After ten days to two weeks the bags of wood chip–bran substrate are white with mycelium. Holes are then punched in the plastic bag or the bag opened to lower the carbon dioxide levels in the bags, thus causing the mushrooms to grow out of the holes. The humidity must be kept high in the cropping room as the mushrooms develop. When the mushrooms are nearly full grown (right) they should be harvested.

CHAPTER 8
EDIBLE MUSHROOMS

A number of excellent, edible fungi grow wild in Hawai'i: *Auricularia*, the Ear Fungus, also called Pepeiao in Hawaiian; *Laetiporus*, the Chicken-of-the-Woods or Sulfur Shelf; *Volvariella*, the Paddy Straw Mushroom; and *Pleurotus*, the Oyster Mushroom, are all prized edibles (see the bibliography for mushroom cookbooks).

Hot Chicken with Wood Ear
(recipe by Lilinoe Cranford of Hilo)

2 cups shredded dried Wood Ear Fungus
4 cloves garlic, finely chopped
6 chicken thighs, sliced into slivers
2 cans water chestnuts, drained and slivered
1 tablespoon oyster sauce
1 tablespoon chili pepper paste (to taste)
1 teaspoon shoyu sauce
1 teaspoon salt
Chicken broth or water

Rehydrate 2 cups shredded dried Wood Ear Fungus in cold water for about 1 hour. Stir-fry garlic and chicken until chicken is browned. Add water chestnuts, Wood Ear Fungus, seasonings, a little chicken broth or water, and stir-fry for another 5 to 10 minutes. Serve hot.

Serves 4

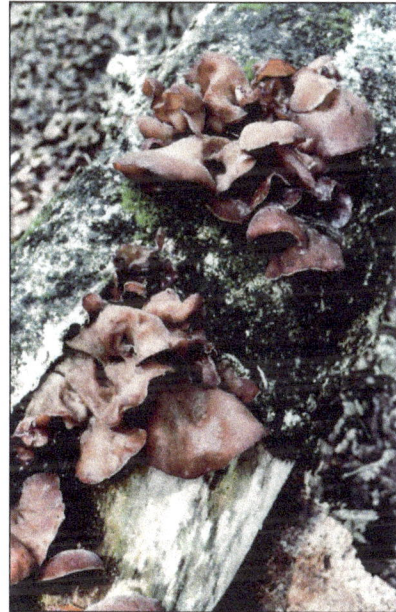

Pepeiao, *Auricularia cornea*, is a rubbery but crunchy-crisp member of the jelly fungi. This Ear Fungus is common in the wet, windward forests of Hawai'i. Pepeiao proliferates on fallen mango and kukui nut branches and logs, but will grow on all kinds of fallen wood, even bougainvillea. The fruiting bodies are cleaned, sliced, and added to soups and gravies where they soak up flavors and add a crispy texture to the dish (see Wet Windward Alien Forests for a full description).

Wood Ear and Chicken Velvet Soup
(recipe by John Chan of Hilo)

$1/3$ cup shredded dried Wood Ear Fungus
1 skinless chicken breast
2 egg whites
White pepper
Pinch of salt
1 can chicken broth
3 cups water
1 tablespoon cornstarch or tapioca starch
Chopped green onion or cilantro for garnish

Rehydrate $1/3$ cup shredded dried Wood Ear Fungus in cold water for about 1 hour. Skin the chicken breast, cut into small cubes, mince finely, then pound with a broad knife blade to obtain a smooth pasty texture. A food processor may be used to achieve similar results. Add 1 tablespoon water, 1 egg white, a dash of white pepper, and a pinch of salt to the minced and pounded chicken. Mix rapidly until the chicken becomes light and airy. Add 1 can chicken broth and 3 cups water into a pot. Bring to a boil and add the Wood Ear Fungus, then reduce to medium heat and simmer for 15 minutes. Beat remaining egg white and drip into simmering broth. Stir gently several times. Using a tablespoon, shape the minced chicken into small balls and drop into simmering broth. After the last tablespoon of chicken is added, simmer for several minutes until chicken is just cooked. Be careful: overcooking will cause the chicken to lose its smooth texture. Thicken soup with cornstarch or tapioca starch prior to serving. Serve hot or cold with green onion or cilantro garnish. Add a drop or two of oil or chile oil if desired.

Serves 4

White Wood Ear Dessert
(recipe by Lo-Li Chih of Hilo)

10 oz. fresh White Wood Ear Fungus
2–4 tablespoons maple syrup
2 cups water
1 small jar cherries

Put cleaned fresh White Wood Ear Fungus, maple syrup, and water into a covered container. Place the container into a steamer and steam at medium heat for about 1 hour. Remove from steamer, add cherries, mix, and serve hot.

Serves 2

Tremella fuciformis, a white foliose jelly fungus, has a texture much like pepeiao and is prized as a component of oriental soups. In Chinese traditional medicine, the White Wood Ear is believed to be helpful for high blood pressure and blood artery problems. It is nutritious for the lungs, heart, and brain (see Wet Windward Alien Forests for a full description).

Coconut Curried Sulfur Shelf
(recipe by Dennis Desjardin)

2 cloves garlic coarsely chopped
1 shallot coarsely chopped
1 tablespoon coarsely chopped fresh ginger
1 tablespoon finely chopped fresh lemongrass
1 tablespoon vegetable oil
400 ml coconut milk (1 can)
3 teaspoons red curry paste
1 teaspoon brown sugar
2 cups fresh Sulfur Shelf Fungi cut in small cubes
    and parboiled
1 cup coarsely chopped bok choy
Salt or 1 teaspoon fish sauce
1/4 cup coarsely chopped cilantro leaves

Sauté the garlic, shallot, ginger, and lemongrass in oil for about 3 minutes. Add the Sulfur Shelf Fungi and sauté for another 2 minutes. Add the coconut milk, red curry paste, and brown sugar and simmer for 5–7 minutes or until the liquid is reduced by about 30 percent. Add the bok choy, salt (or fish sauce), and simmer for about 1 minute. Add the cilantro leaves just before serving. Serve hot with jasmine rice.

Serves 4

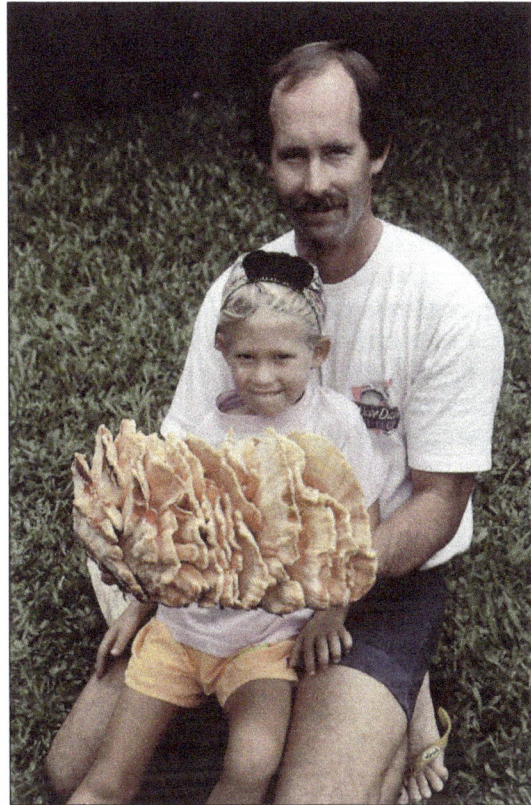

The Sulfur Shelf, *Laetiporus sulphureus*, also called Chicken-of-the-Woods because of its tender consistency, is an excellent edible fungus. This golden-orange to bright red wood-rotting species appears in overlapping brackets on both fallen and standing koa and ohi'a trees. Sulfur Shelves on *Eucalyptus* are best avoided, since there are reports of stomach upsets from these collections (see *Eucalyptus* Forests for a full description).

Pumpkin and Mushrooms
(recipe by Michaelyn Etrata and Family of Kaua'i)

1 cup pork, chopped into $^1/_2$ inch cubes
3 cloves garlic, chopped
2 cherry tomatoes
$^1/_2$ onion, sliced thinly
1 cup diced pumpkin
1 cup chopped okra
1 cup long beans, cut to about 1 inch long
$^1/_2$ cup sliced bitter melon
2 cups fresh Paddy Straw Mushrooms, sliced
$^1/_2$ cup dried shrimp
2 tablespoons fish sauce (to taste)

Combine pork and garlic. Saute until pork is well done; discard excess oil. Add the cherry tomatoes and onion to pork and cook at medium heat for a few minutes. Then add all vegetables, mushrooms, shrimp, and fish sauce, and cover. Simmer until vegetables are tender. Most of the water will be from the vegetables. You may add up to $^1/4$ cup of water if desired, but less water is better to ensure flavor. Serve hot.

Serves 4

Mushrooms and Bitter Melon Soup
(recipe by Michaelyn Etrata and Family of Kaua'i)

2 cups fresh Paddy Straw Mushrooms, sliced
$1^1/_2$ cups water
3 teaspoons salt (to taste)
3 cups bitter melon leaves

Add mushrooms, water, and salt to a pot and bring to a boil. When soup boils, adjust heat to medium and remove accumulated foam on top of soup. Add bitter melon leaves. The soup is ready when bitter melon leaves are tender. Serve hot.

Serves 4

Volvariella volvacea, the Paddy Straw Mushroom, has been collected from bagasse piles (leaves of sugarcane and mud washed off the cane at the mill) by Filipino field workers for years. As the sugar industry closes in Hawai'i, bagasse is no longer available, but this mushroom still appears in wood-chip and compost piles, especially in the hot, rainy summer months. The primordia, dug from within the compost, are especially prized for cooking (see Compost Piles and Wood Chips for a full description). Cleaning the mushrooms immediately after harvest ensures quality. Take the dull side of a knife and rub any debris off the mushroom. Never use a wet knife. Oyster Mushrooms can be used instead of Paddy Straw Mushrooms in the three Etrata family recipes.

Pancit and Mushrooms
(recipe by Michaelyn Etrata and Family of Kaua'i)

1 cup chopped pork or chicken
3 cloves garlic, chopped
2 cups fresh Paddy Straw Mushrooms, sliced
1 cup green beans, sliced
1 cup sliced carrots
2 cups chopped cabbage
2 (8 oz.) pkgs. Pancit noodles
Salt to taste
Lime wedges, for garnish

Combine pork or chicken and garlic. Sauté until meat is well done; discard excess oil. Add all other ingredients, salt to taste, and cook until vegetables and noodles are tender. Serve hot with lime wedges on the side.

Serves 4

Stuffed Wild Mushrooms
(recipe by Richard Matsunaga of Hilo)

12 large whole Almond Mushrooms
1 cup crabmeat
15 water chestnuts, chopped
1 garden burger, chopped
1 tablespoon chopped celery
1 tablespoon chopped onion
3 tablespoons light mayonnaise
3 tablespoons Egg Beater
2 tablespoon grated Parmesan cheese
1 tablespoon white wine
Garlic butter, melted

Agaricus subrufescens, the Almond Mushroom, exudes a strong almond odor and adds an interesting almond extract flavor to food. This species usually appears in compost piles and grass clippings (see Compost Piles and Wood Chips for a full description).

Preheat oven to 375°. Clean the mushrooms, remove stems, hollow out underside of cap, and set aside. Mince the removed mushroom portions and add to the remaining ingredients (except garlic butter). Mix well. Dip mushroom caps in garlic butter, then fill with stuffing mixture. Sprinkle with liberal amounts of Parmesan cheese, place on a greased baking sheet, and bake for 15 minutes. Serve hot or cold.

Serves 4

Stir-fried Mushrooms Javanese Style
(recipe by Guy Dority of Hilo)

1/4 cup sliced onion
1 clove garlic, chopped (or 1 tsp. bottled crushed garlic)
1 fresh green semi-hot chile, sliced thin diagonally
1 tablespoon peanut oil
1/2 lb. fresh Oyster Mushrooms, sliced
1/2 teaspoon shrimp paste
1 tsp. tamarind, dissolved in 1 tablespoon water
1 salam leaf
1 piece of laos or galanga root, sliced

(The last four ingredients are available at Asian groceries.)

Stir-fry the onion, garlic, and chile in peanut oil for 1 minute. Add all other ingredients, mix well, and stir-fry for 3 minutes. Serve hot.

Serves 2

The premier Oyster Mushroom in Hawai'i is *Pleurotus cystidiosus*, a thick, meaty species that grows into flattened brackets nearly 1 foot in diameter in the wild. It is common on living guava trees in the wet, windward valleys of Maui and the Big Island. This species is easily grown at home on wood chips (see Guava Thickets for a full description).

GLOSSARY

The following definitions are our own or are taken from the *Dictionary of the Fungi* (Hawksworth, Kirk, Sutton, and Pegler, CAB International, United Kingdom 1995).

Adnate—gills broadly attached (perpendicular) to the stipe.

Adnexed—gills narrowly attached to the stipe apex.

Agaricales (agaric, agaricoid)—gill fungi; mushrooms and toadstools.

Amyloid—becoming blue to grayish blue in Melzer's reagent.

Anamorph—asexual (imperfect) form of life cycle.

Annulus—a ringlike or skirtlike partial veil surrounding the stem.

Apophysis—a swelling on the stem (e.g., in some species of *Geastrum*).

Asci—the cell in which karyogamy and meiosis occurs and in which spores are formed in the Ascomycetes.

Ascomycete—one of the Ascomycota, a phylum of fungi that produce asci and ascospores.

Areolate (areolae)—cracking into small angular areas.

Basidia—the cell in which karyogamy and meiosis occurs and on which spores are formed in the Basidiomycota.

Basidiomycete—one of the Basidiomycota, a phylum of fungi that produce basidia and basidiospores.

Campanulate—bell-shaped.

Capillitia—thick-walled hyphae found in the gleba of puffballs.

Caulocystidia—sterile (nonfertile) cells formed on the stem surface.

Cheilocystidia—sterile (nonfertile) cells formed on the gill edge.

Chordate—heart-shaped.

Clamp connections—knoblike projections arising adjacent to the crosswalls between cells in a hypha.

Clavate—clublike; narrowing in direction of base.

Conical—shaped like a cone with an acute apex.

Conidium—asexual spore of Ascomycetes.

Convex—curving outward; rounded.

Coprophilous—fungi living on dung.

Coralloid—much branched; like coral in form.

Cortina (cortinate)—a partial veil, frequently weblike, covering the mature gills.

Cystidia—sterile cells, frequently of distinctive shape, occurring on the surfaces of the fruit body; (pileo-) on the pileus surface, (cheilo-) at edges of lamellae, (pleuro-) at side of lamellae, (caulo-) on the stipe.

Daedaleoid—anastomosing to mazelike gills, as in *Daedalea*.

Decurrent—gills running down the stipe.

Deliquescent—becoming liquid after maturing; autodigesting.

Dextrinoid—becoming red to reddish brown in Melzer's reagent.

Disc—the center of the cap.

Effused—stretched out flat.

Endoperidium—inner layer of the peridium.

Epigeal—on the earth; above ground.

Exoperidium—outer layer of the peridium.

Fairy ring—fungal rings in grass and woods with fruiting bodies at the outer edge of the ring.

Fibrillose—covered with silklike fibers.

Fimbriate—delicately toothed or fringed.

Floccose—delicately cottony.

Foliose—leaflike.

Fornicate—arched; having the fruitbody arched over the cuplike mycelial layer.

Furfuraceous—covered with branlike particles; scurfy.

Gasteromycetes—class of Basidiomycetes that do not actively discharge their spores.

Germ pore—a porelike thinning of the wall at the distal end of the spore.

Gills—radiating, platelike structures on which spores are produced.

Glabrous—lacking ornamentation; not hairy.

Gleba—spore-bearing mass of the class Gasteromycetes.

Glutinous—sticky; covered with gluten.

Granulose—surface covered with small granules.

Hallucinogenic—containing pharmacologic compounds that when ingested produce sensory illusions.

Heterotrophic—using organic compounds as primary source of energy.

Hygrophanous—changing color with moisture loss.

Hygroscopic—drawing in or folding of the endoperidium under drying conditions.

Hymenium—the spore-bearing layer of a fruitbody.

Hypha—one of the filaments of a fungus.

Hypogeous—growing below ground; fungi having subterranean sporocarps.

Imbricate—partly covering one another like tiles on a roof.

Inamyloid—unreactive in Melzer's reagent.

Indusium—a netlike structure hanging from the top of the stem under the head of a stinkhorn.

Insititious—inserted; attached directly without obvious basal mycelium.

Intervenose—veined in the interspaces between the gills.

Lamellae—the scientific term for gills.

Lecythiform—shaped like a bowling pin with a ball on top.

Lignicolous—living on or in wood.

Magic mushrooms—hallucinogenic fungi.

Melzer's reagent—an iodine, potassium iodide, chloralhydrate solution used in microscopic analysis.

Mitriform—shield-shaped.

Mushroom—an agaric fruiting body, especially an edible one.

Mycelium—a mass of hyphae.

Mycology—the scientific study of fungi.

Mycorrhiza—a symbiotic, nonpathogenic, or weakly pathogenic association of a fungus and the roots of a plant *(fungus root)*.

Operculum—a covering; a lid.

Papilla—a small rounded to conical outgrowth on the cap.

Pellucid—translucent.

Peridiole—a division of the gleba having a separate wall; the "eggs" of Bird's-nest Fungi.

Peridium—the wall or limiting membrane of a fruitbody.

Peristome—an edging around an opening; as in *Geastrum*.

Pileocystidia—sterile (nonfertile) cells formed on the cap surface.

Pileus—the hymenium-supporting part of the fruiting body (the cap of the mushroom).

Pleated—radially grooved.

Pleurocystidia—sterile (nonfertile) cells formed on the gill sides.

Plicate—folded into pleats.

Polypore—a tough fruitbody with poroid spore-bearing surface.

Pruinose—having a frostlike or flourlike surface covering.

Pseudoperidioles—false peridiole.

Pubescent—having soft hairs.

Pyriform—pear-shaped.

Recurved—curved backward.

Reflexed—growing out from the margin.

Resupinate—flat on the substrate with the hymenium on the outer side.

Reticulate—like a net; netted.

Rhizoids—a rootlike structure.

Rhizomorphs—a rootlike aggregation of hyphae.

Rugulose—delicately wrinkled.

Saccate—like a sac or bag.

Sessile—lacking a stem; with cap attached directly (laterally or centrally) to the substrate.

Spore print—the deposit of spores obtained by placing a mushroom cap on a sheet of paper or glass slide.

Sporodochia—a cushion-shaped cluster of conidiophores and conidia in Ascomycetes.

Squamules (squamulose)—a small scale; having small scales.

Stipe—a stalk; a stem.

Striate—marked with delicate lines, grooves, or ridges.

Strict—narrow and upright.

Sulcate—grooved (more deeply than striate, less deeply than plicate).

Teleomorph—sexual (perfect) form in the life cycle.

Tomentose—having a covering of soft, matted hairs; downy.

Turbinate—top-shaped.

Umbilicus (umbilicate)—a dimple; having a central dimple on the cap.

Umbo (umbonate)—a broad outgrowth; having a broad central outgrowth on the cap.

Undulate—wavy.

Universal veil—a layer of tissue that encloses the entire mushroom primordium; some or all of the tissue disappears as the mushroom grows and expands.

Velutinous—thickly covered with delicate hairs; like velvet.

Viscid—slimy, sticky.

Volva—the remnants of the universal veil on the base of the stem; often sacklike or of annular rings.

Zonate—having concentric lines often forming alternating pale and darker zones.

COMMON AND SCIENTIFIC NAMES OF MUSHROOMS AND TREES OF HAWAI'I

Almond Mushroom *(Agaricus subrufescens)*
Artist's Conk *(Ganoderma applanatum)*
Bagasse Mushroom *(Volvariella volvacea)*
Beaked Earthstar *(Geastrum pectinatum)*
Bird's-nest Fungus *(Cyathus* spp.)
Black Wattle *(Acacia mearnsii)*
Blewit *(Lepista nuda)*
Bottlebrush Tree *(Melaleuca* spp.)
Chicken-of-the-Woods *(Laetiporus sulphureus)*
Charcoal Tree *(Trema orientalis)*
Cone Head *(Conocybe lactea)*
Coral Fungus *(Ramaria* spp.)
Creeping Crumble Cap *(Coprinus disseminatus)*
Dead Man's Foot *(Pisolithus arhizus)*
Dunce Cap *(Conocybe lactea)*
Dye-maker's False Puffball *(Pisolithus arhizus)*
Ear Fungus *(Auricularia* spp.)
Earthball *(Scleroderma* spp.)
Earthfan *(Thelephora terrestris)*
Earthstar *(Geastrum* spp.)
False Shaggy Mane *(Podaxis pistillaris)*
Flowerpot Parasol *(Leucocoprinus birnbaumii)*
Formosa Koa *(Acacia confusa)*
Fly Agaric *(Amanita muscaria)*
Golden Scruffy *(Cyptotrama asprata)*
Green-spored Parasol *(Chlorophyllum molybdites)*
Honey Mushroom *(Armillaria* spp.)
Inky Cap *(Coprinus* spp.)
Ironwoods *(Casuarina* spp.)
Japanese Parasol *(Coprinus plicatilis)*
Jelly Fungus *(Tremella, Auricularia, Dacryopinax* spp.)
Karaka Nut *(Corynocarpus laevigatus)*
Kombucha (a yeast/bacterial curd used for medicinal purposes [Manchurian mushroom])
Manchurian Mushroom (kombucha)

Manele *(Sapindus saponaria)*
Meadow Mushroom *(Agaricus campestris)*
Mica Cap *(Coprinus micaceus)*
Monterey Cypress *(Cupressus macrocarpa)*
Monterey Pine *(Pinus radiata)*
Morels *(Morchella esculenta)*
Moss Agaric *(Rickenella fibula)*
Oyster Mushrooms *(Pleurotus* spp.)
Paddy Straw Mushroom *(Volvariella volvacea)*
Paperbark *(Melaleuca* spp.)
Puffballs *(Bovista, Calvatia, Lycoperdon, Vascellum* spp.)
Redwood *(Sequoia sempervirens)*
Reishi *(Ganoderma lucidum)*
Salt-and-Pepper Shaker Earthstar *(Myriostoma coliforme)*
Scarlet Cup Fungus *(Sarcoscypha mesocyatha)*
Shaggy Mane *(Coprinus comatus)*
Shiitake *(Lentinula edodes)*
Slash Pine *(Pinus elliotii)*
Slippery Jacks *(Suillus* spp.)
Soapberry *(Sapindus saponaria* [Manele])
Split-gill Mushroom *(Schizophyllum commune)*
Spring Polypore *(Polyporus arcularius)*
Starfish Stinkhorn *(Aseroe rubra)*
Stinkhorns *(Aseroe, Mutinus, Phallus, Pseudocolus* spp.)
Sugi Pine *(Cryptomeria japonica)*
Sulfur Shelf *(Laetiporus sulphureus)*
Tumbling Puffball *(Bovista pila)*
Turkey Tail *(Trametes versicolor)*
Waxy Cap *(Hygrocybe* spp.)
Wood Ear *(Auricularia* spp.)
Wooly Cap *(Coprinus cinereus)*
Yellow Parasol *(Leucocoprinus birnbaumii)*

HAWAIIAN TERMS

Haleakala—large volcanic mountain on East Maui; literally "House of the Sun."

Hapuʻu—Hawaiian endemic tree ferns (*Cibotium* spp.).

Hapuuae—mushroom growing on hapuʻu tree ferns (e.g., *Hygrocybe hapuuae*).

Hoale koa—bushy shrub common on dry, lowland slopes on all islands; literally "foreign koa."

Kiawe—an introduced tree to dry coastal areas, *Prosopsis pallida*.

Kipuka—an island of native vegetation surrounded by newer lava flows.

Koa—an endemic leguminous tree, *Acacia koa*.

Kokeʻe—mountainous region of West Kauaʻi; includes Kokeʻe State Park.

Kopiko—a group of small, endemic understory trees; *Psychotria* spp.

Lamalama—mushroom "glowing like the sun," *Hygrocybe lamalama*.

Laulaha—common and widespread mushroom, *Rhodocollybia laulaha*.

Mamane—an endemic leguminous tree, *Sophora chrysophylla*.

Manele—an endemic Hawaiian tree, *Sapindus saponaria*.

Mauna Kea—large volcanic mountain on the Big Island; literally "white mountain."

Mauna Loa—large volcanic mountain on the Big Island; literally "long mountain."

Menehune—mischievous fairylike gremlin in Hawaiian lore.

Naio—an indigenous Hawaiian tree, *Myoporum sandwicense*.

Noelokelani—pink rainforest mushroom whose color resembles that of the pink rose of Maui; literally "pink rose in the mist," *Hygrocybe noelokelani*.

Ohiʻa lehua—major forest tree in Hawaiʻi with red, orange, or yellow flowers, *Metrosideros polymorpha*.

Pakelo—mushroom that is "slippery like a fish," *Hygrocybe pakelo*.

Peleae—any mushroom named after Pele, the Hawaiian goddess of the volcano, *Pholiota peleae, Humidicutis peleae*.

Pepeiao—the Ear Fungus, *Auricularia cornea*.

Poilena—the Yellow-headed Mushroom, *Humidicutis poilena*.

Puaena—the Radiant Mushoom, *Hygrocybe puaena*.

Waolipo—the mushroom "growing in the dark depths of the forest," *Hygrocybe waolipo*.

BIBLIOGRAPHY

HAWAIIAN NATURAL HISTORY AND CONSERVATION

Bioscience, April 1988. Vol. 38. *Hawaii's Unique Biology.*

Carlquist, S. 1980. *Hawaii. A Natural History.* Pacific Tropical Botanical Garden, SB Printers, Inc., Honolulu, Hawai'i.

Cuddihy, L. W., and C. P. Stone. 1990. *Alteration of Native Hawaiian Vegetation.* University of Hawaii Cooperative National Park Resources Studies Unit, Honolulu, Hawai'i.

Gagne, W. C., and L. W. Cuddihy. 1990. Vegetation. Pp. 45–114. In: *Manual of the Flowering Plants of Hawaii.* Eds. W. L. Wagner, D. Herbst, and S. Somer. Bishop Museum and University of Hawaii Presses.

MacDonald, G. A., and A. T. Abbott. 1979. *Volcanoes in the Sea: The Geology of Hawaii.* University of Hawaii Press.

Rock, J. F. 1974. *The Indigenous Trees of the Hawaiian Islands.* Pacific Tropical Botanical Garden.

Stone, C. P., and J. M. Scott. 1985. *Hawaii's Terrestrial Ecosystems, Preservation and Management.* University of Hawaii Cooperative National Park Resources Studies Unit, Honolulu, Hawai'i.

———, and D. B. Stone. 1989. *Conservation Biology in Hawai'i.* University of Hawaii Cooperative National Park Resources Studies Unit, Honolulu, Hawai'i.

Wagner, W. L., and V. A. Funk. 1995. *Hawaiian Biogeography.* Smithsonian Institution Press.

———, D. Herbst, and S. Somer. 1990. *Manual of the Flowering Plants of Hawaii.* Bishop Museum and University of Hawaii Presses.

EARLY STUDIES OF HAWAIIAN FUNGI

Arnold, H. L. 1944. *Poisonous Plants of Hawaii.* (Reprint Ed., 1982) C. E. Tuttle Co., Rutland, VT.

Berkeley, M. J., and M. A. Curtis. 1851. Descriptions of new species of fungi collected by the U. S. Exploring Expedition. *Amer. J. Sci. & Arts,* 2nd Ser. 11: 39–95.

Burt, E. A. 1923. Higher Fungi of the Hawaiian Islands. *Ann. Missouri Bot. Gard.* 10: 179–189.

Cobb, N. A. 1906. Fungus maladies of the sugar cane. *Hawaiian Sugar Pl. Assoc. Exp. Sta., Div. Pathol. & Physiol.,* Bull. 6: 1–254.

———. 1908. Fungus maladies of the sugar cane. *Hawaiian Sugar Pl. Assoc. Exp. Sta., Div. Pathol. & Physiol.,* Bull. 6: 5–103.

Curtis, M. A., and M. J. Berkeley. 1862. Fungi. *U. S. Exploring Expedition 1838–1842,* 17: 193–203.

Hennings, P. 1900. Fungi. Pp. 1–38. In: Beiträge zur kenntuiss der vegetation des süd-und Ostasiatischen Monsungebietes. Ed. O. Warburg. *Monsunia* 1: 1–297.

Lloyd, C. G. 1898–1919. *Mycological Notes*, vol. 1–5, nos. 1–60, and Letters, nos. 1–69. Publ. by the author, Cincinnati, OH.

Peck, C. H. 1907. New species of fungi. *Bull. Torrey Bot. Club* 34: 97–104.

Stevens, F. L. 1925. Hawaiian fungi. *Bernice P. Bishop Mus. Bull.* 119: 1–189.

Reviews of Groups of Fungi from Hawai'i

Anastasiou, C. J. 1964. Some aquatic fungi imperfecti from Hawaii. *Pac. Sci.* 18: 202–206.

Brodie, H. J. 1972. The Nidulariaceae or bird's nest fungi of the Hawaiian Islands. *Can. J. Bot.* 50: 643–646.

Goos, R. D. 1970a. Phalloid fungi in Hawaii. *Pac. Sci.* 24: 282–287.

———, and J. H. Anderson. 1972. The Meliolaceae of Hawaii. *Sydowia* 26: 73–80.

Smith, C. W., and P. Ponce De Leon. 1982. Hawaiian geastroid fungi. *Mycologia* 74: 712–717.

Plant Pathogenic Fungi from Hawai'i

Farr, D. F., G. F. Bills, G. P. Chamuris, and A. Y. Rossman. 1989. *Fungi on Plants and Plant Products in the United States*. American Phytopathological Society Press, St. Paul, MN.

Chun. W. K. C. 1965. Fungus diseases and the competitors of the cultivated mushroom in Hawaii. Master's thesis, HAWN Qiii, H3, no. 207.

Meredith, D. S. 1969. Fungal diseases of bananas in Hawaii. *Pl. Dis. Reporter* 53: 63–66.

Parris, G. K. 1940. A check list of fungi, bacteria, nematodes, and viruses occurring in Hawaii and their hosts. *Pl. Dis. Reporter Suppl.* 121: 1–91.

Raabe, R. D., I. L. Conners, and A. P. Martinez. 1981. Checklist of plant diseases in Hawaii. *Hawaii Institute of Tropical Agriculture and Human Resources, Univ. of Hawaii, Information Text Series* 22: 1–313.

———, and E. E. Trujillo. 1963. *Armillaria mellea* in Hawaii. *Pl. Dis. Reporter* 47: 776.

USDA. 1960. Index of Plant Diseases in the United States. *United States Department of Agriculture, Agriculture Handbook* no. 165: 1–531.

The Fungal Kingdom—General Texts

Alexopoulos, C. J., C. W. Mims, and M. Blackwell. 1996. *Introductory Mycology,* 4th ed., John Wiley & Sons, NY.

Deacon, J. W. 1997. *Introduction to Modern Mycology,* 3rd ed., Blackwell Scientific Publications, Boston.

Kendrick, B. 1992. *The Fifth Kingdom.* 2nd ed., Focus Information Group, Newburyport, MA.

Moore, R., W. D. Clark, D. S. Vodopich. 1998. *Botany,* 2nd ed., WCB/McGraw-Hill, NY.

Moore-Landecker, E. 1996. *Fundamentals of the Fungi.* 4th ed., Prentice-Hall, Englewood Cliffs, NJ.

Raven, P. H., R. F. Evert, S. E. Eichhorn. 1999. *Biology of Plants.* 6th ed., W. H. Freeman, NY.

Webster, J. 1980. *Introduction to Fungi.* 2nd ed., Cambridge University Press, Cambridge.

STUDIES OF MYCORRHIZAL FUNGI OF HAWAI'I

Gemma, J. N., and R. E. Koske. 1990. Mycorrhizae in recent volcanic substrates in Hawaii. *Amer. J. Bot.* 77: 1193–1200.

Koske, R. E. 1988. Vesicular-arbuscular mycorrhizae of some Hawaiian dune plants. *Pac. Sci.* 42: 217–229.

————, and J. N. Gemma. 1990. VA mycorrhizae in strand vegetation of Hawaii: evidence for long distance codispersal of plants and fungi. *Amer. J. Bot.* 77: 466–474.

SELECTED MUSHROOM FIELD GUIDES

Arora, D. 1986. *Mushrooms Demystified.* 2nd ed., Ten Speed Press, Berkeley, CA.

————. 1991. *All that the Rain Promises and More....* Ten Speed Press, Berkeley, CA.

Barron, G. 1999. *Mushrooms of Northeast North America.* Lone Pine Publishing, Vancouver, BC, Canada.

Bessette, A. E. 1988. *Mushrooms of the Adirondacks.* North Country Books, Utica, NY.

————, and W. J. Sundberg. 1987. *Mushrooms.* Macmillan Publishing, NY.

Bougher, N. L., and K. Syme. 1998. *Fungi of Southern Australia.* University of Western Australia Press, Nedlands, Western Australia.

Fuhrer, B. 1993. *A Field Companion to Australian Fungi.* The Field Naturalist Club of Victoria, South Yarra, Australia.

Grgurinovic, C.A. 1997. *Larger Fungi of South Australia.* The Botanic Gardens of Adelaide and State Herbarium.

Hongo, T., and M. Izawa. 1994. *Mushrooms of Japan.* Yama-Kei Publishers, Tokyo, Japan.

Horn, B., R. Kay, and D. Abel. 1993. *A Guide to Kansas Mushrooms.* University Press of Kansas, Lawrence, KS.

Huffman, D. M., L. H. Tiffany, and G. Knaphus. 1989. *Mushrooms and Other Fungi of the Midcontinental United States.* Iowa State Press, Ames, IA.

Imazeki, R., Y. Otani, T. Hongo. 1988. *Fungi of Japan.* Yama-Kei Publishers, Tokyo, Japan.

Lincoff, G. H. 1981. *The Audubon Society Field Guide to North American Mushrooms.* Chanticleer Press, NY.

McKenny, M., and D. E. Stuntz. 1987. *The New Savory Wild Mushroom.* University of Washington Press, Seattle, WA.

Metzler, S., and V. Metzler. 1992. *Texas Mushrooms.* University of Texas Press, Austin, TX.

Miller, O. K. 1980. *Mushrooms of North America.* Chanticleer Press, NY.

Pacioni, G. 1981. *Simon & Schuster's Guide to Mushrooms.* G. Lincoff, ed., Simon and Schuster, NY.

Phillips, R. 1981. *Mushrooms and Other Fungi of Great Britain & Europe*. Toppau Printing, Hong Kong.

———. 1991. *Mushrooms of North America*. Little and Brown, Boston.

States, J. S. 1990. *Mushrooms and Truffles of the Southwest*. University of Arizona Press, Tucson, AZ.

Stevenson, G. 1994. *New Zealand Fungi*. Canterbury University Press, Christchurch, New Zealand.

Van der Westhuizen, G. C. A., and A. Eicker. 1994. *Field Guide-Mushrooms of Southern Africa*. Struik Publishers, Cape Town, South Africa.

Weber, N. S., and A. H. Smith. 1985. *A Field Guide to Southern Mushrooms*. University of Michigan Press, Ann Arbor, MI.

Young, T. 1994. *Common Australian Fungi*. University of New South Wales Press, Sydney, Australia.

MUSHROOM IDENTIFICATION AND NOMENCLATURE

Kirk, P. M., and A. E. Ansell. 1992. *Authors of Fungal Names*. International Mycological Institute.

Kornerup, A., and J. H. Wanscher. 1978. *Methuen Handbook of Colour*. 3rd ed. Eyre Methuen, London.

Largent, D. L.. 1986. *How to Identify Mushrooms to Genus I: Macroscopic Features*. Mad River Press, Eureka, CA.

———, and T. J. Baroni. 1988. *How to Identify Mushrooms to Genus VI: Modern Genera*. Mad River Press, Eureka, CA.

———, D. Johnson, and R. Watling. 1977. *How to Identify Mushrooms to Genus III: Microscopic Features*. Mad River Press, Eureka, CA.

———, and H. D. Thiers. 1977. *How to Identify Mushrooms to Genus II: Field Identification of Genera*. Mad River Press, Eureka, CA.

COOKING WITH MUSHROOMS

Fischer, D. W., and A. E. Bessette. 1992. *Edible Wild Mushrooms of North America*. University of Texas Press, Austin, TX.

Jordon, P., and S. Wheeler. 1995. *The Ultimate Mushroom Book*. Smithmark Publishers, NY.

Miller, H., 1993. *Hope's Mushroom Cookbook*. Mad River Press, Eureka, CA.

GROWING MUSHROOMS AT HOME

Stamets, P. 2000. *Growing Gourmet & Medicinal Mushrooms*. 3rd ed. Ten Speed Press, Berkeley, CA.

———, and J. S. Chilton. 1983. *The Mushroom Cultivator*. Agarikon Press, Olympia, Washington.

Medicinal Mushrooms

Hobbs, C. 1996. *Medicinal Mushrooms, An Exploration of Tradition, Healing, & Culture.* 3rd ed., Interweave Press, Loveland, CO.

Poisonous Mushrooms

Ammirati, J. F., J. A. Traquair, and P. A. Horgen. 1985. *Poisonous Mushrooms of the Northern United States and Canada.* University of Minnesota Press, Minneapolis, MN.

Benjamin, D. R. 1995. *Mushrooms: Poisons and Panaceas.* W. H. Freeman and Company, NY.

Bresinsky, A., and H. Besl. 1990. *A Colour Atlas of Poisonous Fungi.* Wolfe, London.

Lincoff, G., and D. H. Mitchel. 1977. *Toxic and Hallucinogenic Mushroom Poisoning.* Van Nostrand Reinhold, NY.

Hallucinogenic Mushrooms

Merlin, M. D., and J. W. Allen. 1993. Species identification and chemical analysis of psychoactive fungi in the Hawaiian Islands. *J. Ethnopharmacology* 40: 21–40.

Stamets, P. 1996. *Psilocybin Mushrooms of the World.* Ten Speed Press, Berkeley, CA.

Technical Literature on Hawaiian Mushrooms and Other Fungi

Baker, G. E. 1964. Fungi in Hawaii. *Hawaiian Bot. Soc. Newsletter* 3 (4): 23–28.

———. 1977. The prospect for mycology in the Central Pacific. *Harold L. Lyon Arboretum Lecture No. 8:* 1–51.

———, P. H. Dunn, and W. S. Sakai. 1979. Fungus communities associated with leaf surfaces of endemic vascular plants of Hawaii. *Mycologia* 71: 272–292.

———, and R. D. Goos. 1972. Endemism and evolution in the Hawaiian biota: fungi. Pp. 409–431. In: *A Natural History of the Hawaiian Islands. Selected Readings.* Ed., E. A. Kay. University of Hawaii Press, Honolulu, HI.

Desjardin, D. E. 1993. *Incrustocalyptella hapuuae* sp. nov. and *Favolaschia minima* from native forests of Hawai'i. *Mycologia* 85: 1017–1019.

———, and T. J. Baroni. 1991. A new species of *Pouzaromyces* from the Hawaiian Islands. *Mycologia* 83: 832–835.

———, R. E. Halling, and D. E. Hemmes. 1999. Agaricales of the Hawaiian Islands. 5: the genera *Rhodocollybia* and *Gymnopus*. *Mycologia* 91: 166–177.

———, and D. E. Hemmes. 1997. Agaricales of the Hawaiian Islands. 4: Hygrophoraceae. *Mycologia* 89: 615–638.

———, and D. E. Hemmes. 2001. Agaricales of the Hawaiian Islands. 7: Notes on *Volvariella, Mycena* sect. Radiatae, *Physalacria, Porpoloma,* and *Stropharia. Harvard Pap. Bot.* 6: 85–103.

———, and E. Horak. 1999. Agaricales of Indonesia. 1: a new cyphelloid genus (*Lecanocybe lateralis* gen. et sp. nov.) from Java and the Hawaiian Islands. *Sydowia* 51: 20–26.

———, G. J. Wong, and D. E. Hemmes. 1992. Agaricales of the Hawaiian Islands. I. Marasmioid fungi: new species, new distributional records, and poorly known taxa. *Can. J. Bot.* 70: 530–542.

Doyle, M. F. 1985. A floristic survey of the fleshy fungi from the Hawaiian Islands with notes on common marasmioid fungi from southern Illinois. Master's thesis, Department of Botany, Southern Illinois University, Carbondale, IL.

Dring, D. M., J. Meeker, and R. D. Goos. 1971. *Clathrus oahuensis,* a new species from Hawaii. *Mycologia* 163: 893–897.

Gilbertson, R. L., and D. E. Hemmes. 1997a. Notes on fungi on Hawaiian tree ferns. *Mycotaxon* 62: 465–487.

———. 1997b. Notes on Hawaiian Coniophoraceae. *Mycotaxon* 65: 427–442.

Goos, R. D. 1970b. A new genus of the Hyphomycetes from Hawaii. *Mycologia* 62: 171–175.

———. 1977. An addition to the bird's nest fungi of the Hawaiian Islands. *Can J. Bot.* 55: 2761–2763.

———. 1978. Comparative observations of Hyphomycetes of Hawaii and Central America. *Kavaka* 6: 31–35.

———. 1980. Some helicosporous fungi from Hawaii. *Mycologia* 72: 595–610.

Hesler, L. R. 1969. North American species of *Gymnopilus. Mycol. Mem.* 3: 1–117.

Horak, E., and D. E. Desjardin. 1993. Agaricales of the Hawaiian Islands. 2. Notes on some *Entoloma* species. *Mycologia* 85: 480–489.

———, D. E. Desjardin, and D. E. Hemmes. 1996. Agaricales of the Hawaiian Islands. 3: The genus *Galerina* and selected other brown-spored agarics. *Mycologia* 88: 278–294.

Miller, O. K. Jr., D. E. Hemmes, and G. J. Wong. 1996. *Amanita marmorata* subsp. *myrtacearum*—a new subspecies in *Amanita* sect. Phalloideae from Hawaii. *Mycologia* 88: 140–145.

Peterson, K. R., D. E. Desjardin, and D. E. Hemmes. 2000. Agaricales of the Hawaiian Islands. 6: Agaricaceae I. Agariceae: *Agaricus* and *Melanophyllum. Sydowia* 52: 204–257.

Redhead, S. A. 1979. *Physalacria subpeltata* sp. nov. from Hawaii. *Mycotaxon* 10: 46–48.

———, and J. Ginns. 1980. *Cyptotrama asprata* (Agaricales) from North America and notes on the five species of *Cyptotrama* sect. Xerulina. *Can. J. Bot.* 58: 731–740.

Rogers, J. D., Y. M. Ju, and D. E. Hemmes. 1992. *Hypoxylon rectangulosporum* sp. nov., *Xylaria psidii* sp. nov., and comments on taxa of *Podosordaria* and *Stromatoneurospora. Mycologia* 84: 166–172.

———. 1997. *Xylaria moelleroclavus* sp. nov. and its *Moelleroclavus* anamorphic state. *Mycol. Res.* 101: 345–348.

Singer, R. 1975. The neotropical species of *Campanella* and *Aphyllotus* with notes on some species of *Marasmiellus. Nova Hedwigia* 26: 847–896.

———. 1976. Marasmieae (Basidiomycetes-Tricholomataceae). *Fl. Neotrop. Monogr.* 17: 1–347.

Ueki, R. T. 1973. The order Agaricales Clements in Hawaii. Undergraduate Honors Thesis, Department of Botany, University of Hawaii, Honolulu, HI.

———, and C. W. Smith. 1973. The genus *Crepidotus* in Hawaii. *Can. J. Bot.* 51: 1251–1254.

Hawaiian Rust Fungi

Gardner, D. E. 1994. The native rust fungi of Hawaii. *Can. J. Bot.* 72: 976–989.

———. 1997. Additions to the rust fungi of Hawai'i. *Pac. Sci.* 51: 174–182.

———. 1988. Revisions to endemic Hawaiian rusts. *Mycologia* 80: 747–749.

———. and C. S. Hodges, Jr. 1989. The rust fungi (Uredinales) of Hawaii. *Amer. J. Bot.* 77: 1193–1200.

Lichens

Smith, C. W. 1993. Notes on Hawaiian parmelioid lichens. *The Bryologist* 96: 326–332.

Mycetozoans—Slime Molds

Eliasson, U. H. 1991. The myxomycete biota of the Hawaiian Islands. *Mycol. Res.* 95(3): 257–267.

Landolt, J. C., and G. J. Wong. 1998. Dictyostelid cellular slime molds from Hawai'i. *Pac. Sci.* 52: 98–103.

Olive, L. S. 1975. *The Mycetozoans.* Academic Press, NY.

Spiegel, F. W., and D. E. Hemmes. 1999a. Protostelids and other simple mycetozoans of the island of Hawai'i. Third International Congress on the systematics and ecology of myxomycetes. Beltsville, MD, Abstract Volume, p. 19.

———. 1999b. Protostelids associated with tree ferns in Hawai'i. Fourteenth International Botanical Congress, St. Louis, MO, Abstract Volume p. 488.

Stephenson, S. L. 1985. Myxomycetes in the laboratory II: moist chamber cultures. *Amer. Biol. Teacher* 47: 487–489.

———, and H. Stempen. 1994. *Myxomycetes, A Handbook of Slime Molds.* Timber Press, Portland, OR.

ABOUT THE AUTHORS

DON E. HEMMES was first introduced to the wonders of fungi as an undergraduate at Central College of Iowa where he worked on the cellular slime molds with Don Huffman. Later he studied under Hans Hohl at the University of Hawai'i at Manoa (M.S., Ph.D. 1970) and as a postdoctoral researcher at the University of Zürich, and with Salamon Bartnicki-Garcia at the University of California, Riverside. Don taught General Biology and Cell Biology at the University of Hawai'i at Hilo for over 40 years. After serving as Chairman of the Biology Department and Natural Sciences Division, Hemmes is currently Professor Emeritus, living in Hilo, Hawai'i. He has been awarded many teaching awards including the Regent's Excellence in Teaching Award and the W. H. Weston Award from the Mycological Society of America for teaching excellence in mycology. In 1999 he was selected as Professor of the Year for Hawai'i by the Council for the Advancement and Support of Education and the Carnegie Foundation. He was honored as Fellow of the Mycological Society of America in 2004 for his research on Hawaiian Fungi and served as President of the Mycological Society of America in 2007-2008.

Dennis Desjardin's interest in mushrooms started at an early age as he accompanied his parents on forays into the mushroom-rich forests of northern California. After stints as a professional musician and carpenter Dennis returned to college and studied with Harry D. Thiers at San Francisco State University (M.S. 1985) and Ronald H. Petersen at the University of Tennessee (Ph.D. 1989). He also had the privilege of being trained by the renowned mycologists Drs. Alexander H. Smith, Rolf Singer, Meinhard Moser and Egon Horak. He is currently Professor of Biology at San Francisco State University. Dr. Desjardin has published over 140 refereed scientific papers on the taxonomy and evolution of mushroom-forming fungi in which he described 260 new species and 7 new genera. He has active research projects in the Hawaiian Islands, Micronesia, Thailand, Malaysia, Indonesia, Brazil, the African islands of São Tome and Principe, and has developed a recent interest in the origin and evolution of bioluminescent fungi. Dennis is co-author of the new field guide *California Mushrooms* (Timber Press, 2015).

INDEX

A

Agaricus, 49
 campestris, 49
 comptuloides, 27
 comtulus, 27
 lanatorubescens, 111
 rotalis, 43, 83
 subrufescens, 18, 34, 89, 189
Agrocybe, 39
 aegerta, 128
 cylindrica, 128
 parasitica, 128
 pediades, 28, 56
 aff. procera, 36
 retigera, 28
 semiorbicularis, 28, 56
Almond Mushroom. See Agaricus subrufescens
Amanita
 marmorata, 31, 38, 89, 115, 125,
  175–176, 179
 muscaria, 16, 110, 176, 182
Anellaria
 phalaenarum, 51
 sepulcralis, 51
Anthurus javanicus, 40
Arcyria denudata, 168
arid leeward habitat mushrooms
 coastal, 94–97
 montane, 98–103
Armillaria, 129
 nabsnonia, 153
 aff. ostoyae, 153
 sinapina, 129
Artist's Conk. See Ganoderma applanatum
Ascocoryne sarcoides, 155
Ascomycetes, 154
Ascomycota, 6
Aseroe rubra, 136
Atelocauda
 angustiphylloda, 161
 digitata, 160
 koae, 160

Auricularia, 185
 cornea, 78, 185, 186
Australian pine trees, 82, 122

B

Bagasse Mushroom. See Volvariella volvacea
Basidiomycota, 6
basswood trees, 60
Battarraea phalloides, 102
Battarraeoides digueti, 96
Beaked Earthstar. See Geastrum pectinatum
Big Island, places to find mushrooms on,
  13–14
Bird Park, 13–14
Bird's-nest Fungus, 194. See also Cyathus
  pallidus; Cyathus stercoreus
Black Poplar Mushroom. See Agrocybe aegerita
Blewit. See Lepista nuda
bog habitat mushrooms, 156–157
Bolbitius
 coprophilus, 35
 variicolor, 54
 vitellinus, 54
Bottlebrush trees, 31
Bovista pila, 113
bracket fungus, 96
British soldier lichen, 163

C

Callistosporium
 luteoolivaceum, 131
 species (undescribed), 131
Calvatia gigantea, 57
Camarophyllopsis, 150
 hymenocephala, 150
Campanella
 alba, 63
 aff. eberhardtii, 63
Cantharellula humicola, 68
casuarina trees, 82, 122
Caterpillar Fungus. See Cordyceps sinensis
cattle ranch habitat mushrooms, 48–57

Ceratiomyxa fruticulosa, 167
Chaetocalathus liliputianus, 73
charcoal trees, 60
Chicken-of-the-Woods. *See Laetiporus sulphureus*
Chlorophyllum molybdites, 5, 26, 57, 89, 93, 177
Chytridiomycota, 6
Cladonia, 163
Clavulinopsis corniculata, 112
Club Fungi, 6
coastal habitat mushrooms. *See also* mountain
    habitat mushrooms
  casuarina, 82–89
  coconut, 90–93
coconut trees, 90
Collybia, 84
  look-a-like species, 131
  subpruinosa, 129
compost pile habitat mushrooms, 10, 11, 32–43
Cone Head. *See Conocybe lactea*
Conical Waxy Cap. *See Hygrocybe conica*
conifer forest habitat mushrooms, 104–113
Conocybe
  filaris, 133
  fragilis, 46
  gracilenta, 133
  aff. hadrocystis, 46
  lactea, 24, 25
  rickenii, 56
Copelandia
  bispora, 181
  cambodginiensis, 181
  cyanescens, 50, 181, 182
  tropicalis, 181
Coprinus, 61
  cinereus, 32, 33
  comatus, 95
  cothurnatus, 54
  curtus, 34, 61
  disseminatus, 61
  lagopus, 32
  macrorhizus, 33
  micaceus, 127
  aff. picaceus, 55
  plicatilis, 25
  stercoreus, 55
  truncorum, 127
Coprinus disseminatus, 34
coprophilus mushrooms, 35

Coral Fungus, 194. *See also Ramaria fragillima*
Cordyceps sinensis, 174
Crater Rim Trail, 13
Creeping Crumble Cap. *See Coprinus disseminatus*
Crepidotus, 170
  citrinus, 72
  roseus, 72, 121
  stromaticus, 72
  sulphurinus, 72
  uber, 73
Cup Fungi, 6
Cyathus
  pallidus, 42, 47
  stercoreus, 57
cypress trees, 104
Cyptotrama asprata, 62
Cystolepiota species (undetermined), 152

D

Dacryopinax spathularia, 2, 79
Dead Man's Foot. *See Pisolithus arhizus*
Dermocybe clelandii, 116
Descolea, 116
  alienata, 131
Descomyces, 116
  albellus, 121, 124
  albus, 121, 124
Diachea leucopodia, 165
Dictyophora
  cinnabarina, 30, 43, 88
  multicolor, 88
Didymium verrucosporum, 169
Disciseda, 100
  anomala, 100
  verrucosa, 100
Dunce Cap. *See Conocybe lactea*
Dye-maker's False Puffball. *See Pisolithus arhizus*

E

Ear Fungus, 194. *See also Auricularia cornea*
Earliella scabrosa, 76
Earthball, 179, 194. *See also Scleroderma cepa;*
    Scleroderma verrucosum
Earth Fan. *See Thelephora terrestris*
Earthstar, 98, 194.
    See also Geastrum aff. welwitschia;
    Geastrum pectinatum; Myriostoma coliforme

Endoraecium acaciae, 161
Entoloma
  blue-stemmed species of, 68
  cibotiicola nom. prov., 153
  fibrosum, 153
  mariae, 153
  aff. *placidum,* 68
  purum, 69
  stylophorum, 69
  umbiliciforme, 29, 81
Entomophthora, 171
eucalyptus forest habitat mushrooms, 114–121
eucalyptus trees, 31

F

fairy rings, 4–5
False Shaggy Mane. *See Podaxis pistillaris*
ferns, hapu'u tree, 126, 142
flowerpot habitat mushrooms, 44–47
Flowerpot Parasol. *See Leucocoprinus birnbaumii*
Fly Agaric. *See Amanita muscaria*
Fomitopsis nivosa, 2
forest habitat mushrooms. *See also* grassland
    habitat mushrooms; trees
  arid leeward coastal, 94–97
  coastal casuarina, 82–89
  coconut, 90–93
  conifer, 104–103
  eucalyptus, 114–121
  guava thicket, 58–59
  mesic montane native, 126–141
  montane casuarine, 122–125
  wet montane native rainforest, 142–155
  wet windward alien, 60–81
fountain grass, 94
Fringed Polypore. *See Polyporus arcularius*
Fuligo septica, 165
fungi. *See* Hawaiian fungi

G

Galerina
  atkinsoniana, 144, 145
  decipiens, 144, 145
  hynorum, 144
  nana, 145
  paludosa, 157
  velutipes, 20, 47, 64

Ganoderma
  applanatum, 138
  australe, 125, 138
  lucidum, 173, 174
Geastrum, 100
  berkeleyi, 86, 87, 135
  campestre, 101
  corollinum, 101
  fimbriatum, 87
  fornicatum, 101
  hungaricum, 101
  javanicum, 135
  aff. *morganii,* 135
  pectinatum, 86, 87
  velutinum, 135
  aff. *welwitschia,* 93
  aff. *welwitschii,* 81, 86
Gemmed Puffball. *See Lycoperdon perlatum*
Giant Puffball. *See Calvatia gigantea*
Gloeophyllum
  striatum, 96, 103
  trabeum, 103
Gloiocephala epiphylla, 20, 66
Golden Scruffy. *See Cyptotrama asprata*
golf course fairway mushrooms, 36
Gomphus pallidus, 59
grassland habitat mushrooms, 48–57.
    See also forest habitat mushrooms;
    lawn habitat mushrooms
Green-spored Parasol. *See Chlorophyllum*
    molybdites
Grifola frondosa, 174
guava thicket habitat mushrooms, 58–59
gunpowder trees, 60
Gymnopilus
  subtropicus, 22, 47, 65, 89, 121
Gymnopus
  luxurians, 43, 85
  menehune, 43, 84, 85
  subpruinosus, 129
Gyrodontium versicolor, 141

H

Halawa Valley, 13
hallucinogenic Hawaiian mushrooms,
    181–182, 200
hapu'u tree ferns, 126, 142

Hawaiian fungi, 2–6, 159–171.
  See also jelly fungi
  bibliography for, 196–197, 200–202
  rainforest, 142
  relationship with lichen, 162
  tea made from, 173–174
Hawaiian Islands
  abbreviations used in this book for, 21–22
  bibliography for, 196
  Hawaiian terms that describe, 195
  map of, 11
  mushroom species unique to, 130, 142
  places to find mushrooms on, 13–14
Hawaiian mushrooms. *See also* Hawaiian fungi
  art objects made with, 77, 138
  bibliography for, 199–201
  common and Hawaiian names for, 194, 195
  culturing at home, 183–184, 199
  determining edibility of, 180
  field guides for, 15, 198–199
  glossary for, 191–193
  hallucinogenic, 181–182, 200
  health benefits of, 140, 173–174, 200
  identification of, 15–20, 199
  on man-made materials, 2, 3–4, 79
  official rules about, 14
  poisonous, 175–180
  recipes with, 185–190, 199
  seasonality of, 9–11
  selected places where found, 11–14
  species, diagnoses of, 20
  species, number of, 8–9
  species found only on Hawai'i, 130, 142
  tea made from, 140
Hawaiian mycologists, 6–9
Hawai'i Volcanoes National Park, 13–14
Headless Stinkhorn. *See Mutinus elegans*
Heliocybe sulcata, 99
Hemimycena tortuosa, 107
Hemitrichia
  calyculata, 168
  serpula, 167
Hen-of-the-Woods. *See Grifola frondosa*
hoale koa, 94
Hobsonia mirabilis, 155
Hohenbuehelia atrocaerulea, 65
Honey Mushroom, 129
Ho'omaluhia Botanical Garden, 12

Horsehair Fungus. *See Marasmius androsaceus*
Hosmer's Grove, 13
Humidicutis, 147
  marginata, 147
  peleae, 147, 157
  poilena, 147
Hydropus
  marginellus, 64
  semimarginellus, 64
Hygrocybe, 147, 150
  cantharellus, 149
  conica, 29, 110
  conicoides, 29
  constrictospora, 146, 148
  graminicolor, 148
  hapuuae, 149, 152
  laeta, 148
  lamalama, 146, 157
  mexicana, 47
  noelokelani, 19, 148
  ovinus, 150
  pakelo, 146
  psittacina, 146
  puaena, 149
  relative abundance of, in Hawaiian
    rainforests, 10
  squarrosa, 150
  subovinus, 150
  waolipo, 150
hyphae, 3–4
Hypholoma fasciculare, 39, 179

I

Inky Cap, 194. *See also Coprinus cinereus*
Inonotus specius (undetermined), 138
ironwood trees, 82, 122

J

Japanese Parasol. *See Coprinus plicatilis*
Jelly Fungus, 60, 194.
  See also Auricularia cornea;
    Tremella fuciformis

K

Kahaualea Natural Area Reserve, 14
Kamakou Forest Preserve, 12–13
karakanut trees, 129

Kauaʻi, places to find mushrooms on, 12
Kaumahina Wayside Park, 13
kiawe trees, 94
Kipuka Puaulu (Bird Park), 13–14
koa trees, 126, 159
Kokeʻe State Park, 12
Kombucha, 173
Koʻolau Mountain Range, 12
kukui nut trees, 60
Kukuiolono State Park, 12

L

Laccaria
    fraterna, 107, 117
    proxima, 107, 117
Lactocollybia epia, 85, 93
Laetiporus, 185
    sulphureus, 120, 187
Lamproderma
    arcyrionema, 169
    scintillins, 167
Lanaʻi, places to find mushrooms on, 13
lava flows, lichen on, 159, 162, 163
lawn habitat mushrooms, 24–31, 36.
        See also compost pile habitat mushrooms;
        flowerpot habitat mushrooms;
        grassland habitat mushrooms; trees
Lentinula edodes, 174
Lentinus
    bertieri, 74
    ciliatus, 74
Lepiota
    besseyi, 18, 43, 83
    humei, 36
    look-a-like species, 91
Lepista
    nuda, 27
    subalpina, 130
    tarda, 27, 43, 57
Leucoagaricus
    hortensis, 36
    leucothites, 49, 177
    look-a-like species, 91
    meleagris, 35
    naucinus, 49, 177
Leucocoprinus
    birnbaumii, 43, 45, 178

fragillissimus, 25
lilacinogranulosus, 44
look-a-like species, 123
luteus, 45
species (undescribed), 123
Leucopaxillus gentianeus, 111, 121
lichens, 159, 162–163, 201
Limacella species (unidentified), 91
Ling Zhi. See Ganoderma lucidum
Lycogala epidendrum, 167
Lycoperdon, 100
    perlatum, 154

M

MacKenzie Park, 14
Macrolepiota rachodes, 26
Magic Mushrooms. See Copelandia cyanescens
mamane, 98
Manchurian Mushroom, 173
mango trees, 60
Marasmiellus
    hapuuae nom. prov., 151
    pacificus, 63
    palmivorus, 92
    segregabilis, 151
    troyanus, 92
Marasmius
    androsaceus, 109
    anisocystidiatus, 70
    exustoides, 70
    pseudobambusinus, 71
    radiatus, 81, 124
    thwaitesii, 71
Maui, places to find mushrooms on, 13
meadow habitat mushrooms, 48–57
Meadow Mushroom. See Agaricus campestris
medicinal mushrooms, 173–174, 200
menehune (fairy) rings, 4–5
Merulius tremellosus, 140, 170
mesic montane native forest habitat mushrooms,
        126–141
Mica Cap. See Coprinus micaceus
Microporus flabelliformis, 77
molds, 2–6, 159, 164–169
Molokaʻi, places to find mushrooms on, 12–13
monkey pod trees, 60
montane. See mountain habitat mushrooms

Morchella esculenta (Morels), 13, 154
Moss Agaric. *See Rickenella fibula*
mountain habitat mushrooms.
　　See also coastal habitat mushrooms
　　arid leeward, 98–103
　　casuarine forest, 122–125
　　native forest, 126–141
　　wet native rainforest, 142–155
Mouse Feces on a Stick. *See Xylaria apiculata*
mulberry trees, 60
Munro Trail, 13
mushrooms. *See* Hawaiian mushrooms
Mutinus
　　bambusinus, 41
　　elegans, 41
Mycena, 149
　　alphitophora, 66, 89
　　brunneospinosa, 66
　　epipterygia, 152
　　hapuuae, 151
　　marasmielloides nom. prov., 151
　　metata, 108
　　papyracea, 123
　　pura, 108
　　sanguinolenta, 109
　　spinosissima, 66, 67
mycetozoans, 159, 164–169, 202
mycology and mycologists, 6–9
Myriostoma, 100
　　coliforme, 100

N

Naematoloma fasciculare, 179
naio, 98
Netted Stinkhorn. *See Dictyophora cinnabarina*
noni trees, 60

O

O'ahu, places to find mushrooms on, 12
ohi'a trees, 126, 142
Onygena corvina, 99
Orange-gilled Waxy Cap. *See Humidicutis*
　　marginata
Oyster Mushrooms, 4, 183, 185. *See also*
　　Pleurotus cystidiosus; Pleurotus djamor
　　look-a-like species, 65
　　recipes with, 188, 190

P

Paddy Straw Mushroom. *See Volvariella volvacea*
Pala'au State Park, 12
Panaeolus
　　antillarum, 51
　　campanulatus, 51
　　cyanescnes, 50
　　papilionaceus, 51
　　semiovatus, 52
　　sphinctrinus, 51
　　subbalteatus, 52
Paperbark trees, 31
Parmeliella mariana, 163
Parrot Waxy Cap. *See Hygrocybe psittacina*
pasture habitat mushrooms, 48–57
Paxillus
　　corrugatus, 134
　　curtisii, 134
　　panuoides, 106
Pele, mushroom species named for, 144, 147
Pepeiao (Wood Ear), 194. *See also Auricularia*
　　cornea
Peziza arvernensis, 42
Phaeolus schweinitzii, 139
Phallus, 40
　　rubicundus, 40
Phellinus
　　gilvus, 77, 103, 125
　　kawakamii, 88
　　robustus, 103
Phlebia tremellosus, 140
Pholiota, 10
　　peleae, 144
Physarum
　　bogoriense, 169
　　globuliferum, 166
　　melleum, 169
　　nutans, 168
Pig Ears. *See Gomphus pallidus*
pine trees, 104
Pisolithus
　　arhizus, 118
　　tinctorius, 118
Pleurotus, 183, 185
　　cystidiosus, 58, 183, 184, 190
　　djamor, 91
Podaxis pistillaris, 95
poisonous mushrooms, 175–180

Polipoli Springs State Recreation Area, 13
Polyporus arcularius, 74, 75, 89
Porpoloma bambusarum, 68
Protista, 6
Psathyrella
   fuscofolia, 132
   hydrophila, 132
   aff. *singeri,* 92
Pseudocolus
   fusiformis, 40
   schellenbergiae, 40
Pseudocoprinus, 61
Psilocybe
   coprophila, 53
   cyanescnes, 50
   semiglobata, 53
Puccinia vitata, 161
Puffballs, 194. *See also Battarraeoides digueti;*
   Bovista pila; Calvatia gigantea; Lycoperdon
   perlatum; Pisolithus arhizus; Tulostoma
   dumeticola; Tulostoma involucratum;
   Vascellum floridanum
      desert-stalked, 98
      differences from Earthballs, 179
      look-a-like species, 95
Pulveroboletus xylophilus, 93
Puʻu Makaʻala Natural Area Reserve, 14
Pycnoporus
   cinnabarinus, 76, 90
   sanguineus, 76, 89, 90
Pyrrhoglossum pyrrhum, 133

R

rainforests
   effect of fungi on, 3
   mushrooms that grow in, 142–155
   seasons when mushrooms grow, 10–11
Ramaria
   fragillima, 59
   aff. *myceliosa,* 137
Ramariopsis
   corniculata, 112
   kunzei, 112
redwood trees, 104
Reishi. *See Ganoderma lucidum*
Rhodocollybia
   laulaha, 130, 143

relative abundance of, in Hawaiian
   rainforests, 10
Rhodocybe hawaiiensis, 125, 130
Rickenella fibula, 62
Rigidoporus
   microporus, 75
   ulmarius, 139
rust fungi, 159, 160–161, 202

S

Salt-and-Pepper Shaker Earthstar. *See Myriostoma*
   coliforme
Sarcodon atroviridis, 117
Sarcoscypha
   coccinea, 141
   mesocyatha, 141
   occidentalis, 141
Scarlet Cup Fungus. *See Sarcoscypha mesocyatha*
Schizophyllum commune, 134
Scleroderma, 179
   cepa, 119
   verrucosum, 119
Setchelliogaster, 116
   tenuipes, 116
Shaggy Mane. *See Coprinus comatus*
Shaggy Parasol. *See Macrolepiota rachodes*
Shiitake. *See Lentinula edodes*
slime molds, 159, 164–169, 202
Slippery Jacks, 194. *See also Suillus brevipes*
sphagnum bog habitat mushrooms, 156–157
Splitgill Mushroom. *See Schizophyllum commune*
spores, 5
   of *Galerina velutipes,* 20
Spring Polypore. *See Polyporus arcularius*
Starfish Stinkhorn. *See Aseroe rubra*
Stemonitis fusca, 166
Stereocaulon vulcani, 162
Stereum hirsutum, 120
Stinkhorns, 194. *See also Anthurus javanicus;*
   Aseroe rubra; Dictyophora cinnabarina;
   Mutinus elegans; Phallus rubicundus;
   Pseudocolus fusiformis
   strawberry guava thicket habitat mushrooms,
      58–59, 60
Stropharia
   rugosoannulata, 37
   semiglobata, 53
   variicolor, 37

sugi pine trees, 104
Suillus
    brevipes, 31, 105
    granulatus, 105
    salmonicolor, 31, 105, 106
Sulfur Cap. *See Hypholoma fasciculare*
Sulfur Shelf. *See Laetiporus sulphureus*
Sulfur Tuft. *See Hypholoma fasciculare*

T

Tetrapyrgos nigripes, 67
Thelephora terrestris, 113
Trametes versicolor, 140, 174
tree ferns, hapu'u, 126, 142
trees. *See also* names of specific trees
    alien to Hawai'i, 31, 60, 82, 94, 129
    bogs under, 157
    conifer, alien to Hawai'i, 104
    native Hawaiian, 90, 126
Tremella
    boraborensis, 78
    fuciformis, 79, 186
Trichia favoginea, 168
trumpet trees, 60
Tubifera microsperma, 166
Tulostoma, 96, 97
    dumeticola, 97
    fimbriata, 102
    involucratum, 97
Tumbling Puffball. *See Bovista pila*
Turkey-tail. *See Trametes versicolor*

U

Usnea australis, 162

V

Vascellum
    floridanum, 31
    lloydianum, 31
    subpratense, 31
Volvariella, 185
    volvacea, 38, 188, 189

W

Wa'ahila Ridge Park, 12
waiawi habitat mushrooms, 58–59
Waihou Springs State Recreation Area, 13
Waikamoi, 13
Waxy Cap, 194. *See also Humidicutis marginata;*
        Hygrocybe conica; Hygrocybe psittacina
wet montane native rainforest mushrooms, 142–155
wet windward alien forest mushrooms, 60–81
White Wood Ear Fungus. *See Tremella fuciformis*
witches' broom, 159, 161
wood-chip habitat mushrooms, 10, 11, 32–43, 44
Wood Ear, 194. *See also Auricularia cornea*
wood surfaces, mushrooms that grow on, 2, 4, 79
Wooly Cap. *See Coprinus cinereus*

X

Xanthoparmelia coloradoensis, 163
Xylaria
    apiculata, 81
    moelleroclavis, 80
    psidii, 58

Y

Yellow Parasol. *See Leucocoprinus birnbaumii*

Z

Zygomycota, 6

E P B M — We hope you enjoyed this title from Echo Point Books & Media

Before Closing this Book, Two Good Things to Know

Buy Direct & Save

Go to www.echopointbooks.com (click "Our Titles" at top or click "For Echo Point Publishing" in the middle) to see our complete list of titles. We publish books on a wide variety of topics—from spirituality to auto repair.

Buy direct and save 10% at www.echopointbooks.com

DISCOUNT CODE: EPBUYER

Make Literary History and Earn $100 Plus Other Goodies Simply for Your Book Recommendation!

At Echo Point Books & Media we specialize in republishing out-of-print books that are united by one essential ingredient: high quality. Do you know of any great books that are no longer actively published? If so, please let us know. If we end up publishing your recommendation, you'll be adding a wee bit to literary culture and a bunch to our publishing efforts.

Here is how we will thank you:

- A free copy of the new version of your beloved book that includes acknowledgement of your skill as a sharp book scout.

- A free copy of another Echo Point title you like from echopointbooks.com.

- And, oh yes, we'll also send you a check for $100.

Since we publish an eclectic list of titles, we're interested in a wide range of books. So please don't be shy if you have obscure tastes or like books with a practical focus. To get a sense of what kind of books we publish, visit us at www.echopointbooks.com.

If you have a book that you think will work for us,
send us an email at editorial@echopointbooks.com

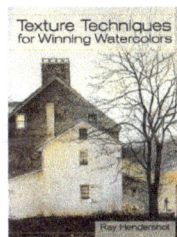

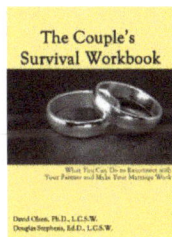

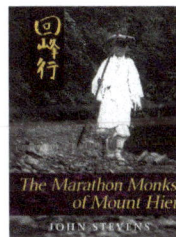

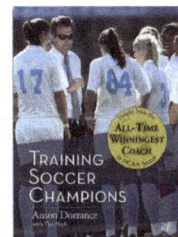

www.ingramcontent.com/pod-product-compliance
Lightning Source LLC
Chambersburg PA
CBHW041017280326
41926CB00094B/4659